W9-COI-310

Race and Remembrance

AFRICAN AMERICAN LIFE SERIES

A complete listing of the books
in this series can be found online
at wsupress.wayne.edu

Series Editors
Melba Joyce Boyd
Department of Africana Studies
Wayne State University

Ronald Brown
Department of Political Science
Wayne State University

Race and Remembrance

A MEMOIR

Arthur L. Johnson

WAYNE STATE
UNIVERSITY PRESS
DETROIT

Library of Congress Cataloging-in-Publication Data

Johnson, Arthur L., 1925–
Race and remembrance : a memoir / Arthur L. Johnson.
    p. cm. — (African American life series)
Includes bibliographical references and index.
ISBN 978-0-8143-3370-9 (cloth : alk. paper)

1. Johnson, Arthur L., 1925– 2. African American civil rights workers—Michigan—
Detroit—Biography. 3. Civil rights workers—Michigan—Detroit—Biography.
4. African Americans—Civil rights—Michigan—Detroit—History—20th century.
5. National Association for the Advancement of Colored People—History—20th
century. 6. National Association for the Advancement of Colored People—Officials
and employees—Biography. 7. Civil rights movements—Michigan—Detroit—
History—20th century. 8. Detroit (Mich.)—Race relations—History—20th century.
9. Detroit (Mich.)—Biography. I. Title.

F574.D453J64 2008
323.092—dc22
[B]

Grateful acknowledgment is made
to the MGM Grand Casino Detroit
and Dr. William F. Pickard for
their generous support of the
publication of this volume.

Designed by Omega Clay
Typeset by Keata Brewer, E. T. Lowe Publishing Company
Composed in Warnock Pro and Gotham

*This book is dedicated to Chacona Winters Johnson,
my faithful companion, wife, friend, and critic for the past
twenty-seven years. She has helped to keep me humble,
made days of sadness shorter, and hours
of joy everlasting.*

"I do not know what happiness is, and I do not think it is important that we be happy. But it is important that you find your work and do it as if you were sent into the world at this precise moment in history to do your job. If happiness can be achieved, it will be found in a job well done and in giving and not in receiving."

—Dr. Benjamin E. Mays, *Born to Rebel: An Autobiography*

Contents

Foreword

A Magnificent Life and Journey: Dr. Arthur L. Johnson

Great lives, in their encounters with successes and failures, hope and despair, glory and tragedy, heights and depths, and faith and doubt, disclose much about the vitality and creative power, the meaning and mystery of the human spirit at its best. Such is the case of Dr. Arthur L. Johnson, who has been a dear friend of mine since we were freshmen at Morehouse College in 1944.

This book is powerful, illuminating, insightful, honest, straightforward, and inspiring. It is about Art Johnson and his times and multidimensional institutional involvements, opportunities, and challenges. It tells us much about the battles he has fought; the social, civic, educational, public policy, and political struggles in which he has been involved; the institutions and forces that have nurtured and sustained him as well as those that have oppressed and crushed him; his contributions and achievements; his pains and sufferings; his sorrows and joys; his inner strength and reserves; his fears, tears, and doubts; his triumphs over tragedies; his sensitivities in the face of brutal insensitivities, heartlessness, institutional and barbaric evils; his persistence and determination in confronting entrenched, institutionalized wrongs, perversities, degradation, humiliation, and dehumanization; his inordinate integrity, decency, and warm humanity; and his loving, gentle, giving, and forgiving spirit.

Ultimately, this book is about the human mind, heart, spirit, and will.

It is also about social and institutional change and continuity, power struggles and moral purposes, strategies and tactics, rebellion and affirmation, American ideals and realities, protests and celebration of the status quo, individual rights and community responsibilities, "the children of light" and "the children of darkness."

Arthur Johnson was born in Americus, Georgia, in 1925, in the heart of the Old South, in the days of rabid Jim Crow segregation and discrimination with its controlling ideology of white supremacy and superiority. Brutal racism was the order of the day and night. Significantly, Americus is in south Georgia, near Plains, the birthplace of the thirty-ninth president of the United States, Jimmy Carter.

At the age of twelve, Arthur moved to Birmingham, Alabama, a city made famous during the civil rights movement for its horrible bombings, "Bull" Connor and his fire hoses and police dogs, and its efforts to avoid social, institutional, and historical change.

Early in the days of his youth, Arthur, somehow and for some reason, developed, deep in his heart and bones, a lifelong passion for racial and social justice and equality, and the inclusivity of human rights and dignity for all of God's children. The passion gripped him, and he gripped the passion. He became a social activist in high school. His social activism intensified and accelerated at Morehouse College, where he was the founder of the institution's chapter of the NAACP.

At Morehouse, he, like Martin Luther King Jr., Lerone Bennett Jr., Bob Johnson, Charles V. Willie, and countless others, came under the magical influence, prophetic power, and majestic and transcendent spell of Dr. Benjamin Elijah Mays, whose creative and inexhaustible moral and intellectual restlessness and passionate commitment to social justice, righteousness, and the Kingdom of God are legendary. The powerful, transformative impact and humanistic commitment captured him and, to this day and hour, never let him go. They never shall.

Arthur Johnson graduated from Morehouse in 1948. In 1949 he received a master's degree in sociology from Atlanta University, having written a thesis titled "The Social Theories of W. E. B. DuBois." In 1949–50 he was a research fellow in sociology at Fisk University.

In July 1950, at the tender age of twenty-four, Dr. Johnson became the executive secretary of the Detroit branch of the NAACP at an annual salary of $3,000. To his surprise, he was in for a new awakening about the depths, universality, and tyranny of racism in the Motor City. He discovered massive racial discrimination and segregation in housing, restaurants, hotels, bars, the entertainment industry, hospitals, and the police department. He found it in the banking business in loans and mortgages, in "redlining" by insurance companies, and in Jim Crow practices in government and politics. "The practices of discrimination and segregation in health care," he writes, "were not much different in Detroit than in the Jim Crow South."

With his passionate commitment to social justice and racial equality, Arthur went to work to battle and disarm the Goliath of racism in Detroit. His efforts were indefatigable and virtually nonstop. As the executive secretary of the NAACP, Arthur became a national leader of the civil rights movement. He became a vital agent and instrument of social and historical change in Detroit and on the national landscape. He was thoughtful, courageous, fearless, determined, and crafty. Through it all, he maintained his integrity, incorruptibility, honor, decency, character, and clear socioethical vision and humanistic commitment. He maintained close communication and warm ties with his Morehouse classmate and friend Martin Luther King Jr.

In a variety of capacities, Arthur Johnson's peerless leadership continued to influence Detroit for the better on many fronts—racially, politically, culturally, civically, and educationally—and in law enforcement, the administration of justice, and in other areas.

In this luminous and constructive book, Dr. Johnson, as a sociologist and moralist, gives a searching and compelling analysis of racism and its various manifestations, dimensions, and terrible consequences. One of his chapters contains a subheading entitled "Racism in the Bloodstream."

Dr. Johnson's account of some personal tragedies is riveting, courageous, insightful, and inspiring. His marriage to Chacona in 1980 was profoundly redemptive and fulfilling. Their mutual love, devotion, and caring are an experience of beauty and special joy to behold.

For his significant human service, contributions, and achievements, Dr. Johnson has been the recipient of a long list of honors, awards, and citations—including several honorary degrees. Beyond history, in the bosom of eternity, Arthur Johnson's grandmother, whom he idealized, and who in his formative years was his guardian angel and role model, must be happy and proud of his magnificent life and journey.

Samuel DuBois Cook
President Emeritus, Dillard University

Acknowledgments

I hesitated in developing a list of acknowledgments, knowing that such a list was bound to contain a number of omissions, but I wanted to go as far as I could in recognizing the contributions of others to the development of my own thought, actions, professional life, and sense of well-being. My debt to these individuals—scholars, teachers, family members, students, friends, and colleagues—encompasses a list that I could never say is complete.

My commitment to this project began with a deep sense of obligation to others, and I wish I could cite by name everyone who has played a helpful role in this endeavor. My readers will need to be kind in judging errors and omissions. With considerations of this character, I feel I must recognize the following: Damon J. Keith, Rachel Keith, Melvin and Celess Chapman, Julian and Julia Pate, William Pickard, Colin Cromwell, Alex Parrish, Charles Boyce, Catherine Blackwell, Brazeal Dennard, Mable and Joseph Winters Sr., Tom Jeffs, Frederick Matthaei Jr., Eugene Miller, Samuel DuBois Cook, George Gullen, Lerone Bennett Jr., Paul Freeman, Charles Vert Willie, Peter and Julie Cummings, Lillian Bauder, Alfred Glancy, Clim McClain, Betty Canty, Joya Person, Sylvia Shearer, David Baker Lewis, Dave Bing, Jack Robinson, Joe Coles, Katherine Barnhart, Mildred Jeffrey, Coleman A. Young, Frederick G. Sampson, Leon Atchinson, Stanley Winkelman, Walter Chivers, Walter Douglas, Richard Rogel, Eugene Driker, Trudy and Abe Ulmer, Richard Levy, Laverne Ethridge, Connie Baker, Gwen Shannon, Marilyn Dillard, Benjamin E. Mays, Lionel Swan, Nathaniel Tillman, Kemper Harrell, Nettie Jones, Sam Logan, Nicholas and Doris Hood, James Wadsworth, Sue Slack, Larry Doss, Norman Drachler, Alan E. Schwartz, Edward Turner, Mamie and W. A. Thompson, Dennis Archer, Sue Mosey, Charles Adams,

Jennifer Granholm, Alice and Julius Combs, Charles Whitten, John Whittington, Jesse Jai McNeil, Irene Graves, David Adamany, W. E. B. DuBois, Ira de A. Reid, Shirley and Norman McRae, Richard Bilaitis, Robert Perkins, Lawrence Givens, David Lawrence, Sammy Davis Jr., Dick Gregory, Shirley Stancato, Myrlen Washington, Corinne Houston, Rebecca Davis, Martin Luther King Jr., Duke Ellington, Langston Hughes, Walter Evans, Josephine Baker, Rosa Parks, Aileen Cromwell, Ansley Cromwell, Colin Cromwell Jr., Irvin Reid, Arthur Jefferson, Alberta Blackburn, Jane Robinson, Marc Stepp, William McGill, Terry A. Gardner, Marvin Jones, Louis Jones, and the Walter P. Reuther Library of Labor and Urban Affairs.

All of these friends and fellow travelers have played a special role, touching my life, providing special support, and opening doors and windows to some of life's highest possibilities. To all of them—along with my wife, Chacona; my children Averell, Wendell, Brian, Angela, Carl, and David; my mother and grandmother; and the grandeur of a Morehouse education—I owe everything. I would also like to express my gratitude to my brother James; my sisters Shirley Ellis, Elizabeth Reid, and Winifred Harrison; and my grandchildren Rachel Sewell, Brian Johnson Jr., Wendell Johnson Jr., Alexandra Sewell, Olivia Sewell, Jason Watkinson, Don'aa Ellis, Erika Dillard, and Leia Sewell.

I will always feel a deep sense of indebtedness to Wayne State University Press for its diligent and valiant role in bringing this project to fruition.

A Special Acknowledgment

I wish to acknowledge with deep gratitude the indispensable role of Steve Palackdharry in researching, organizing, and writing this memoir. From the beginning of this endeavor, I have felt the pulse of Steve's good heart and strong mind.

Introduction

Charles V. Willie
Graduate School of Education, Harvard University

I am honored to prepare this introduction to invite you to read and reread this marvelous memoir about the life and times of Arthur L. Johnson. From a humble beginning, he has lived a good life, confronting the good and the bad and overcoming both. His life is a living example of the civil rights song "We Shall Overcome." And, of course, he was one of the local shapers and designers of that freedom movement in Detroit.

Arthur Johnson tells us that he had only two pairs of britches when he entered Morehouse College in 1944 and had to work as a waiter while studying as a student. After four years, he graduated with a Bachelor of Arts degree in sociology; and after another year of study, he received a Master of Arts degree in sociology from Atlanta University. The following year, he was a research fellow in sociology at Fisk University. Then, he shook the dust of the South off his shoes and went to Michigan in 1950 as executive secretary of the Detroit branch of the National Association for the Advancement of Colored People (NAACP). Detroit was his point of no return. He has been a resident of this city for more than half a century. Both the city and Arthur's job were challenging experiences. However, Arthur was equal to these challenges because of his philosophy of life.

Arthur Johnson is a person who prefers to light a candle rather than curse the darkness. He has chosen to build coalitions and partnerships among racial, ethnic, and socioeconomic groups rather than crush the opposition. Nevertheless, he was not reluctant to use direct action against intransigent malefactors. He would not cooperate in his own oppression. He preferred to negotiate but was not reluctant to demonstrate.

Arthur Johnson admired Benjamin Elijah Mays, his college president, who reminded "his boys" that the future is always with those who take the high road—the high road of truth, social justice . . . love of humankind, and concern for the advancement of all. Arthur has understood Aristotle's distinction between "making a good living" and "making a good life." While people who make a good living may have wealth, power, and influence, those who make a good life become persons-for-others, redeeming the poor and afflicted and making no peace with oppression. When asked to assess his twenty-seven years as president of Morehouse College, Dr. Mays said, "We believe that . . . we helped to instill in many a Morehouse student a sense of his own worth and a pride that thereafter enabled him to walk the earth with dignity" (*Born to Rebel*, 194). Arthur was one of "Bennie's boys" who developed a sense of his worth at Morehouse College and who did what he had to do with dignity.

Arthur Johnson understood John Rawls's notion of "justice as fairness." Rawls believed that since none of us earns our starting place in life, we are obligated to give compensating opportunities to those who have missed out. With an undergraduate minor concentration in political science and with empathy for the oppressed, Arthur understood very well these principles of political philosophy and applied them every day of his life.

In biblical literature, we are told in the book of Genesis that Jacob wrestled with an angel all night and was blessed for his tenacious activity. Arthur had to wrestle with evil every day in his life and sometimes was cursed for his tenacious activity to resist it. However, he, too, eventually was blessed with all kinds of awards and beautiful experiences, such as membership on the board of directors of the Detroit Symphony Orchestra, the Detroit Institute of Arts, the Detroit Science Center, and the Art League of Michigan; and as the founder of the Detroit Festival of the Arts. Although some rain has fallen into his life, as it has in the lives of us all, Arthur did not let it wash away the enduring beauty of life manifested in music and art, love and justice.

Despite his recognition of the importance of political action, Arthur Johnson has been a true believer in education. It was fitting that he should end his professional career with an appointment in higher education at Wayne State University, a very fine public and urban educational institution in Detroit. He served Wayne State as vice president for university relations and as a professor of educational sociology for nearly a quarter of a century. One year after Arthur retired in 1998, he received an honorary Doctor of Humane Letters Degree from Wayne State University. He had received a similar honor—the Doctor of Humane Letters Degree—in 1979 from his alma mater, Morehouse College in Atlanta, Georgia.

It is interesting to note that Wayne, a state university, is located in the North, and Morehouse, a private college, is located in the South. As a result, Arthur's good work has been recognized in all regions of this nation by public and private enterprises and by people in a variety of racial, ethnic, and socioeconomic groups.

While the visual part of Arthur's work has been centered largely in Detroit, the honors he has received for good work well done indicate the universal effects of his contributions in promoting the general welfare. During the 1990s, Arthur received the Horace L. Sheffield Jr. Bridge Builders Award and the Detroit Urban League's Distinguished Warrior Award. Further indications that Arthur has had a "many splendored" career is the range of diversity in the kinds of organizations and associations that have heaped honors upon him: the Greater Detroit Chamber of Commerce, the Greater Detroit Interfaith Round Table, the Detroit Bar Association, and the Hospice of Southeastern Michigan.

While I have mentioned some of the reasons why one ought to read this book, I would be remiss if I did not tell the reader about Arthur's wonderful writing style. He is a good storyteller by way of the written word. The stories are chock-full of facts but never dull. A vivid picture is presented of Arthur's childhood in his family of orientation with a mother, a stepfather, and a grandmother—the latter being the great stabilizer for him. After reading about the fundamental role Arthur's grandmother played in his life, all proposals for schools for boys only without women teachers should be reexamined in view of the effect a grandmother can have on a grandson as revealed in this memoir.

Arthur is able to share with the reader how it feels to be caught in the middle of a race riot trying to counsel frightened white government authorities and angry black rebelling citizens because he was there betwixt all sorts and situations, trying to find a common interest and negotiate fair public policies.

With a front seat on urban sociology and urban history derived, in part, from being part of the confidential advisory cabinet to the first black mayor of a big city in the United States, Arthur provides valuable information in his memoir about city life and community organization.

A major value of this book is that it records happenings in an urban community from two different perspectives: the bureaucracy perspective and the grassroots perspective. Arthur Johnson realized that most cities operate as a bureaucracy in which there is a hierarchical structure of authority and a formal body of rules for governance. Arthur insisted that people of color should be major players in Detroit bureaucracies, but he also recognized the value of grassroots social action from the bottom up in urban communities. And for this reason, he built a local chapter in Detroit into one of the most effective chapters of the NAACP in the United States. A careful reading of the Johnson memoir will reveal how to deal coterminously with top-down decision-making systems and bottom-up policy-making movements.

It is fair to classify Arthur Johnson as one of this nation's finest applied sociologists who believes that it is possible to attain justice for all in a democratic nation-state.

The stress of fulfilling public responsibilities and civic duties as well as personal and family responsibilities is visited several times in this memoir, and ways in which religion may be of assistance during times of trouble are mentioned, too.

A few decades ago, I developed a new name for people like Arthur Johnson. I call them intercessors. Their role is essential in urban communities. It is a role that advocates negotiation and mediation for the purposes of attaining justice and turning an enemy into a friend, as mentioned by Martin Luther King Jr., one of Arthur's classmates at Morehouse College. The intercessor helps to find ways to solve social problems. For what he has done in Detroit and in the state of Michigan, Arthur should receive a double blessing for the radical social changes he has helped to promote.

I hope this introduction has invited you to read the remarkable story of one who was born when segregation of racial populations in the United States was legal and who successfully devoted most of his adult life to promoting integration for all.

William Zinsser, a writer, editor, and teacher and the author of *Writing about Your Life* (2004), advises the writer of memoirs that if you think small, you'll wind up finding a big saga. This is precisely what Arthur Johnson has done. However, he does not tell it all if such information would hurt others, and he does not try to get even with his enemies. He focuses on particular events that represent what George Herbert Mead would call "the generalized other." Finally, Zinsser reminds us that "to write well about your life you only have to be true to yourself." This is precisely what Arthur Johnson has done.

Race and Remembrance

CHAPTER 1

Early Years

I was born in Americus, Georgia, in 1925 to Clara Stewart and Arthur Allen. My birth was out of wedlock, and my biological father was never a part of my life. Nor was I ever curious about what he was like. My mother never spoke of him, and I learned his name by accident. When I was ten, I found a notation in the family Bible indicating "Arthur Allen" as my father. For many black families at this time, the only record of family history was a note jotted in the Bible. This inscription was in my maternal grandmother's handwriting, and I asked her about it. She told me that I met my father only once, when I was three years old. She and I were walking in downtown Americus when a man approached us and spoke to her. He heard me say that I wanted an ice cream, and he bought one for me. My grandmother did not reveal to me that this man was my father until she related the story of the encounter. I did not recall the meeting, and I accepted her judgment that it was best for me not to know who Arthur Allen was.

My mother was seventeen years old when I was born. A few years later, she married James Johnson, who was five years older than she was. He worked as a janitor for the Elks Club downtown. It was a place where members of the white power structure gathered. My mother worked as a domestic servant for a white family. Her mother, Elizabeth McFarland, was also a domestic servant. My grandmother was the strong and steadfast mentor of my youth, and without her, I would have undoubtedly fallen into despair from the cruelty of my stepfather and the racism of Americus.

James Johnson was a mean-spirited man who habitually belittled my mother and me through verbal and physical abuse. He resented

1

me because I was not his own, and he wanted me to fail to justify his spite. My mother was unable to stand up for herself or for me. The only time I felt safe at home from my stepfather's brutality was when my grandmother was present. Her quiet strength and self-assurance seemed to disarm him. I wanted to emulate her, hoping one day that I could defeat my fear in the face of hatred.

When I was six, my mother and stepfather moved to Birmingham, Alabama, so he could look for work in the coal mines and steel mills. They left me behind in the care of my grandmother. Though I knew I would miss my mother, I was thrilled to be with my grandmother and rid of my stepfather. Free from his tyranny, I began to come into my own under my grandmother's loving tutelage.

I idolized my grandmother. I considered her my patron saint. She was slight of build and carried herself gracefully and with great dignity. She embodied a shining goodness that accentuated her beauty. She was dark-skinned and evinced some Native American features in her face and eyes. Even when she disciplined me, she had a compassionate visage. She sometimes joked about a telling difference between herself and her daughter—my mother. She said that my mother tended to laugh when she saw a minor accident befall another person, for example, if someone badly stumbled walking downtown. My grandmother would only feel concern for the other's embarrassment. It was a difference in self-confidence that enabled my grandmother to empathize. My grandmother lived to be a vital ninety years old. She is living proof to me that the quality of one's life is determined by how much one cares about the well-being of others.

My grandmother, her ten-year-old daughter Vera, and I lived in a small wooden house on Academy Street, which was in an impoverished, all-black neighborhood not far from the center of town. Americus was a typical small southern city. Of the nearly 9,000 residents in 1930, more than half were black. The stark lines and strictures of segregation were enforced by the constant threat of violence meant to instill fear and submission in the black populace. I saw the Ku Klux Klan march through the streets of downtown in their

This is the only remaining picture that I have of my grandmother, Elizabeth McFarland. It was taken at her eighty-fourth birthday party in Birmingham, Alabama, in October 1971. She died six years later.

hooded regalia. I heard stories of black men lynched for some alleged indiscretion toward a white female. I learned even as a boy, as did all black males, that racism was not just about skin color but had an inflammatory sexual dimension. When walking downtown, I had to be especially careful with my gaze and demeanor.

Downtown was one of the few places where the separate and unequal lives of blacks and whites intersected. Thus, it was a venue where the implicit threat of violence was publicly reinforced. I did not go downtown too often, and so most of my days in Americus, I did not see a white face.

In our two-room home, the front room doubled as the bedroom and living area. It contained a single bed in which my grandmother, Vera, and I all slept. The back room was the kitchen and dining area. My grandmother paid the rent and supported us by working as a domestic servant. She did the cooking, cleaning, and laundry for a white family. She labored long, hard hours for a pittance, but there was a benefit to her work that allowed us to live well in one respect. After making dinner for the white family and doing their dishes, my grandmother was allowed to bring a pan of food home for us. As a result, we never went hungry. Other poor blacks on our block subsisted on beans with a slab of bacon and perhaps a piece of pork or chicken occasionally. White families had full-course meals for supper: meat, potatoes, bread, vegetables, black-eyed peas, and corn on the cob. Every day I looked forward to dinner, not only because we ate well, but also because during that hour, we lived the "good life" that was otherwise reserved for the privileged. To this day, the one thing I am class conscious about is food.

I started first grade when I was six. McCay Hill School was a block away, and Vera and I would walk there together. Though she was my aunt, Vera was only four years older than I, and I thought of her like a sister. All the students, teachers, and administrators at McCay were black. The school taught grades one through nine. There was no high school for blacks in Americus at that time. The white power structure considered further education for blacks both unnecessary and dangerous: unnecessary because they deemed blacks intellectually deficient, and dangerous because they understood that knowledge empowers. These dual motives are contradictory, but of course, racism is not about reason. It is about power.

McCay was poorly equipped, terribly understaffed, and overcrowded. There was no maintenance staff, and the students themselves did the janitorial work. However, despite the deprivations, the education we received at McCay was remarkable. Teachers and administrators were determined to triumph over the inequities of segregation. They cared about the children and were committed to developing the highest possible aspirations in their students. They wanted us to know that even though the dominant society wanted them to fail as educators, they would persevere and work harder. They expected us to do the same.

My grandmother reinforced the life lessons taught at McCay. She could read and write fairly well despite her limited schooling. She had beaten the system designed to discourage blacks from bettering themselves, and she instilled in me a desire and responsibility to develop my mind. I also understood that I was an extension of her best hopes, and I felt duty-bound to honor her love for me by striving to excel and to make her proud.

My grandmother's love virtually erased the feelings of pain and neglect caused by my stepfather's brutality and my mother's inability to change the situation. I did not feel the sting of poverty even though I was quite aware that we were poor. There were blacks on our street better off than we were. They had homes with more rooms, better furnishings, and radios. Still, I thought in many respects that I was in an ideal living situation, and I did not feel anything important was lacking. Despite my grandmother's meager wage, she put a roof over our heads and good food on our table. She bought medicine when we were sick, and books and clothing for school. She also managed to bring Christmas joy and little surprises in the midst of our poverty. That our home was headed by a single mother did not set us apart from other families. Out-of-wedlock births and female-headed households were prevalent in the neighborhood. Good and steady jobs for black men were rare. Even when couples got married, the commitment did not last. These were the facts of life for poor blacks—the legacy of slave masters who denied the legitimacy of familial bonds between slaves.

What gave the neighborhood a sense of community was its devotion to the school and to the church. Every Sunday I would walk down Academy Street with my grandmother to Mt. Olive Baptist Church. The church had about 150 members. Reverend C. W. Woodall was pastor. Mt. Olive is where I was exposed to music. My motivation to appreciate music came from my grandmother. She loved the gospels, hymns, and great spirituals and was utterly transported by them. My schoolteachers also nurtured an appreciation of music that again derived from their own church roots. Reverend Woodall, my grandmother, and my teachers asked me to think about the message in the music—of redemption from suffering and the hope of a better life—and take this message to heart. Over the years, my love of music has deepened, but one thing has not changed. It is still a deeply immersive experience to me that resounds with freedom.

Though we lived in the isolation and segregation of Americus, I was able to develop an understanding that blacks elsewhere were engaged in the struggle to fight racism and to achieve successes that challenged the white power structure. I learned this in school and through other experiences in the neighborhood. The greatest black hero of the time was the boxing champion Joe Louis. When he fought, everyone on the block would gather in the homes with radios. We celebrated his victories in the ring over white opponents as victories for our entire race. He was an emblem of extraordinary individual courage, and we saw him as a black man who single-handedly defeated a mighty system that wanted to beat him down.

When I was eight, I started a small business selling the *Pittsburgh Courier* door to door on my street. The *Courier* was the national standard-bearer of African American journalism. It advocated political policies that would improve the lives of blacks, and it called on all blacks to become active in changing society and shaping their destiny as a people and as individuals. The weekly paper featured columns by black intellectuals such as W. E. B. DuBois and Dr. Benjamin Mays, both of whom, as it turns out, would play significant roles in my intellectual development later. These writers spoke about the great movement on the horizon and the importance of education in preparing to participate in it. I was too young to understand most of what DuBois and Dr. Mays were saying, but nonetheless I began to feel that I could beat the system by doing what they asked of me. These were big thoughts for a black child in the segregated South of 1933, and they are a measure of how my grandmother's guidance allowed me to take possession of myself.

When I was twelve, I suffered an injury that would affect me the rest of my life. I owned a BB gun that my grandmother bought for me after I promised I would be careful with it. And I was. Then one day the daughter of the black woman from whom we rented our two rooms found the gun, pointed it at my face, and fired from close range. The BB made a small hole in my right pupil and knocked me to the floor. My eye bled profusely and the pain was unbearable, but my grandmother did not take me to a doctor. She did not understand what a doctor could do to treat such an injury, because having grown up in poverty, she was unfamiliar with the world of expert medical attention. As a result of the injury, I lost half the vision in my right eye. I did not see an ophthalmologist until more than a year later. He prescribed glasses for me, which made a world of difference, but I still experienced problems when reading. I developed a habit of tilting my head a certain way to help my eyes focus on the page. These difficulties did not reduce my reading comprehension or my great appetite for the written word, but they did reduce my reading speed.

A few months after my eye injury, my mother arranged for me to come live with her and my stepfather in Birmingham, Alabama. I did not want to leave my grandmother, and she wanted me to stay. But my mother prevailed, and I took the train by myself to Birmingham. Leaving my grandmother was the most traumatic experience of my young life. My heartsickness was further complicated because I had come to like a girl named Katie who lived across the street, and I knew I would never see her again.

In Birmingham, we lived in a three-room shotgun house on Tenth Street in an all-black neighborhood called Pratt City. My stepfather worked as a coal miner. He was a man of average frame and stern countenance. His ill-tempered and abusive behavior had grown worse in the six years since I last saw him. His disrespect for my mother was so great that he did not even attempt to disguise his womanizing. More nights than not, he did not come home.

My stepfather also had little regard for our immediate neighbors on the street. He kept pigs and chickens in the backyard. He also owned a mule, and every morning, even on schooldays, I had to take the mule out to graze. The noise and smell of all the animals offended neighbors, but the public health authorities did not respond to complaints. I was the one who had to tend to the animals and clean up after them. Whenever my stepfather wanted my mother to cook a chicken, he would order me to go to the backyard and wring its neck. I felt sorry for the animal I was forced to kill because my stepfather felt that violence would toughen me. Each time I killed a chicken, however, was just as troubling as the last. Notwithstanding my stepfather's warped view of strength of character, I was growing stronger and felt the day would come when I would be able to stand up to him.

My mother worked as a domestic servant for a white family named Houston. The family had two children, Billy and Emily, who were close to my age. Mr. Houston was a top-level manager with the Southern Bell Telephone Company. Mrs. Houston was a homemaker. I saw the Houstons as a decent family who occasionally did nice things for my mother. They permitted her to bring home a pan of food that served as our supper and would even drive her home some days. I got to know the family because they sometimes invited me to come to work with my mother so I could play with their kids. This was my first opportunity to interact with whites so closely, and I felt as though the family had embraced me. Two incidents, however, changed how I viewed the Houstons, because they conveyed how the Houstons actually viewed me. While riding in the backseat of their car, I overheard Mr. Houston telling his wife a derogatory story about "a nigger woman." Then, when I turned thirteen, Mrs. Houston abruptly stopped inviting me to play with Billy and Emily. I learned from my experiences with the Houstons how deeply racism runs beneath the sheen of southern congeniality.

Another lesson I learned when I was thirteen about racism in Birmingham was stark and vicious. I was walking downtown with one of my stepfather's male relatives who was about five years older than I was. A young white girl walking with her parents stepped across my path and accidentally bumped into me. Instinctively, I put my hand on her shoulder to keep my balance. Just then, her father struck me in the face hard enough to knock my glasses off. He continued hitting me as I lay on the ground trying to protect myself against the blows. No one witnessing the assault attempted to intervene or object. My companion stood frozen in fear. After the attacker walked away and I picked myself off the street, I felt angry and confused that my relative had not tried to stop him. I soon realized, however, that there was nothing he could have done without risking his own life at the hands of white bystanders who also felt entitled to violently punish a black person for any violation of southern racist mores, no matter how slight and unintentional that violation might be.

At home in Birmingham, my family never discussed the racial indignities each of us faced on a daily basis. The culture of oppression was so complete that there was a pervasive sense of helplessness among its victims. Black parents did not want to agitate their children because they knew how dangerous any act of defiance would prove to be. "Be good," my mother always reminded me when I left the house, and I knew that this was not moral advice. She had great faith in my moral compass. Rather, it was a note of pragmatic accommodation. She wanted me to be proud of myself and yet not let pride be my undoing in a society where blacks were expected to internalize inferiority and express due deference to each and every white person no matter what the circumstances were. It was a difficult balance to achieve, especially with my emerging consciousness that it should be my life's pursuit to fight racial injustice.

I went to Parker High, the largest black high school in the world. Parker was a source of great pride in the black community in Birmingham. The school had a group of devoted and highly skilled black teachers who had a sense of mission and spoke with a single voice: You are not only as good as white students anywhere but you are better—because you need to be better to make it in American society. Parker had rigorous academic standards and enforced strict discipline. Girls wore blue dresses. Boys wore ties. The staff did all they could to rouse the conscience of the students. History teachers made us promise to register to vote when we turned twenty-one and then to try to vote despite the poll taxes, literacy tests, and intimidation tactics used to disenfranchise blacks in the South. Parker sought to prepare us to become part of the generation that would change things. I still remember many of my teachers at Parker with reverence. My English teacher, Mrs. White, would read the classics aloud to us with great feeling, flair, and insight. Once she told the rest of the class that she wished they would study the English language as diligently as I did. I felt embarrassed to be singled out, but her acknowledgment encouraged me to challenge myself even more.

Parker High was about eight miles from my home, and I would take the electric street trolley there and back. My experience on these trips invariably followed the same pattern. Boarding the trolley, I would find a seat at the back of the car where blacks were consigned to ride. Then, as the trip proceeded and the car would fill up, the conductor would come to the back and say to me, "Boy, get up." I would have to surrender my seat to a white passenger even though we both paid the same fare. Though I was seething inside, the memory of my mother's words would calm me: "Be good."

Weekdays after school and all day on Saturday, I worked in a haberdashery downtown owned by a Jewish couple, Maurice Bombshell and his wife. My duties were sweeping and dusting, and occasionally, I ran errands for the store owners. On Saturdays, I would pick up lunch for the Bombshells at the corner drug store, which had an old-style soda fountain offering ice cream, sodas, and sandwiches. I would step up to the counter, place my order, then stand and wait, since blacks were not permitted to sit. Frequently, the service people asked me to move away from the counter so as not to draw attention to the fact that I, a black boy, was being served. Each time this happened, my indignation would build a little more, until one day when I could not tolerate the insult anymore and left the drug store without receiving the Bombshells' lunch order. I explained to Mr. Bombshell that I didn't want to go to that drug store ever again because they didn't know how to treat me. Though I felt Mr. Bombshell was a good man, I was still afraid that he would make me endure the humiliation of returning to the drug store. To my great relief, Mr. Bombshell said to me compassionately, "That's all right, Arthur, you don't have to do it." That moment, as much as anything else in my whole life, gave me a sense that I was not alone. Almost a decade later, after I became leader of the Detroit NAACP, I returned to Birmingham and called Mr. Bombshell. I asked if I could see him. He said he would be happy to receive me, although there was risk involved, since his next-door neighbor was the head of the Ku Klux Klan. When I arrived, Mr. Bombshell and I embraced each other as old friends, and I said to him: "I have come to thank you for helping me on one fateful day to preserve my dignity and self-respect."

I was my mother's only child until after I came to Birmingham. Then she and my stepfather started a family, and I would eventually have a stepbrother and three stepsisters. For much of my time in Birmingham, my mother was pregnant or nursing and needed some extra help. Vera came from Americus to live with us for a while. She was still like a sister to me, and I felt very protective of her. One day I was in the kitchen with my mother, and I could see Vera and my stepfather outside arguing. Suddenly, he shoved her to the ground, grabbed her arm, and dragged her violently along the dirt and then up the broken wooden steps to the porch, where he deposited her. I thought I would go crazy watching him hurt her, but I still felt powerless to stop him. I knew, however, that to become the man I wanted to be, I would one day have to stand up to him.

One morning my stepfather came home after staying out all night, and, as was his pattern, he walked into the kitchen to pick up his lunch box that my mother was preparing. As usual, his manner was surly and swaggering. He sat down at the dining table where I was eating breakfast and demanded to know what I was doing with the money I was making from my job at the haberdashery. I looked directly in his face and said defiantly that I was using the money to take care of myself. He got up, stood over me, and tried to intimidate me, but I maintained my gaze and showed no fear at all, knowing that he preyed on weakness. Instead of striking me, he turned away. That moment changed everything. I had come to embody my grandmother's strength. From that day, he did not dare abuse me, and I feared him no more.

Not long after this turning point, my grandmother wrote to say that she would be coming to stay with us for an extended time. On the day she arrived, I rushed from school and ran into the house. She was seated in the kitchen. I ran to her, fell into her lap, and wrapped my arms around her. I wept uncontrollably. For the first time, I felt that I had come home in Birmingham. I had always associated tears with sadness. To my surprise, I discovered that tears could also express great joy.

Now that I had freed myself from my stepfather's brutality, I desperately wanted the same for my mother. I spoke to my grandmother about this and found out that she, too, wanted her daughter to escape this life of daily degradation. After many discussions, my grandmother and I came up with a comprehensive plan to move my mother to another place where we could live and she would be safe. We presented the plan to my mother, and she seemed open to the possibility. When the decisive moment arrived, however, she could not go through with it, and I was terribly disappointed. It seemed quite apparent to me how different I was from her. In time, however, I would come to forgive my mother's weakness and sympathize with her dilemma. Now when I think of her, one memory more than others tends to linger. I am seated at the table in her kitchen. There is only the two of us. She has worked a long day as a domestic servant, and she fixes me a plate of the food she has brought home. My mother sits with me and quietly watches me eat without thought of her own hunger. At the end of the day, this simple offering redeemed for her the hard work, sacrifices, and indignities.

After dinner, I would finish my homework and then read books by black authors that I got from the small, segregated public library at the edge of downtown. At the black library, I discovered W. E. B. DuBois's autobiography, *Dusk of Dawn.* I was familiar with his writing from his columns in the *Pittsburgh Courier,* which I continued to read diligently. One could not read *Dusk of Dawn* and come away unchanged. DuBois wrote about the need to develop a "Negro intelligentsia" who would become the leaders of the black community and defeat the system of racial oppression. DuBois called this prospective vanguard "the talented tenth." The brilliance of DuBois's thought and the poetry of his writing captured me. I began reading many other black writers and poets, discovering a world of artistic and intellectual African American expression. Richard Wright's *Native Son* haunted me. I also read works by Julia Mood Peterkin, Langston

My stepfather, James Johnson, flanked by my mother, Clara *(right)*, and his sister *(left)* outside our home in Birmingham, Alabama, in 1944.

Hughes, James Weldon Johnson, Claude McKay, and Paul Lawrence Dunbar. My mind became consumed with the issues of race and the devastating consequences of racism.

I became involved with the Southern Negro Youth Conference, which was headquartered in Birmingham and which sought an end to Jim Crow. I decided to pass out pamphlets from the organization to other students at Parker. This caught the attention of the principal, William Bennett Johnson, who asked to speak to me in his office. He cautioned me about my involvement with the Southern Negro Youth Conference since it was tied to various Communist groups. He did not want to douse my activism but asked me to be discreet for my own safety and the safety of others at the school.

My desire and confidence to be a leader were growing. In my neighborhood, I was asked to serve on the neighborhood council. The council had fifteen members, and not only was I the only teenager, I was also the only male. Senior year at Parker, I ran for class president and won. My new stature in school captured the interest of a few young women. Though I was socially self-assured in other ways,

I was painfully shy about dating. Part of the reason, undoubtedly, was how much my stepfather tried to make me feel inadequate as a man. In a typical incident, he once demanded that I help him with a small garden he tended away from the house. He asked me to hoe, and after a while, he snatched the tool from my hand and said dismissively, "You act like a girl." He was relentless in these kinds of taunts. And so, when a pretty young woman at school asked me to take her to the prom, my anxiety made me hesitate. She then promised that if I chose her as my date, she would wear the most beautiful dress of any girl at the prom. I told her that I was not planning to go to the prom because I did not know how to dance. Still, her insistence and attractiveness won me over, and I agreed to take her. On the day of the prom, however, my anxiety grew so intense that I became physically sick and was unable to leave my house.

The other major worry I had during my senior year was about my future education. I had no idea where to go to college and how I could afford it even if I could find a college that accepted black students. A few months before graduation, my math teacher announced to the class that a professor from Morehouse College in Atlanta would be speaking in the school library at two o'clock and that male students were invited to attend, since Morehouse was a college for black men. I had never heard of Morehouse. I listened intently as Professor Nathaniel Tillman described the culture and philosophy of Morehouse and how the college was preparing tomorrow's leaders. Professor Tillman was a Shakespearean scholar and chairman of the Department of English. He was soft-spoken, graceful in manner, and marked by a warm, unpretentious smile. When he finished speaking, I knew the next destination I wanted my life to take me.

I applied to Morehouse and was admitted on the strength of my transcripts. I then wrote the college a letter stating that I would not be able to come unless I had a job and asking if the college would help me find employment. The college wrote back that I had been selected to serve as a waiter in the dining room. The letter spelled out the basic expenses of attending Morehouse and how my job would help

My mother, Clara, and my stepfather, James Johnson, in 1961.

defray some of the cost. Tuition was $50 a semester. Room, board, and laundry were another $27 a month. Even with the job, I could not afford these costs. My grandmother provided the rest of the money I needed to attend Morehouse. Over the years, she had accumulated some savings from her meager earnings as a domestic servant. She offered me all that she had as a pure act of love.

I graduated from Parker High in 1944. I was the first in my family to finish high school. After the ceremony, my stepfather astonished me by handing me a graduation gift. It was a wristwatch—something I did not own and something he felt I would need in college. I do not know what motivated him to give a present. Perhaps it was a small gesture of remorse. I kept the watch, but the gesture was empty to me. In a few months, I would begin a phase of my life in which his role would be nominal and strictly on my terms.

I cannot deny my stepfather's formative influence in my life. I learned to define myself against him. In some cases, it was a relatively inconsequential matter. For example, he loved to eat watermelon, and to this day, I will not touch the fruit. In other ways, he cast a larger shadow that forced me to step into the light. I learned from him to fight fear and to suffer pain without feeling defeated. I learned to stand strong with pride and never allow anyone to compromise my dignity again. These lessons would serve me well in the future, ironically, in my struggles against perpetrators and defenders of racism.

CHAPTER 2

Dear Old Morehouse

No institution has touched my life as much as Morehouse College in Atlanta. Morehouse is unique in its place in higher education in America. As the years have passed, my understanding of the debt I owe this small and proud men's college grows ever deeper. The words of the Morehouse hymn that I sang as a student have even more meaning to me now:

> Dear old Morehouse, dear old Morehouse,
> We have pledged our lives to thee;
> And we'll ever, yea forever
> Give ourselves in loyalty.
> True forever, true forever,
> To old Morehouse may we be;
> So to bind each son the other
> Into ties more brotherly.
> Holy Spirit, Holy Spirit,
> Make us steadfast, honest, true,
> To old Morehouse, and her ideals,
> And in all things that we do.[1]

At the end of my freshman year at Morehouse College in 1945, I boarded a bus at nightfall in Atlanta to return to Birmingham for the summer. I felt emboldened by the lessons I was learning at Morehouse, which strengthened and informed my determination to fight racism. I resolved that I would sit in the front section of the bus that was reserved for whites. The three-hour trip went through rural

1. J. O. B. Moseley, "Dear Old Morehouse."

17

Georgia and Alabama, places where a young black man would not be safe alone and at night, particularly if he were branded a trouble-maker. So I was aware that my decision was fraught with danger.

As the trip began, I recalled how I was always forced to surrender my seat at the back of the trolley car to a white person when I traveled to and from Parker High in Birmingham. Those daily incidents were humiliating, and I wanted to make a stand to redress the past. I recalled the words of Dr. Benjamin Mays, the president of the college, during one of his speeches to the students at Morehouse. He urged us to maintain our self-respect and courage in the face of racial injustice. He also related an experience where he was ordered to get off a bus for refusing to yield to segregation.

Sometime during the trip, the driver demanded that I move to the back of the bus where other blacks were seated. I refused. The driver said that he did not want trouble, but if I persisted, he would stop the bus at the side of the road and wait until I got off. I was hoping that other blacks on the bus would support my defiance. To my dismay, however, they were upset with me for disrupting their trip. A black man in back angrily shouted, "Why don't you just get up!" I was mortified and shaken as I retreated to take my place among black passengers who seemed as disapproving of my actions as the white passengers. As the trip continued, I questioned the wisdom of my decision under these circumstances. I had just started the intellectual revolution that is Morehouse and I thought, I must learn to choose my battles.

Morehouse, a small school of about 350 students, was located a few miles from downtown Atlanta. As a freshman, I was required to attend a series of lectures by Dr. Mays on the theme of Free Men in a Semi-Free World. The Tuesday morning lectures were delivered in the small chapel in Sale Hall, which later came to be known as the "Chapel of the Inward Journey." I was a sociology major, following the lead of my intellectual mentor, W. E. B. DuBois, and so I spent much of my academic day at Sale Hall, where most of the liberal arts classes were held. President Mays was at home in the pulpit. He was an ordained minister who had received his doctorate in religion from the University of Chicago. In his lectures, he argued that it was our duty not to accept any form of racial segregation imposed upon us. He insisted that although we lived under a system of racial oppression, we should not permit anyone to enslave our minds and that each of us was responsible for his own intellectual freedom. Dr. Mays preached an academic gospel of discipline, hard work, and excellence. "If you are behind in the race," he said, "you must run faster than the man ahead of you if you are to catch up." Morehouse Men must be intrepid leaders bent on changing the system. "Everywhere I turn, I find the monster of fear," he said. "If you are to stand for a just cause, you must be courageous."

Dr. Mays lived what he taught in all respects. I so admired him that I was determined to make his lessons incarnate. I immediately boycotted the Fox Movie Theater, where blacks had to sit in the balcony, as well as other establishments in Atlanta that practiced segregation. My classmates were equally affected by Dr. Mays's eloquence and example. He inspired us to strive for leadership, and it was his manner of leadership that we strove to emulate. The noted historian Lerone Bennett Jr., who graduated from Morehouse in 1949, has referred to Dr. Mays as the "schoolmaster of the civil rights movement." In Mays's twenty-seven-year tenure as the president of Morehouse, he influenced thousands of young black men to commit their futures to the cause.

Dr. Mays came to Morehouse in 1940. When I arrived with the class of 1948, he was in the prime of his highly effective leadership. The intellectual culture on campus, an expression of his vision, was electric. The conscience of the nation was beginning to stir over issues of racial oppression. The Truman administration created the President's Committee on Civil Rights in the wake of what was regarded as a national scandal: black soldiers from the South who had served their country in World War II came home to discrimination, racist threats, and lynchings. The president's committee marked the first time the federal government had investigated the issue of civil rights since 1890. Its report, released in 1947, called for significant reforms in voting rights and employment practices to create a more just society. The report was a milestone for a nation in transition. It encouraged civil rights activists and enraged southern racists.

The mission of Morehouse, President Mays repeatedly emphasized, was to train leaders to take up and advance the gathering movement. Morehouse considered itself not only the most prestigious black college in the country but also one of the nation's elite institutions of higher learning, bar none. Almost all the students came from poor families and poorly funded segregated schools, and yet Morehouse made us believe that we were as good as, if not better than, white college students from privileged backgrounds, and that a Morehouse education ranked with one from Harvard, Princeton, or Yale. Morehouse knew we had to take this belief to heart if we were to accomplish the mission that awaited us.

Because of the rigorous academic expectations at Morehouse, I was assigned to take a remedial reading course in addition to my required course load. The problem was with my reading speed, which was still hindered by my eye injury. Ironically, this injury was the reason I was in college at this time rather than drafted into the military to serve in World War II. The problems with my reading speed did not keep me from doing well in my regular classes, and I was disappointed that the college had placed me in the remedial class. It was a blow to my intellectual ego and seemed at odds with the student leadership positions I had begun to assume.

As a freshman, I organized the Morehouse chapter of the black fraternity Phi Beta Sigma. I became the first president, and I sought a way to distinguish our fraternity from the others on campus that were stronger and better established. So, we took a firm stance against the practices of hazing. We declared that no one wanting to become a member of Phi Beta Sigma would be subjected to hazing, and we condemned the hazing practices of other fraternities. In addition, we emphasized that Phi Beta Sigma was dedicated to scholarship and community service.

HOMECOMING WITH BENNIE MAYS

One O'Clock P.M.

November 14, 1976

MATADOR ROOM
PASCHAL'S MOTOR HOTEL
830 Martin Luther King, Jr. Drive, S.W.
Atlanta, Georgia

A signed flier from the 1976 event honoring Dr. Benjamin Mays, the legendary president of Morehouse College in Atlanta.

Also as a freshman, I decided to start the first chapter of the NAACP at Morehouse. Becoming active in the NAACP had been on my mind for a while. I knew that DuBois had cofounded the organization and had been editor of its influential magazine, *The Crisis.* Since I was a boy, I had read stories about the feats of the NAACP in the *Pittsburgh Courier.* The *Courier* and the *Chicago Defender,* both black-owned papers, were regarded by the black community as the record of truth about the struggle. Walter White, the NAACP executive secretary, wrote a syndicated column that regularly appeared in the *Courier.* Under White's leadership, the NAACP led the fight against the practices of lynching, segregation, poll taxes, and all-white political primaries. His close friendship with Eleanor Roosevelt gave the NAACP access to the highest levels of power, and White helped persuade President Truman to create the landmark Committee on Civil Rights. I strongly believed that Morehouse needed an NAACP chapter of its own. I felt that I was psychologically ready to head this student chapter because of how much I had read on the issues and because of the leadership experience I had gained in my high school days. So I wrote to Ruby Hurley, the national secretary for the NAACP Youth Department, advising her of my interest in starting the Morehouse chapter. She endorsed my petition and gave me some general instructions about organizing the chapter and conducting meetings.

The first member I recruited was Victor Backus. Victor had the distinction of being the only white student at Morehouse. I had never been in a class where not every student was black, and I had not had a white friend my age before. Victor and I were both in freshman English, which was taught by Professor G. Lewis Chandler. Professor Chandler liked to challenge his students' ability to write literary criticism through friendly competition. Each Friday he assigned a paper that we had a week to complete. He then would read the best-written paper aloud to the class. Late in the fall semester, Victor's work had been featured many times, and I had yet to win the honor. I desperately wanted my work recognized, so for the first time in my life I stayed up all night, writing and rewriting a critical analysis of a particular poem. When Professor Chandler read my paper to the class, I was elated. I exhibited the proper restraint and humility, but it was nice to get the better of Victor, at least that week.

The Morehouse NAACP chapter met every month in a classroom on campus. We had about fifty members. We would discuss practices of segregation and racism that we encountered in Atlanta and strategize about what could be done. Although these practices were woven into Atlanta's culture, we all recognized that the city had a special character that, in many ways, made it more hospitable to black college students than any other city in the South. There were four major historically black colleges in the city: Morehouse, Spelman, Clark, and Morris Brown. These institutions played a vital role in the economy and prestige of Atlanta. As a result, the city's white leadership worked to build cooperative relationships with black leaders in the academic, religious, and business communities. Morehouse students felt safe at school. The white police force did not encroach on the black campuses to harass students, despite the civil rights activism stirring in the colleges. However, racial segregation and debasement were still prevalent downtown. For example, Rich's Department Store not only enforced rigid segregation, it had a policy that salespersons were to address black customers by their first names and white customers with courtesy titles. The only reason for this policy was to remind blacks of their social inferiority while doing business with them. A successful protest against this policy was led by the pastor of Ebenezer Baptist Church, Reverend Martin Luther King Sr., who was a key civil rights figure in Atlanta. Reverend King was a graduate of Morehouse and his son, Martin Luther King Jr., was in our freshman class.

Martin was only fifteen years old when he enrolled in the college under its early admissions program for advanced students. He and I shared the same class schedule, since we were both sociology majors. Martin was a quiet student and was not a leader on campus. I cannot say that I understood he was marked for greatness when we were fellow students. Because of our common interests and schedule, we became friends, and Martin attended our NAACP meetings. His father was very active in the Atlanta chapter, and during my sophomore year "Daddy King," as he was affectionately called by Morehouse students, approached me with an assignment that was part of a broader NAACP-led effort in Georgia. He asked me to go to three black colleges in the state to speak to students about registering to vote and then voting against Eugene Talmadge in the 1946 gubernatorial primary for the Democratic Party. Talmadge was a notorious white supremacist who had already served three terms as Georgia's governor. After a recent federal court decision struck down the rule allowing "whites only" voting in Democratic primary elections, Talmadge campaigned on a promise to defy the ruling and completely disenfranchise blacks again. I spoke to college students at Albany State, Fort Valley State, and Georgia State, encouraging them to use the new opportunity to vote to defend this opportunity in the future. The overall voter registration drive in Georgia was successful. Nearly 125,000 blacks registered to vote, a number significantly greater than in any other Southern state at the time. As a result, Talmadge lost the popular vote in the primary, despite the widespread fraud, intimidation, and violence perpetrated by his supporters against blacks trying to vote. However, Talmadge was still awarded the election through a formula that gave more weight to white rural counties over the counties where more blacks lived. We had won the battle but lost the war, because the enemy was still able to rig the system.

Talmadge died before he could take office, and his son Herman became the governor. The son was cut from the same cloth—a white sheet. Racists in Georgia stepped up their intimidation and violence against civil rights activists and black voters. The racial climate in the state was now even more hostile. I learned a valuable lesson from the great civil rights leaders in Atlanta during this time. They understood and accepted the painful reality that white racists predominated in numbers, power, and resources. We could never fight back using any of the enemy's tactics. We had to define our movement in opposition to the enemy's mindset. Under this reality, black leaders had to survive with honor and be alert for any opportunity that might emerge to use the limited economic and political power in the black community to effect change. Black leaders needed to be constantly vigilant and strategic in their thinking. I embraced this lesson in Atlanta, and it would guide my activism from then on.

My role in the voter registration drive was one of the few times I was able to participate in the larger movement outside our campus. I was simply too busy with college life. I joined the debate team as a freshman because it was coached by Professor Nathaniel Tillman. Professor Tillman was the one who drew me to Morehouse when I attended his talk about the college at Parker High. As a sophomore at Morehouse, I took his "Language and Thinking" class, which influenced me more than any other I have ever taken because it changed my approach to critical thought. It taught me how to analyze arguments to find their hidden flaws and biases and to construct counterarguments that exposed those flaws and biases. I would never read a newspaper editorial the same way again. Professor Tillman was the reason the Morehouse debate team excelled and was a source of pride on campus. We used to joke that our success in the debate field made up for the losses on the football field.

Another activity that kept me busy was my job as a waiter in the cafeteria. Without the job, I could not pay my expenses, but the demands of the job, my extracurricular activities, and the difficulty of my classes took a toll on me. I worked all three meals every school day. Meals at Morehouse were served "family style," and it was a waiter's responsibility to put the food and place settings on the table and then help clean up. The work left me little time to eat my own meal, and I was always rushing to the next class. It was especially hard for me to concentrate in the class after lunch, and indeed, I would sometimes doze off at my desk from fatigue. On one such occasion, in a class called "Matter and Energy," Professor B. T. Harvey asked me a question, and a fellow student nudged me awake so I could reply.

I then heard the professor say, "Don't bother. Let him sleep." I felt embarrassed that I had developed a reputation for sleepiness in class and made a vow not to allow my hectic schedule to hurt my grades. I refocused and then crammed for the final. I scored an 87 out of 100 and got a B for the course.

My work as a waiter not only affected my schoolwork, it also compromised my social life. In fact, I quit the job for a while so I could enjoy more time for myself. In my sophomore year, I started dating a young woman who was a freshman at Spelman College. She asked me to escort her to a ball at her school. I declined, insisting that I did not know how to dance and did not intend to learn. However, she stated in no uncertain terms that I was gong to the ball and that I was going to dance with her. She had her way. The relationship developed quickly, and soon she talked of marriage. I told her that I could not consider marriage until after I completed Morehouse and my graduate studies. The relationship cooled after that, and I began to date others, though not as seriously. The extra time I had for my social life did not last long. I returned to my job as a waiter to pay my debts and make ends meet.

The Morehouse dining area was the scene for one of my most dramatic memories of President Mays. As a waiter, I heard all of the student complaints about the food. The students were rarely satisfied, even though most of them, like me, came from homes where three meals a day, of any sort, was not an affordable family practice. One day the students decided to protest the quality and portions of their lunch. They pounded on the tables, shouted their grievances, and scraped full plates of food into the trashcan. The other waiters and I stood by and watched. During the protest, Dr. Mays came into the cafeteria. The room fell silent. He calmly walked to the trashcan, leaned over, and began to lift out every full slice of bread. He counted each one aloud and placed it on the counter. With each successive number, the sense of shame among the students seemed to ratchet up. At the end, President Mays had tallied eighty-seven slices of bread. He then spoke to the assembly. He censured the conduct of the students and told us that we needed to keep our focus on what was truly important. He lamented our waste of energy and the waste of food. He reminded us that people, and children in particular, were dying from starvation around the world, and that to be so disconnected from this tragedy was sinful. Finally, he pointed out that the school did its best to provide three meals a day with a variety of foods. This surpassed what our families at home were able to enjoy. Moreover, it was the sacrifices our families made that enabled us to be here. After Dr. Mays's speech that day, the students never again protested the food they received during my remaining time at Morehouse.

During summer breaks, I worked full time to pay tuition and room and board for the next school year. Before my sophomore year, I first worked as a janitor in the Sears, Roebuck department store in downtown Birmingham. I mopped floors every night from midnight until nine in the morning. I then went back to Atlanta and worked on the maintenance staff at the Federal Reserve Building. The staff was divided into teams of two. My partner and I worked from 5 p.m. to 2 a.m. It was our responsibility to clean all the restrooms in the building. My partner was a black man who was about twice my age and who worked this job as his living. After he cleaned the face bowls and fixtures, he would towel them dry so that not a single drop of water remained. I asked him why he went to such lengths to make sure that things were spotless. He said that it was a matter of pride in his work. I learned a valuable lesson from him. Work is meaningful, at its best, when you do more than what is required for no other reason than that it is your work.

In the summer before my junior year, I worked on the Cullman Brothers' tobacco farms in Simsbury, Connecticut. Cullman Brothers had a standing arrangement with Morehouse allowing it to recruit black students for summer work. Martin Luther King and other students I knew had already worked on the farms, and I signed up in the spring of 1946, relieved that I would not have to search for work when the school year ended. I had never been outside of Georgia and Alabama, and I looked forward to the adventure. About fifteen of my fellow students and I took the train from Atlanta to Simsbury. The big tobacco fields were covered in gauze to diffuse the light that fell on the "shade tobacco" plants. We worked long and laborious days during the week picking the crop, hauling it away, and then stitching and hanging the leaves to dry. At the start of picking season, the leaves were low to the ground, and we would have to slide on our butts in the mud from stalk to stalk. In the next round of picking, we would walk on our knees. By the end of the season, the plants were seven feet tall, and we could pick the leaves standing up.

A few weeks after we arrived, the Morehouse men started discussing amongst ourselves the rights of migrant laborers. As our discussions progressed, we decided that we needed to prepare a proposal that stated our demands for better working conditions. Since I was a member of the Morehouse debate team and led the NAACP chapter, the group elected me to research and write the proposal and then take it to management. We all chipped in some money, and I hired a driver to take me to Hartford. I went to the state agency that regulated migrant labor and read about our rights and how to file a possible complaint against Cullman Brothers. Shortly after I returned, I presented our argument to management. It agreed to make the necessary changes to meet our demands. As a result, our workload and hours became tolerable. I decided that I would like to return to this job next summer, since I had come to enjoy exploring the East Coast. However, when I applied for the job during the following school year, Cullman Brothers informed the college that I was no longer suitable to work for the company.

During that summer in Simsbury, some of my classmates and I would use our days off to travel. The racial attitudes in New England were a breath of fresh air to all of us from the Deep South. The movie theaters in Simsbury were not segregated, and for the first time in our lives we could actually sit where we wanted and next to white patrons. We hired a car and driver to take us to Boston to watch Canada Lee perform in *Othello*. Lee was a trailblazing African American actor in film and on stage. I was exhilarated to see Lee perform the lead role, speaking the

My Morehouse classmate Alexander Horton *(right)* and myself at the Cullman Brothers' tobacco farms in Simsbury, Connecticut, in the summer of 1946.

immortal words of Shakespeare in front of an audience who cared only about the power of the art and not the color of the skin of those on stage and in attendance. We went to the Tanglewood Music Festival in Lenox, Massachusetts. Serge Koussevitzky led the Boston Symphony Orchestra in a spirited performance of *Don Juan* by Richard Strauss. The Berkshires were much more than a backdrop. Everything was in harmony: the orchestra, the audience, and the breathtaking surroundings. I had developed an appreciation for classical music because of a class at Morehouse taught by Professor Kemper Harreld. Professor Harreld was head of the music department and a distinguished concert violinist in his own right. My experience at Tanglewood deepened my appreciation of classical music into an abiding love.

When the work on the tobacco farm ended, I did not make the return trip with my Morehouse classmates. Instead, I took a train to New York City. I walked around Manhattan, surveying the faces of people from all over the world and gazing up at the skyscrapers. Because I needed to save my money for the coming school year, I did not stay long, but I wanted to step foot in New York before I rode back to the Deep South. I took a seat in the segregated car on the train from New York to Atlanta. I read for a while and then noticed a man shifting cards on a cardboard box while three others watched and wagered. I left my seat and inquired about the game. The man said it was called "three card monte." The three cards were the jack of spades, jack of clubs and the ace of spades. The game started with the cards face up. The man then turned the cards over and deftly rearranged them with his hand. The object was to follow the ace and then point it out after the man had finished. I watched the game closely for many rounds and thought that I had discovered the secret of the man's method. I was convinced that I could outsmart him. After all, I was a leading Morehouse student and, after my summer travels, a man of the world. I had no idea that I was being drawn into a confidence game. I started by betting the small amount of cash I was carrying. When I lost that, I asked for credit. Soon I was deep in debt, and the man insisted on payment. I told him that only money I had was a check made out to Morehouse College from my summer employer, Cullman Brothers. He demanded the check and I handed it over. It was for $350, which was to cover tuition plus room and board for my junior year. The instant I gave him the check, my heart sank to my gut and my mind went blank. I returned to my seat and everything began to whirl. I thought I would go crazy from the jarring impact of what I had done. In one foolish and arrogant moment, I had thrown away three months of hard work and, worst of all, perhaps my very future.

Back on campus, I decided after several days that I had only one option. I made an appointment with President Mays to ask for financial aid from the college to remain in school. When I approached his office, the walk from his door to the chair in front of his desk seemed like a steep uphill climb. I told him that I had lost all of the money I had made. I did not explain how. I did not lie, but I could not bear to admit to Dr. Mays how irresponsibly I had acted. After gently admonishing my carelessness, he said, "What a terrible thing," and he placed a call to the bursar. Dr. Mays related my narrative to the bursar and asked what could be done to help me. Dr. Mays listened to the bursar's reply with a puzzled look. "What did you say?" he asked. After a few moments, Dr. Mays smiled and said, "My goodness, that's remarkable." Dr. Mays then told me that $350 had been deposited into my student account. The check that I had lost had been mailed to the college, and I was officially enrolled for my junior year.

My last two years at Morehouse were focused on sociology. I had determined that I wanted to pursue a master's and doctorate in the field. My ultimate goal was to become a professor and to research the issue of race. The chairman of the sociology department at Morehouse was Professor Walter Chivers. No other black sociologist trained as many black sociologists of the next generation as he.[2] He taught "situational sociology." We learned how to examine a particular situation and understand the broader social processes at work. Martin King was also in this class. Years later, he commented that Professor Chivers's analysis of segregation helped shape his subsequent thinking about how to fight this system of injustice.

The Tuesday morning lecture series in the chapel in Sale Hall was still a vital part of our education. Distinguished Morehouse alumni would speak about what it meant to be a "Morehouse Man." These speakers included "Daddy King," Martin's father; John Wesley Dobbs, who was regarded as the unofficial mayor of Atlanta's black community and who was a leader in the movement for black suffrage; Dr. Mordecai Johnson, president of Howard University; Howard Thurman, the great Christian theologian and preacher; and Dr. Ira de A. Reid, chairman of Atlanta University's sociology department. These speakers sought to articulate and instill a set of expectations of excellence in intellect and ethics that defined the Morehouse Man. This set of expectations was the heart of the Morehouse culture

2. See Charles V. Willie, "Walter R. Chivers—An Advocate of Situation Sociology," *Phylon Quarterly* 43, no. 3 (1982): 242.

or "mystique." Morehouse knew what its student body needed, and every important educational factor circulated through its heart. We took great pride in the mystique that surrounded us and that we internalized. We also learned to tease ourselves about our self-assuredness, and it was said, you can always tell a Morehouse Man, but you can't tell him much. Nevertheless, we never doubted that the ego-building the college undertook was right. It was right for the place. And it was right for the times. We understood that the mission ahead was rife with adversity that would try our mettle. In these moments of doubt and discouragement, we could rely on the tradition we embodied and feel assured that we belonged to a whole far greater than the sum of its parts.

In my junior year, I attended lectures on sociology at Atlanta University. It was the oldest graduate school in the nation serving black students. From the day I was admitted to Morehouse, I knew that I wanted to pursue graduate work in sociology at Atlanta University. The head of the department was W. E. B. DuBois. Unfortunately, DuBois left the university just when I arrived at Morehouse. As a result, I saw my intellectual hero only once. When I was a freshman, DuBois spoke at Ebenezer Baptist Church. He was introduced by the pastor, "Daddy King." DuBois was returning to work for the NAACP after a ten-year estrangement from the organization he co-founded. His appearance at Ebenezer expressed that reconciliation. Four years later, however, DuBois would once again break from the NAACP because of a bitter ideological dispute with Walter White and other NAACP leaders. DuBois had become deeply disillusioned with the pace of progress in fighting racism and segregation in the United States. He advocated radical strategies that were at odds with the more pragmatic approach of the NAACP, which sought to change the system through civil disobedience, consciousness raising, legal challenges, and suffrage. I sympathized with the merits of DuBois's argument and never left his intellectual side, even as my involvement with the NAACP deepened.

Dr. Ira Reid replaced DuBois at Atlanta University. He encouraged me to attend the lecture series on campus, which featured some of the foremost social scientists of the time. I saw the great anthropologist Margaret Mead present her research on "primitive cultures." Dr. Reid was an eminent sociologist in his own right, and I was still determined to enroll in Atlanta University after graduating from Morehouse. I was accepted into the master's program and began to think about my thesis. I knew that I would be writing about aspects of DuBois's theories related to race.

Graduation day at Morehouse arrived in June of 1948. My mother and grandmother came from Birmingham the day before commencement. They had not been to Morehouse before and had never stepped foot on a college campus. They spent the night in a room in student housing. I remembered how strange it felt when I first arrived at Morehouse and unpacked my things in the room I shared with two others at Graves Hall. So many things were new to me, even the simplest conveniences. For example, I had never taken a shower before, since we only had bathtubs at home. The simple pleasure of a long, hot shower was something I relished every day at Morehouse. Being in a dorm room must have felt even stranger to my mother and grandmother, but I was glad that they, who never dreamt of higher education for themselves, got to live like college students for one night and glimpse what they had dreamt for me. In the morning, I escorted them to commencement. The ceremony was held outside, amid the buildings that held so many memories and now bore witness to this closing act. The weather that morning was perfect, and the event began with music. The Morehouse Glee Club, led by Professor Harreld, sang with one voice.

President Mays spoke first. He said that the class of 1948 was the best that Morehouse had produced in his tenure, and he expected its members to go far. His prediction was prophetic. In our class was Martin Luther King Jr., who became the first black to win the Nobel Peace Prize; Samuel DuBois Cook, who became the first African American professor at a white college in the South when he joined the faculty of Duke University; Robert E. Johnson, who became executive editor and associate publisher of *JET* magazine; Charles Vert Willie,

My Aunt Vera
(McFarland) and
myself in April 1948,
two months before
my graduation from
Morehouse College.
Vera was only four
years older than I, and
I thought of her as a
sister. We maintained
this close relationship
for our entire lives.

who became an eminent sociologist and a professor at Harvard; and many others who made significant contributions to their professions and to the struggle.

Dr. Mordecai Johnson, the president of Howard University, was the commencement speaker. He urged us to see the world: "Let no barriers of race stop you from thinking with a world view." I knew that I would take this advice to heart. I was far removed from the isolation of Americus, but I was closer to my grandmother than ever before. This moment belonged to her as much as me. My name was called. I walked across the stage, saw my grandmother and mother in the crowd, and tears began to flow down my face. President Mays handed me my diploma. After commencement, my grandmother, mother, and I embraced and emptied ourselves in tears. No words were spoken. The feelings ran too deep. There are moments of triumph that events undo. Even in my young life, I had already known many such experiences. Then there are moments of triumph that time cannot rescind. They forever transcend the present and the person. They embody the determination of the generations who came before and of those whose faith in you became your own. All these things gathered at this stage, on this brilliant summer morning.

Before I entered Atlanta University, Dr. Reid departed. Dr. Mozell Hill took his place and would supervise my master's. The university helped me secure a summer research job before my program began. I went to Statesboro, Georgia, to study the high incidence of venereal disease in the black community there. My research involved considerable investigation. I interviewed infected residents to identify who were the principal carriers of the disease. Health authorities in Statesboro established a rapid treatment center. Those who were identified as carriers were forcibly detained at the center and given injections of penicillin by white nurses. One the one hand, I was disturbed by the violation of the rights of these black patients, but on the other hand, these individuals knew they carried the disease and continued to spread it, creating an epidemic. And so, even though I was distrustful of the authorities' treatment of blacks, I accepted the intervention. These decisions are difficult, and it would not be the last time that I would have to weigh the intervention of authorities who had a history of flouting the rights of blacks in order to control a situation that threatened to devastate the black community.

I had a scholarship to attend Atlanta University, but I still needed steady work to get by. Dr. Hill understood this and asked me if I would like to take over a sociology course he taught at Spelman College. He arranged an interview for me with Spelman's president, Florence Read, who was a white woman leading a historically black college for women. The interview was demeaning. President Read never invited me to be seated and asked imperious questions from behind her desk. I returned to Dr. Hill and expressed my anger about being treated so rudely. He spoke to President Read on my behalf, and she agreed to give me the teaching job.

I completed my master's degree at Atlanta University in a year and a half. Then, in the fall of 1949, I took a research fellowship and student-teaching position at Fisk University in Nashville, Tennessee. Though I seemed to be ensconced in academia, a deep-seated restlessness was intensifying, and I began to question my career path. The call of social activism as a primary pursuit was growing stronger. My activities in the NAACP had given me many connections in the organization. After founding the Morehouse chapter, I attended youth conventions at the state and national levels. I became president of the Georgia NAACP Youth Conference and organized an intercollegiate council of the NAACP in Atlanta. In the course of these activities, I met many NAACP leaders, including Gloster B. Current, who was once executive secretary of the Detroit branch and was now the national director of NAACP branches. In the spring of 1950, Current visited Atlanta University and informed Professor William Boyd that he was seeking someone for the leadership vacancy in Detroit. Dr. Boyd was one of my former teachers, and he asked Current if he remembered meeting me. Dr. Boyd also expressed that, in his judgment, I was the best candidate for the job. Current then called me at Fisk University, and I told him that I was very interested in the position. He said that two board members of the Detroit branch, Dr. and Mrs. W. A. Thompson, would interview me in Nashville and that if things went well, they would arrange for me to come to Detroit and interview further. Indeed, things went well, and a trip to Detroit was in order.

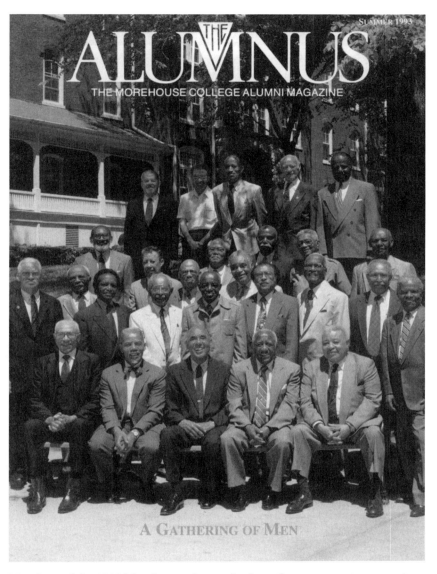

Members of the 1948 Morehouse class at the forty-five-year reunion event in 1993. I am at the far left in the second row from the top. (Photo courtesy of Morehouse College)

Though I knew intuitively that the Detroit NAACP job was the right choice for me, I was still torn. I went back to Atlanta University and had a long talk with Professor Hill. He understood my decision but was regretful because he felt that I had something important to contribute to the field of sociology, and that this would be lost if I left school. He urged me to consider a compromise plan. I should spend three years in the job and then return to writing my doctorate, incorporating the real-life lessons I had learned in Detroit into my research. The plan appealed to me because it resolved the conflict I was feeling. But little did I know that Detroit was not a way station on my life's journey. It was the destination that would define the rest of my life.

CHAPTER 3

Detroit NAACP

I boarded a train from the Deep South to Detroit. We stopped in Cincinnati, which falls on the Mason-Dixon Line, where trains headed north were no longer segregated, in theory if not in practice. Except for the summer I worked on the tobacco farm in New England, I had not spent time in the North, so I was not sure what to expect about the practices of racism and segregation in Detroit. I only knew that it would be my job to fight against them.

I came to Detroit alone. I had no relatives or friends here. When I arrived in the city on July 2, 1950, I was twenty-four years old. My starting salary to lead the Detroit NAACP was $3,000 a year. The minimum wage in 1950 was 75 cents an hour. I knew that I would be working long hours for much less than minimum wage, but money did not concern me. I was resolute and idealistic, and excited by the challenge. To be an effective leader of the Detroit branch, I would have to build strong and trusting relationships in the community. I was confident I could do so and that I would learn as I went along.

I arrived at the Michigan Central Depot, a couple of miles from downtown. My first memory of Detroit was of watching a black woman working as a porter struggling with a large suitcase. The image caught my attention because it deviated from the traditional gender roles in the South. My grandmother or mother would have not thought of a porter's job as women's work. Three black women who were on the Detroit NAACP board picked me up at the depot. They drove me to the black YMCA downtown. I stayed in a room there for two months while I searched for better accommodations that I could afford. Eventually, I rented a room in the home of the Scott family in Virginia Park, a black neighborhood on the city's west side.

The office of the Detroit NAACP was on the second floor of a two-story building at St. Antoine and Vernor, at the edge of a vibrant black commercial and entertainment district called "Black Bottom" or "Paradise Valley." A small room in our office suite was subleased to the Eastside Merchants Association, an organization of Jewish merchants committed to building good relations between the Jewish merchants and the African American community. The organization was led by Samuel J. Lieberman. Many times, I asked the organization to pay its rent in advance to help us meet our financial responsibilities, and the Eastside Merchants Association always obliged.

The Detroit branch of the NAACP had about 5,000 members when I arrived in 1950. Detroit's membership total made it the largest branch in the nation, as it had been since the NAACP started local branches in 1912. The Detroit branch was also the only one with an executive secretary, which was the top executive position in the organization. Gloster B. Current was the first, followed by Edward M. Swan. I was the third. Both Current and Swan had strong reputations and deep ties in the Detroit civil rights community, even before becoming executive secretary. I did not, but I think I was offered the job for several reasons. I had some NAACP leadership experience and a degree from Morehouse, which was already known as an intellectual cradle of civil rights activism. Second, I was willing to work for a very modest salary. And finally, some on the board may have felt that my youth disposed me to be more compliant to their interests. Even though we all shared the same mission, as in any organization, there were egos and politics behind the scenes. It would not be long before some of these political conflicts would come to a head.

In 1950, Detroit was the fourth-largest city in the nation. More than 1.8 million people lived in the city, the highest population the city would ever have. Eighty-four percent of the residents were white. Detroit was the epicenter of the Great Migration from the South, drawing both whites and blacks to the promise of good-paying jobs related to the auto industry. Detroit was also the birthplace of the burgeoning American middle class. The rate of home ownership in

Detroit was higher than in any other city in the country. The economic vitality of the city was a major reason why it boasted the largest NAACP branch.

The branch was also regarded as one of the most active and important in the nation, and again, much of this was related to economics. Generally speaking, in the history of the civil rights movement, the blacks who were most involved were self-employed professionals who made their living from a black clientele and, therefore, whose livelihood could not be directly threatened by white opponents of the struggle. These professionals included ministers, doctors, lawyers, and undertakers. Black doctors and lawyers were restricted in their practices by a system of discrimination that prevented them from having white clients and institutional access. A large cadre of activist black professionals evolved in Detroit because they served a black community that economically benefited from the robust manufacturing sector. As a result, the city was one of the most important centers of African American life in the nation. Still, of the 300,000 blacks in Detroit in 1950, only a tiny percent were members of the NAACP, and I knew that we had to increase our presence in the community if we were to address the problems of segregation, discrimination, and police brutality. These problems were in many ways quite similar to those in the Deep South. The principal difference was the heightened component of violence in the South used to enforce Jim Crow.

Our branch office had a staff of two: my secretary, Barbara Helms, and myself. We were strapped for money and needed to increase our membership to keep the office going. A young man, Samuel Simmons, frequently volunteered to help in the office and was eventually hired as my assistant. Samuel taught me to drive, since I had never had the opportunity or necessity to learn before. I then bought a used car and was able to get around the Motor City by myself. This was no small matter. It enhanced my efforts both to raise our membership and to do hands-on civil rights work in the community.

My membership campaign focused on the black churches. The church was crucial not only because it was the most powerful institution in the black community but because it did not have to answer to the white-controlled power structure. In this respect, the system of racial segregation created an opportunity to develop black institutions that could challenge the system. Ministers invited me to speak to their congregations about the NAACP's work. I tried to encourage the worshippers to subscribe to our $2 annual membership fee, half of which we sent to the national office. It was not an easy sell, and I was disappointed that the black community did not do more to support us. The community understood that the NAACP was the strongest organization of its kind and was out front fighting systemic racism and segregation. However, it was difficult to raise consistent funds for the long-term struggle.

I chose Tabernacle Missionary Baptist Church to be my place of worship. Tabernacle was located on the west side and attracted many of the leading black civil rights activists in the city. At Tabernacle, I got to know a young lawyer named Damon Keith. He was born on the west side and was determined to establish a law practice in the city that would fight racial injustice. Damon and I soon became best friends, and this friendship would become one of the most significant relationships of my life. Damon was very active in the NAACP and took the lead in some of our most important initiatives. We both understood the value of mentorship, and we cultivated an inner circle of older and wiser friends who advised us on strategy and tactics.

Our chief advisor was Joe Coles, who worked as a field investigator for the Mayor's Interracial Committee. Joe counseled us about how to work within the system and still be faithful to our cause and ideals. He always emphasized that strategy must be a vital part of courageous action. We must outthink an enemy that believed it was inherently smarter than we were. In our discussions, we would bring forth and debate different plans for winning the battles we faced against the white power structure. We would also discuss the strengths and weaknesses of various black leaders in town and how to deal with conflicts of interest and personality. Joe did not hesitate to criticize

Damon's and my actions and intentions. We listened without objection and sought to better ourselves for a cause much greater than ourselves.

Damon and I were amenable to advice, but we were also strong-willed, and sometimes our stubbornness would get the best of us. In the early years of our friendship we would occasionally get angry and not speak to each other for two or three weeks at a time. Fortunately, we soon outgrew this immature behavior and came to count on our friendship as an inspirational constant throughout the struggles, triumphs, and life changes that nearly sixty years of being together in the same city would bring.

One of the first issues I pursued in Detroit was housing segregation. The Detroit NAACP had achieved a historic legal victory in this area before my arrival. In 1948, the branch took up the cause of a black couple, Orsel and Minnie McGhee, who were prevented from buying a home in an all-white west-side neighborhood because of racially restrictive covenants. These covenants were specifically written into real estate deeds and proclaimed that only whites could purchase and occupy the properties. Blacks, Jews, Hispanics, and Asians were effectively excluded from neighborhoods that sought to permanently maintain their lily-white status. The Detroit NAACP took the McGhee case all the way to the United States Supreme Court, where it was combined with two other restrictive covenant cases that the Court agreed to hear. The lead case was *Shelley v. Kraemer,* out of St. Louis, Missouri. Thurgood Marshall argued the case for the NAACP before the Court, which then declared racial covenants unconstitutional. On paper, it was a victory against housing segregation; in practice, however, things were entirely different. Authorities in Detroit refused to enforce the Supreme Court decision. Detroit newspapers wrote detailed articles instructing and encouraging white homeowners to circumvent the law and keep blacks out. This was indicative of how the mainstream media in Detroit was but an extension of the white institutional power structure. This structure had one principal goal: to maintain the social, economic, and political advantages

Meeting on the *Sipes v. McGhee* restrictive covenants case. *Left to right:*
Edward Turner, president of branch; Attorney Francis Dent; Attorney
Constance Baker Motley of the NAACP Legal Defense and Educational Fund;
Attorney Willis M. Graves; myself. Detroit, 1952.

of the white population by restricting the rights and opportunities of
black people.

Race and neighborhood purity were the fundamental political
issues in Detroit. The campaigns for mayor and common council
centered on white fear of black progress. Albert Cobo took office in
1950, the year I arrived, for the first of his two elected four-year terms
as mayor. Cobo was a racist. His supporters expected him to stand
firm against the equality and encroachment of blacks. Cobo made
it clear that the city's official policy was segregation in public housing. Blacks would not be permitted to live in public housing units in

white neighborhoods, even though federal funds were used to build the units and federal law prohibited discrimination. The NAACP took the lead in fighting the Cobo administration's racist policies. We sued the Detroit Housing Commission in federal court and eventually won a favorable decision. Our guiding strategy in fighting issues of discrimination was to illuminate the law in order to fight an unjust system. Victories in court strengthened our cause, but the system was still recalcitrant. Even after the court ruled that public housing must be integrated, the Cobo administration enforced segregation in existing units and cancelled the construction of other buildings.

The housing crisis for blacks was acute and getting worse. The black population in the city was growing, but blacks were confined to live in particular areas, and black neighborhoods were specifically targeted for "urban renewal"—or, as we referred to it, "urban removal." With the full encouragement and financial support of the federal government, new highways were planned that necessitated the destruction of black districts. Paradise Valley, the commercial and cultural heart of black Detroit, was to be leveled to create Interstate 75. Blacks had no choice but to crowd into already overcrowded neighborhoods where landlords took advantage of demand by charging extortionate rents for substandard housing.

The discrepancy between housing availability for whites and blacks was staggering. From 1945 to 1955, about 100,000 private housing units were built on vacant land in the city, but only 2 percent of those units were available to nonwhite residents, even though, in 1955, almost a quarter of the city's population was black. Blacks had a greater need for public housing but had less access to these subsidized units. The waiting list for blacks was more than 6,000 names long, whereas there was virtually no waiting list for whites. On the housing issue alone, the pressure and frustration in the black community was mounting.

Black families who moved into white neighborhoods often faced violence and intimidation from the residents. When problems arose, the police, other authorities, and the newspapers looked the other way, so families would often call the NAACP for help. There were hundreds of racial incidents in the 1950s and early 1960s involving blacks brave enough to integrate an area. These blacks experienced prolonged harassment, broken windows, and, in extreme cases, bodily harm and arson. In one typical incident, a young black woman named Pedie and her mother moved into a white neighborhood on the west side. On their first evening in the house, about thirty-five white demonstrators gathered outside and repeatedly shouted, "Nigger go home." Pedie called me and I went to her house. As I walked to her door, the angry mob cursed and threatened me. I did not react or show any outward signs of fear. Once inside, I sat with the women for about three hours as we waited for the demonstration to subside. There was little else I could do but let them know that they were not alone. I called the police and they took the position that they could not disperse the crowd or offer protection to the women. Later I went down to the local precinct and spoke to the sergeant in charge. I told him that I would not accept the police excuse that white residents had the right to demonstrate in front of the woman's home and attempt to intimidate her into moving away. I wanted the authorities to know that they were on notice and that the NAACP would be watching and documenting the situation. Again, we knew that the law on the books was on our side, and our goal was to get law enforcement to act according to the law. I continued to check on Pedie and her mother. Eventually, the racist demonstrations and abuse ended when it became evident that the women would not be forced out of their home.

Blacks seeking a home in a white neighborhood also had to overcome the redlining and discrimination practices of the banks. In the fall of 1963, a young black woman came to my office and asked the NAACP to do something about First Federal Savings and Loan, the largest home-loan bank in the city. The woman said that she had been denied a mortgage for $13,000 even though she had $8,000 in savings at the bank and was eminently qualified for the loan. The only possible reason for her rejection was her race and the fact that the home was in a white area.

In addition to its discriminatory lending practices, First Federal had a policy of not hiring blacks for jobs that represented the company to the public. Of the bank's 340 employees, only twelve were black, and all of them worked as porters or janitors. The bank had been in the city for almost three decades and had never hired a black teller or clerk. We tried to negotiate directly with First Federal to change its policies, but the negotiations failed. The NAACP formed a discrimination action committee, and we decided to picket and stage sit-ins. We started picketing in October. The bank's tactic was to wait us out and hope that our will would be broken by the winter cold.

Led by our committee chair Abe Ulmer, we picketed for five months, but it was the sit-ins that ultimately forced the bank to come to terms with our demands. A group of us, including Abe's wife Trudy, would enter First Federal, sit down in the service line, and decline to move. The bank would call the police, and we would force the police to remove us physically since we refused to get up and walk. Our resistance was always peaceful, but the commotion inside and outside First Federal disrupted business and embarrassed the bank in the community. The sit-ins took a toll on us, both physically and financially, since we had to endure the arrests and defend ourselves in court. But we were determined to keep up the campaign for as long as it took. Finally, the bank called in a mediator named Ron Haughton. We reached a settlement in which First Federal pledged to change its discriminatory practices. The bank agreed to hire and train blacks as tellers and other financial jobs. The bank also agreed to end its pattern of racial bias against blacks seeking loans or mortgages.

Another issue we took on was the discrimination against blacks at restaurants, bars, and hotels. The eating and entertainment venues downtown and along Woodward Avenue, the main commercial thoroughfare in the city, refused to serve blacks. A few months after I arrived in Detroit, we set up a restaurant discrimination committee. The chair of the committee was Ernest Dillard. His wife, Jessie, also participated. We met every Friday at 6 p.m. at the black YMCA downtown. We would select the target of our sit-in demonstration for the evening and plot our strategy. The use of sit-ins as a protest tool was experimental, and our committee was one of the first in the country to try this tactic.

The law prohibited restaurants from racially discriminating, but restaurants in the city openly flouted the law. We entered the restaurant we chose and would wait to be served. Inevitably, an hour would go by without a waiter or any restaurant employee offering a menu or any service whatsoever. Then, one of us would get up and ask for the manager or maître d'. We would politely explain to the person in charge that we had been waiting patiently for an hour and that no one has come by to take our order. Invariably, the person would respond that the restaurant was "unable to serve us." We would ask for a more detailed explanation, but in most cases, the person would simply re-iterate the pat company line. Sometimes the person would ask what we wanted to order, and whatever we said would be met with, "Sorry, we don't have that," even though we could see other customers eating the same meals we requested. Our sit-ins caused a measure of tension among the white patrons in the establishment, although there was not a single occasion in all our protests when a patron took our side. The tension was part of our strategy. We wanted to be an embarrassment to the facility.

After the restaurant made it clear that we would not be served, we would leave and use a pay phone outside to call the police and ask that they come right away. What we said to the police on the phone depended on the venue. For example, after our sit-in at the Stage Door Bar, an upscale cocktail lounge on Woodward Avenue, we told the dispatcher that a fight was about to break out at the place. When the police arrived to speak to the management, we explained that the bar was in violation of the law because it refused to serve us. The manager then claimed the he denied us service because we had come to the bar intoxicated and must have had too much to drink at another establishment. We, of course, had not consumed any alcohol. But the manager knew that the law permits bars to refuse to serve customers who, in their own judgment, are drunk. And we knew, going into this protest, that the bar would likely use this excuse to cover its illegal actions. The senior officer at the scene knew it was an excuse, but instead of confronting the manager, he asked us why we wanted to stay when it was evident that we were not wanted. I then politely argued with the officer that it was our right to be served and we wanted the law to be enforced. The officer refused to act, but we had made our point. All of the discussions among the Stage Door management, the police, and ourselves took place in open view of the patrons and disrupted the normal activity at the establishment. It was the only way we could draw attention to the problem and fight this pattern of discrimination.

The restaurant discrimination committee met almost every week for a number of years. As a result, we visited almost every eating and entertainment venue in the city that practiced racial discrimination. We protested many establishments several times. We staged sit-ins at the Arcadia rink, which refused to admit blacks wanting to skate. We sat at the counter at the famous Brown Derby restaurant and asked for cups of coffee. The owner said he didn't have any coffee even though there was a big pot brewing in front of us. So we continued to sit and wait. Eventually, the owner decided to close the place early for the night and lose business rather than serve us. On a number of occasions, restaurant and bar owners took the extreme measure of shutting down for the night rather than dealing with us or the police, even though we all understood that the police would not make the owners abide by the law. The establishments did not want to cope with unwanted attention and agitation.

After nearly two years of protests, some of the major eateries in the city finally began to serve black customers. Meanwhile, the NAACP continued to pressure the major hotels in Detroit about their illegal discrimination practices. These hotels refused to rent their social facilities to blacks for private parties, meetings, and other events. Blacks were also customarily denied the opportunity to rent a room for an overnight stay. We made it clear to the hotels that we would consider legal action if they did not change their policies to comply with the law. Finally, in 1953, the Book-Cadillac Hotel downtown allowed two major black fraternities to hold their respective national conclaves at the hotel. Though it was still a struggle, other hotels eventually followed suit.

Racial discrimination forced blacks in Detroit, as in all major cities, to develop their own commercial district featuring small businesses, restaurants, bars, and entertainment places. Paradise Valley was only a few square miles in area, but it was a city within the city, a teeming convergence of entrepreneurial, cultural, and residential activity. I spent many evenings in Paradise Valley enjoying the pulsating energy of Hastings Street and its arteries. Renowned black musicians and entertainers performed in the Valley's clubs and theaters—names like Paul Robeson, Duke Ellington, Billie Holliday, Nat King Cole, Ella Fitzgerald, Sam Cooke, and Dick Gregory. Indeed, the Valley was a necessary stop for all the great black entertainers of the time. These entertainers and other black celebrities would stay at the Gotham Hotel, which was renowned for its world-class elegance and was the social center and crown jewel of the black community. The lobby was decorated with original paintings of prominent African American leaders in Detroit. In each of the hotel's 200 rooms was a copy of Langston Hughes's *Simple Speaks His Mind.* The Gotham was owned by the black businessman John J. White. It was well known in the black community that White ran a lucrative numbers ring and used some of the proceeds to embellish his hotel. One day in 1952, White walked into my office at the edge of the Valley. He complimented me on the civil rights work the branch was doing and said that he had heard that we were struggling financially. He handed me $1,000 to help meet our operating expenses and said that more would be forthcoming.

A decade later, John White was arrested on gambling charges. The Gotham Hotel was vacant and would soon be leveled, just like the rest of Paradise Valley. The urban renewal program that began under Cobo in 1950 continued under successive white administrations, gradually and irrevocably destroying the heart of the black business community. Black citizens and leadership had no say in the urban renewal program, and the white power structure did not hesitate to sacrifice black neighborhoods for the sake of highways designed to decentralize the city and facilitate suburbanization. In retrospect, I wish that we had fought sooner and more vigorously on the issue. By the time the black community was organized in opposition to the program, it was too late to stop its momentum. In our efforts to achieve integration, we ceded, unwisely, much of what African Americans had already built. We wanted integration to succeed so badly that we neglected to provide staunch support to centers of black enterprise.

The destruction of the Valley devastated black entrepreneurship in the city, and the consequences would resonate long after white flight was virtually complete. The writing was already on the wall in 1950 that the white populace wanted to leave the city rather than interact with blacks in neighborhoods, workplaces, parks, and restaurants. Moreover, those who fled had little regard for the kind of city they left behind. In the next fifty years, the city's overall population would fall by half, and its racial makeup would be reversed. Black leaders in the 1950s and 1960s struggled to desegregate the city and its institutions. Meanwhile, whites were abandoning the city in droves, eventually making Detroit the most segregated metropolitan area in the nation and undercutting our hard-fought victories for social justice.

As soon as it took office, the Cobo administration began to recast city commissions to promote its agenda of segregation. It forced out the only black member of the Housing Commission and gutted the Mayor's Interracial Committee, causing the resignation of some members, including Edward Turner, president of the Detroit NAACP board. The Interracial Committee was created after the city's race riot in 1943. Thirty-four people died in the two days of rioting; twenty-five of them were black. The white police force shot and killed seventeen people, all of them black.[3] The Interracial

3. Vivian M. Baulch and Patricia Zacharias, "The 1943 Detroit Race Riots," *Detroit News*, http://info.detnews.com/history/story/index.cfm?id=185&category=events.

Committee was chartered to study the racial issues that triggered the riot and to make constructive recommendations. The Cobo administration did not want an advisory group that conflicted with its agenda, but it still needed a prominent black leader to serve on the Interracial Committee in order to justify the committee's name. Cobo wanted to appoint Edward Davis to the committee. Davis was the first African American in the country to own an auto dealership. He was well regarded in the black community, and he responded to criticism about his pending appointment by saying that he felt could make a difference on the committee. As the leader of the NAACP, I wanted to state our official position on this controversy. Damon Keith and I met with our friend Joe Coles to discuss a course of action. We were of the same mind: the NAACP must take a strong stand against any black leaders who allowed themselves to be exploited by the mayor's office. Coles warned me that I would likely pay a price for my forthcoming outspokenness. I issued a statement to the Detroit newspapers that read: "No self-respecting Negro citizen can accept assignment to any city commission by Mayor Cobo." The statement became front-page news.

My comments created their own controversy. Some people thought they were too harsh toward Ed Davis and that they could be perceived as an insult to the chair of the Interracial Committee, Father John E. Coogan, a white liberal Catholic priest. Others understood the comments as necessary defiance against the conspicuous racism of the Cobo government. I knew that my actions were in the tradition of my mentors in the civil rights movement. When a situation arises, I was taught, you must strategize around your core principles and then act quickly before the dynamics of the situation change and an opportunity has slipped away. There are opportunities for agitation that build enthusiasm in the movement by reminding people of the struggle's resolute conscience. And so there was no doubt in my mind that I had done the right thing. Nevertheless, I was called in front of the Detroit NAACP board to explain my comments and defend my job as executive secretary.

It was early in my tenure, but I knew that the outcome of this board meeting would determine the tenor and limits of my leadership for a long time. My critics on the board accused me of being too aggressive in confronting the enemy, acting too often on my own, and exceeding the scope of an executive secretary's responsibilities. The president of the board, Ed Turner, defended me. Then, some friends who were active and important members of the branch spoke on my behalf. They included Damon, Horace White, and Joe Coles. Joe went to war for me. He told the board that I was a purposeful young man who had a long way to go and who must be allowed to express himself to stimulate constructive tension in the community. In addition, Joe argued that the board should not criticize and discourage me because the difficult work of civil rights activism required passion, initiative, and self-confidence. Ultimately, Joe's argument prevailed, and the experience invigorated my determination and sense of freedom to pursue the issues on which our office had to be out front.

The major hospitals in Detroit discriminated against black doctors and practiced segregation in the placement of black patients. The hospitals did not permit a black patient to share a semiprivate room with a white patient. They also allocated a certain number of beds to black patients in a segregated ward or floor of the hospital. Henry Ford Hospital, a facility with 560 total beds, allotted thirty-six beds for black patients, all on the same floor. Grace Northwest Hospital had no beds for black patients. Mt. Carmel only accepted black patients into private rooms. Women's Hospital allotted fourteen beds to black obstetrics patients and fourteen beds for other black female patients. These twenty-eight beds were kept separate from the 214 beds reserved for white patients.[4] The pattern of segregation was repeated at almost every major hospital. Because of the restricted number of hospital beds for blacks, there were many cases in which a

4. Women's Committee to End Discrimination in the Medical Services, "A Report on Medical Discrimination in the City of Detroit," 1952. Detroit Urban League Collection, Box 42, Hospital and Medical Center Studies, 1951–52, Bentley Historical Library, University of Michigan.

black patient in need of serious medical attention was denied admission into a hospital because its black quota was filled. In addition, black patients admitted to hospitals received inferior care, resulting in higher death rates and a greater incidence of complications that could have been avoided with more attentive care.[5]

The major hospitals in Detroit generally denied black doctors staff privileges, which refers to the ability to admit patients to a hospital and treat them there. In 1952, of the 250 black doctors in the city, only fourteen had staff privileges. Many hospitals did not even bother to respond to written requests from black doctors for staff privileges. Only six of the more than fifty hospitals in the city had professional relationships with black doctors.[6] Black doctors often had to relinquish care of their patients to white physicians to get those patients admitted to hospitals. This discrimination against black doctors hampered their training and development, and it hurt hospital care for black patients as well, since they were denied the knowledge and consideration of their regular physicians. Moreover, the discrimination reinforced the bitter stereotype that black doctors were inferior to white doctors in expertise. This stereotype was so ingrained in the system that it frequently affected black health-care consumers, who often preferred white doctors. Most Detroit hospitals also refused to train and hire black nurses. As a result, many hospitals had no black medical professionals.

The practices of discrimination and segregation in health care were not much different in Detroit than in the Jim Crow South. Since the large hospitals in Detroit received federal funding, I decided to attack

5. Women's Committee to End Discrimination in the Medical Services, "A Report on Medical Discrimination in the City of Detroit," 1952. Detroit Urban League Collection, Box 42, Hospital and Medical Center Studies, 1951–52, Bentley Historical Library, University of Michigan.
6. Women's Committee to End Discrimination in the Medical Services, "A Report on Medical Discrimination in the City of Detroit," 1952. Detroit Urban League Collection, Box 42, Hospital and Medical Center Studies, 1951–52, Bentley Historical Library, University of Michigan.

the issue by writing the office of the United States Surgeon General, which had the authority to investigate whether the hospitals were in violation of federal law. In cooperation with the Detroit Urban League and other advocacy groups, we collected data and case histories to document the segregation and discrimination. Despite the strength of evidence, I received a reply from the Assistant Surgeon General, Dr. Jack. C. Haldeman, that the government would not withhold funds from a Detroit hospital practicing segregation. I also wrote to hospital administrators in Detroit and informed them that the NAACP would take legal action unless they changed their policies. Our lengthy campaign made some inroads, but it was not until the landmark Civil Rights Act of 1964 that Detroit hospitals turned the corner in respecting the rights of black medical professionals and black patients.

Of all the issues of racial oppression in Detroit, the most volatile was police behavior and brutality toward black citizens. The virtually all-white police force acted like an army of occupation, bent on harassing, intimidating, and abusing blacks. The problem was so pervasive that almost every black adult in the city had a personal experience or observation involving racially motivated police misconduct. The misconduct included: disrespectful, profane, and racist language; unreasonable and humiliating bodily searches in public places; illegal arrests; and violent treatment. Black motorists stopped by the police were habitually taunted. The officers always addressed the black individual by his or her first name. Women were often called "honey child" and asked suggestively, "Where's your husband tonight?" Men were called "boy" and told, "This can't be your car," implying that blacks were incapable of owning nice things. The NAACP also regularly received complaints about the police confiscating money and items of value from the black residents they stopped.

The NAACP became the office of record for complaints of police misconduct against black citizens. When word got out in the black community that someone was making an effort to document incidents of brutality, victims came to my office to tell their stories.

White officers were notorious for beating up black citizens if they perceived any note of protest against offensive treatment. In many of these instances, police trumped up charges of drunkenness, disorderliness, or resisting arrest in order to apprehend innocent blacks who questioned why they were being harassed by the police. These charges were later dropped in court, but there was no redress for the violence inflicted on the innocent victims.

A young man named David Mundy came to my office in May of 1958, two days after he had been beaten by four plainclothes officers. The officers had just left a bar when they spotted David's girlfriend, Jo Ann Watkins, walking alone just after David said goodbye to her. The officers started propositioning Jo Ann as if she were a prostitute. David saw what was happening and came back to help Jo Ann. He asked the four men to stop talking to his girlfriend so rudely. One of men replied, "Do you mean that nigger bitch?" Another one then jumped on his back. David threw him off, and then all four men grabbed him. They then informed David that they were police. David stopped struggling, was handcuffed, and then put in an unmarked squad car. En route to the main precinct downtown, the two officers in back repeatedly hit David and called him "nigger," "monkey," and other racist taunts. One officer said, "We'll give you something to tell the NAACP." The beating continued at the precinct. David was charged with soliciting. He was found not guilty at trial.

A Chrysler autoworker, Mary Stewart, sat in my office a year before David's experience. She said she was driving at night with two girlfriends when they were stopped by a patrol car with three officers. Mary was ordered out of the car. She hesitated and then was forcibly removed from the driver's seat. One of the officers struck her in the face and shoulders with his nightstick, while the other officers restrained her by grabbing her hair and arms. Mary was thrown into the back of the patrol car and taken to the precinct. The desk sergeant asked her what had happened to her face. When Mary explained, the sergeant and the other officers laughed. Mary was taken to Receiving Hospital, where her face was stitched. She was then taken to the lockup at the main precinct. She spent two days in jail on the charge of drunk driving. The charge was later dismissed.

The firsthand accounts of police brutality gave me a unique perspective on the extent of the problem. Over a five-year period between 1956 and 1960, I collected evidence of 149 incidents of police brutality. The beating was so severe in forty-seven of these cases that the black victim required hospitalization. About a third of all police brutality incidents occurred at the precinct. In these cases, police arrested a black person, took the suspect to the precinct, and then beat him or her mercilessly in a detention room or elsewhere at the station. When asked about the incident later, the officers would say dismissively that the suspect accidentally fell out of the chair during interrogation or somehow managed to hurt himself or herself in lockup. For each incident of brutality that was reported to me, I had a photographer take pictures of the injuries sustained by the victim. I sent detailed complaints and evidence to police and city officials. These officials not only turned a blind eye but tacitly endorsed police misconduct as way of repressing the black populace. Offending police officers never admitted to the brutality and were rarely held accountable. In only four cases did the police department admit any wrongdoing on the part of the misbehaving officers.

In addition to notifying officials about police brutality complaints, I would often send a press release and accompanying photos to the major papers and to the *Michigan Chronicle,* a black-owned newspaper in the city led by Longworth Quinn. The major newspapers had a standing arrangement not to cover incidents of police brutality, and invariably, only the *Chronicle* would publish an article. Each time the *Chronicle* told a story, other victims and witnesses of police brutality would step forward and come to my office. They wanted someone to take note of the insult and injustice they suffered, and the NAACP was their only recourse.

In December of 1960, I testified before the United States Commission on Civil Rights. The commission was in Detroit to investigate racial issues in the city. I was asked to speak specifically on the issue of police brutality. After relating stories and statistics about the depth of the problem, I made several proposals for corrective action: First, I argued, an independent citizen review board should be established to adjudicate complaints of police brutality and make binding recommendations to the police department that would punish those officers found guilty of misconduct. Second, the police department needed to hire and promote more black officers. Only 3 percent of the police force was black, and these officers were concentrated in a few precincts and assigned the least significant police work.[7] Third, the department should provide meaningful race-relations training for existing officers. Fourth, the department should raise the educational and training requirements for new hires and increase its salaries to attract better-qualified people. Finally, city officials and community leaders needed to speak out against police brutality and make it clear that it must not be tolerated.

The city and police department would be slow to act on any of my proposals. I did not expect otherwise, because police misconduct and brutality were part of a broad policy to control blacks, contain them in segregated neighborhoods, relegate them to second-class citizenship, and keep them from aspiring toward better opportunities in employment, education, and quality of life. By not censuring the practices of police misconduct and brutality, the white corporate structure gave tacit approval to those entrenched practices. White leadership failed to heed a warning that black leadership brought to their attention: police brutality was causing a volatile rage to simmer in the black community that, if not calmed by significant reform, could one day erupt and engulf the city.

A month after I testified before the Civil Rights Commission, I experienced my own dangerous encounter with racist officers. I was leaving my home on Atkinson Street on the west side, not far from where the

7. G. Nelson Smith, "The Detroit Police Department's Policy and Practice in the Recruitment and Assignment of Police Officers," Detroit Urban League Community Services Department, December 1958. Walter Reuther Library, Wayne State University.

Detroit riot would begin some years later. It was a winter night and I was warming up my car and listening to the radio when a police car drove up next to my parked car and flashed its lights. I rolled down my window, and the officer on the passenger's side of the police car asked me brusquely, "What are you doing here?" I understood immediately that the officers were out to intimidate me, and I was determined not to back down. I responded indignantly, "What do you mean what am I doing here?" The officer quickly got out of his car, grasped the handle of my door, flung the door open, and yanked me out of the car. He twisted me around so that my back was to him and ordered me to put my hands up. The officer then grabbed the bottom of my overcoat and pulled it up over my head as he patted me down. He found my wallet, checked my license, and gave it back to me, perhaps recognizing who I was. I demanded that he explain why I had been accosted. He replied that they didn't have to answer my questions. I asked for their names, and he said, "We don't have to give you our names. Get them any other damn way you want." The officers then got back in their car. But before they could drive off, I walked directly in front of their car and stood so that they would have to run me over if they wanted to leave quickly. I yelled that if they were not going to give me their names, then I would take down their license plate number, go to the precinct, and file a complaint. "We don't give a damn," one of them yelled back.

I acted with a complete lack of fear when I stood in front of the officers' car. I certainly was aware, from all the stories I heard from police brutality victims, that the officers could have driven over me and then made some excuse about how I fell and hurt myself. But at that moment, I was determined to make a stand. I understood implicitly what Martin Luther King Jr. would later declare: "If an individual has not discovered something that he will die for, he isn't fit to live." Standing in front of the police car, I did in part what my anger led me to do and in part what my deepest belief needed me to do. The heightened mix of outrage and honor transcended fear.

After I returned to my car, the officers left right away, and I drove to the eighth precinct station. I was still incensed and resolute.

I thought of a strategy that was not altogether logical or sincere. I wanted to make a scene for the sake of making a scene. Inside the station, I started yelling for the sergeant in charge. I got everyone's attention and continued to carry on. I wanted to demonstrate to both the white officers and black citizens at the station that a black man who had been treated unjustly could come in and raise hell without being afraid to stand up to the system. The sergeant was quick to try to quiet me, and he asked me into his office. I gave him a livid and detailed account of what had happened. I left the precinct feeling that I had proved something to the people who were there and to myself.

Much as I lived with the dangers of being a civil rights leader in Detroit, I also understood that the South was a far more dangerous place for black leaders confronting systemic racism. The assassination of Medgar Evers on June 12, 1963, reminded me of this stark fact in visceral terms. Medgar, the field secretary for the NAACP in Mississippi, worked diligently to establish local chapters and fight Jim Crow under perilous circumstances. I would see Medgar at annual national NAACP meetings, and we kept in close contact. As companions devoted to the struggle, we were brothers.

Medgar helped lead an independent investigation of the murder of Emmett Till on August 28, 1955, in Money, Mississippi. Emmett was fourteen years old when he was savagely beaten and shot to death by racists for allegedly flirting with a white woman. His body was dumped into the Tallahatchie River. The murder provoked outrage among blacks across the country. The Detroit NAACP organized a demonstration for Sunday, September 25, 1955. I invited Medgar to the rally, and he agreed to speak. Two days before our scheduled rally, an all-white jury in Mississippi acquitted Emmett's murderers despite overwhelming evidence of their guilt. The perfunctory verdict intensified the outrage in the black community and amplified interest in our event.

The rally was to be held at 3 p.m. in Bethel African Methodist Episcopal Church. Bethel held 2,500 people, and it became apparent in the morning that the church could not accommodate everyone

Branch president Edward Turner, Medgar Evers, and myself before Medgar's speech in Detroit on September 25, 1955.

A crowd gathers to attend Medgar's appearance at Bethel African Methodist Episcopal Church in Detroit.

that wanted to come. Another church a block away, Scott Methodist, agreed to open its doors. More than six thousand people attended the rally at the two churches. It was the largest mass demonstration by blacks in Detroit history up until that time. Medgar spoke to the crowd about the courage of blacks in the South who were determined to participate in American democracy despite intimidation, sham "literacy tests," and the knifings and shootings of those who refused to surrender their right to vote. He asked the crowd, "Shall we stop now?" In solemn unison, they replied, "No." The Detroit NAACP took up a collection to help Emmett Till's family and to support the investigation into his murder. More than $14,000 was raised. All the money came from black Detroiters, since, as the newspapers noted, not one white person attended the rally to support the cause of ending racial injustice.

I spent time with Medgar and his wife Myrlie before and after the rally. His visibility during the murder investigation had increased the threats on his life, but he remained defiantly fearless. "You can kill a man," he often said, "but you cannot kill an idea." When Medgar was assassinated outside his home in 1963, I was in the midst of a campaign to stage peaceful marches in the virtually all-white Detroit suburbs to protest housing segregation and discrimination. In Warren and Redford, we encountered derisive jeers and racist taunts from angry whites that rivaled what civil rights marchers in the South experienced. The day before we marched in Dearborn, we were alerted that we would be met with violence, though it did not materialize. Since I was the executive secretary of the branch, I stood in the front line of every march and needed to set the example for my fellow marchers. I would not permit myself to be intimidated. We had fear to deal with, but we had to overcome it. When I learned that Medgar had been killed, after the initial shock and grief subsided, the first thing I thought was that although I had been faithful to the principles and obligations of our cause, I had not been exposed to the same dangers as Medgar. I felt chagrined. I had believed, until the moment of Medgar's death, that I was an equal companion in the struggle. But there was a vast difference between Detroit and Mississippi. I thought that I was on the firing line in Detroit and embodied the fearlessness that we in the movement were committed to. But Medgar faced everyday threats that required a level of courage to which I did not have to rise.

Six weeks after Medgar was killed, his widow Myrlie came to Detroit at my behest. The Detroit NAACP led a peaceful march of two hundred protesters against housing discrimination in the suburb of Oak Park. Myrlie and Rosa Parks were the honorary leaders and walked beside me.

In addition to our protests in the suburbs, we picketed apartment buildings in Detroit that refused to rent to African Americans. These demonstrations were organized by an action committee headed by Abe Ulmer, an NAACP member who worked as a Detroit school-teacher. We protested outside an upscale, all-white apartment building on the corner of John R and Kirby in the university cultural center. As a result, the management agreed to rent to several black professionals. We then began to picket an exclusive apartment building near the Detroit River. The protests embarrassed the white tenants, who then used their political contacts to press the new chief of police to intervene and stop our efforts. The tenants claimed their privacy rights were being violated.

The chief of police was George C. Edwards. He was a liberal Democrat who, at the behest of the recently elected mayor Jerome Cavanagh, had left his position as a justice on the Michigan Supreme Court to oversee the Detroit police force. Edwards was highly regarded for his civil rights advocacy, and Mayor Cavanagh brought him in to fulfill a promise to the black community to address the problem of racist police behavior. Cavanagh was first elected in November of 1961, largely on the strength of the black vote. Black leadership in the city, including Damon Keith and myself, rallied support for the Cavanagh campaign among African Americans. The incumbent mayor Louis Miriani had alienated the black community by implementing an aggressive anticrime crackdown in which the police would harass and often arrest any black individual who was deemed

The march against housing discrimination in Oak Park, Michigan, in 1963. In the front row, third from the end on the left, is Abraham Ulmer. Next to him is Rosa Parks, and then Edward Turner. I am on the far right, carrying a sign. Next to me is Myrlie Evers.

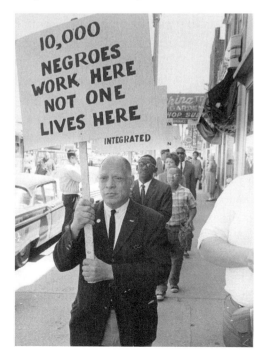

The NAACP-led march in Dearborn in 1963 to protest housing discrimination and segregation. *Front to back:* branch president Edward Turner, myself, Bobby Person, Joya Person.

to be "in the wrong place at the wrong time." Cavanagh, who at the time was a thirty-three-year-old attorney with very little political experience, pledged to end this policy and to build bridges with the black community. In the 1961 election, 30 percent of the electorate was black, and 85 percent of them voted for Cavanagh, propelling him to an upset victory and precipitating a hopeful celebration in the black community.

After Chief Edwards was contacted by the tenants of the all-white apartment building, he personally called on the NAACP board to restrain our action committee from demonstrating against private housing facilities. The board was divided on the issue, but a majority felt that the organization needed to honor the personal appeal from someone who was a strong friend of the black community. I was deeply disappointed with the board's decision. I, too, considered Chief Edwards to be an ally. He had approached me about getting the NAACP's support for raising the wages of Detroit police officers. This was an unprecedented gesture of respect toward our organization from the police administration, and we agreed to endorse the pay increases if it would help improve the department. However, I thought Chief Edwards's request on the apartment issue was unreasonable because it deprived us of the only tactic we had to force the building's owners to end their discriminatory practices. In my fourteen years as executive secretary of the branch, this was the only instance where I felt we compromised our convictions and lost our way in attacking an issue.

The summer of 1963 in Detroit featured the largest civil rights march in American history to that point. The march, called the "Walk to Freedom," was organized by Reverend C. L. Franklin of New Bethel Baptist Church; the future state senator James Del Rio; the UAW president Walter Reuther; Benjamin McFall, owner of a leading funeral home in Detroit; and other community leaders. It was planned for June 23. At the end of the four-mile march down Woodward Avenue to Cobo Hall, Martin Luther King Jr. was to address the crowd.

The NAACP was not involved in planning the "Walk to Freedom." March organizers did not engage the NAACP in the process, and some frictions developed around the perceived snub. Although there was tremendous cooperation among the various sectors of black leadership, there was also competition to be out front on the prominent issues and opportunities facing the moment. This competition was made more intense by a growing controversy among black leaders about whether the NAACP needed to be in the lead on every significant civil rights issue. Some people in the community at that time believed that the NAACP was actually against the march because of the risk that its grand scale might prove to be a disappointment and thus would harm the momentum of the movement. However, I can say categorically that the majority of the branch leadership did not oppose the march, even though some board members were initially skeptical about the idea. As the excitement about the march grew in the community, we understood that it was bound to be a milestone for the city and the nation. We supported the march but had to recognize that we did not have leadership participation in it. Because the branch was at the forefront of the all the issues of segregation, discrimination, and police brutality, not being a part of this landmark civil rights event particularly concerned me, and I knew that I had do something to advance the NAACP's interest.

I came up with the idea that we should print a thousand placards that simply said "NAACP." I got an estimate from a silk-screen company that this rush order would cost $750. I asked the board to convene a closed-door meeting. The board authorized the funds, and we all agreed to keep my strategy a secret. I approached a trusted volunteer, Phil Gordon, to help me get the signs made and then bring them to the staging area for the march. We set the signs out and told marchers that the signs were there for the taking. Within minutes, all one thousand signs were gone.

An estimated 125,000 people marched in the Walk to Freedom. The event was covered by national and international media. When I watched the network news programs that same evening, I saw a sea of NAACP signs toward the front of the march. I was thrilled. Looking at the pictures, viewers could not help but come away with the impression that the NAACP had played a prominent role in organizing the event and making it successful. I did not want to take credit for others' work, but I did not want to see the NAACP shut out of this important coverage.

At the march, I watched the procession from the roof of Cobo Hall. It was a breathtaking experience, and tears of joy welled in my eyes. I believe that every person who marched that day felt that they were making strides toward the African American hope and determination to be free. Up to this time, this was the most powerful statement of civil rights in the nation, and indeed the world. I watched the marchers file into Cobo to hear Martin speak. There was a deep irony at work. This venue, named after a racist mayor, was transformed by a man who would become the iconic voice for racial justice. Twenty years ago on this same day, the worst race riot in U.S. history happened in Detroit. The Walk to Freedom was a model of peaceful protest and racial cooperation.

Martin delivered his "I Have a Dream" speech to the thousands gathered at Cobo. This was the first time Martin gave the address. He would deliver it again two months later before a vast crowd at the Lincoln Memorial in the nation's capital. Martin's voice this day in Detroit was never better. He had worked out the structure, rhythm, and climactic part of the speech so that it moved like a great piece of music. We were all utterly spellbound. He spoke about the difference between segregation in Detroit and the Deep South. "We must come to see," he said, "that de facto segregation in the North is just as injurious as the actual segregation in the South." Ours was a single struggle because "injustice anywhere is a threat to justice everywhere."

I spoke to Martin that night and congratulated him on his triumphant speech. We spoke as old friends, and as usual, I addressed him as "M.L." He wanted my advice on an important matter, but time and his pressing commitments did not permit that conversation then. We agreed to resume our talk after the March on Washington. My former and young classmate at Morehouse College was now, without a doubt, the indisputable leader of the civil rights movement.

Martin and I had remained in touch when I came to the leadership post at the Detroit NAACP. We would see each other when he was in town, and we corresponded and spoke by phone regularly. As he grew into his calling, the demands of his schedule made it increasingly more difficult for him to devote time to friends and their interests. I understood this, though on occasion it was a source of frustration. There were things that Martin could have done to help the NAACP that he chose not to do because he had taken up the challenge of building the Southern Christian Leadership Conference. The NAACP and the SCLC were not altogether complementary organizations in the movement, and we sometimes found ourselves competing for leadership roles, resources, and publicity. Whether or not we wanted to acknowledge it, the unfortunate reality was that each of the various civil rights groups was also a kind of business, and in this business, success was measured by who got what done.

In March of 1958, I wrote to Martin and asked him to appear at an event for the Detroit NAACP's Freedom Fund Campaign. Martin was already scheduled to be in Detroit, and I wanted him to fit us into his schedule. I was very disappointed when Martin declined my invitation, and I wrote him back asking him to "be ever mindful that a helping hand from you is ten, twenty-five, one hundred times more productive than that of countless other friends whose resources and influence can never quite measure up to their interest in this work." Martin responded when he returned to his office in Montgomery, Alabama. He apologized for not being able to attend our event. He continued:

> I do hope you will understand that my non-acceptance was not due to a lack of interest, but to the tremendous pressures of an overcrowded schedule.
>
> My physician has insisted that I slow down or face the tragedy of a physical break down. There are ever so many things that I would like to do, that I would enjoy doing, such as being with you on your Freedom Fund program, but they are physically impossible . . .

Let me commend you for the great work you are doing with the Detroit branch. I am always happy when I hear of your success. You are doing a job, not only for Detroit and the Negro, but for the whole of American democracy. You have my prayers and best wishes for continued success in all of your endeavors.

Sincerely yours,
Martin Luther King, Jr.

Martin's gracious letter disarmed my frustration. It reminded me of the enormous stress he was under and of the strength of our friendship, since he had taken the time to write a candid response.

The Freedom Fund Dinner was in its third year when Martin and I exchanged letters about the event. The NAACP started this campaign in 1956, and it soon became the most important fundraising event not only for the branch but also for the NAACP as a whole. I conceived the idea of the Freedom Fund Dinner in late 1955 after the national chairman of the NAACP, Dr. Channing H. Tobias, had called for the establishment of a one-million-dollar "Fight for Freedom" fund. Each of the branches was asked to create a new fundraising event, with half of the proceeds going to the National Freedom Fund and the other half going to the branch itself. I felt that the black professional community in Detroit was ready to support an elegant and signature dinner event with a ticket price of $100 per couple. To be successful, the event needed to be well-managed and well-marketed and feature, as its keynote speaker, someone greatly admired in the black community. Most of all, the dinner needed to have great social appeal.

My confidence that the idea would succeed was inspired by my organizing experiences and by observations of the dynamics of fundraising events. In 1953, the branch was in acute financial difficulty. In general, we were always strapped for cash, and we lived with this struggle as a routine part of our mission. We had often had a hard time making the rent, and I sometimes would not collect my own modest salary so that my assistant would be paid. But this time, the financial problem threatened our work, and I was quite worried. I

In the Holiday Room of the Gotham Hotel in Detroit, 1953. *Left to right:* Edward Turner, branch president; Walter White, executive secretary of the NAACP; Dr. James J. McClendon; Mamie Thompson; Josephine Baker; Joseph Craigen.

called Josephine Baker, whom I had met on a previous occasion, and told her that the branch was desperate for money. I asked her for a few minutes of her time when she came to town to appear at a private reception at the Gotham Hotel. She graciously agreed. The event drew many black professionals who wanted to see this already legendary and glamorous performer. Also in attendance were Nat King Cole and his wife Maria, Dr. Benjamin Mays, and Walter White. Josephine spoke to the gathering and made a passionate appeal to support the branch and its important work. She said that she would start the process by immediately contributing $100 in cash. Within minutes, every man in the room followed suit. This experience taught me something about the effective use of star power and peer pressure.

I took my idea of an ambitious fundraising dinner to the president of the branch, Ed Turner. He approved it and told me to move forward.

A few board members expressed doubts that the idea could work, but these voices were drowned out by supporters. Though the ticket price was steep, I never doubted that there were enough members of the black community who had the means and the willingness to support the event if it smartly combined allure and obligation. I decided to ask Thurgood Marshall, who was chief counsel of the NAACP, to be the keynote speaker. Thurgood was the most charismatic figure in the NAACP at the time. His work on the landmark *Brown v. Board of Education* case in 1954 had earned him a towering reputation in the black community. When Thurgood agreed to appear at the dinner, the event acquired a prestige and authority that signaled its due importance.

We decided that the first people we should approach about attending the event were black physicians. Accordingly, we needed a prominent medical professional to serve as the first chair of the Freedom Fund Dinner. Our first choice was Dr. DeWitt T. Burton, who had developed Burton Mercy Hospital, which served black patients and physicians. Dr. Burton was one of the strongest members of the branch, but he reasoned that he could be most effective working behind the scenes to get colleagues and clients to support the event rather than serving in an official capacity. His assessment proved to be right. We turned to Dr. Alfred E. Thomas to be the first chair.

The first dinner was scheduled for April 1956. Dr. Thomas assembled a small group of branch executives: Moses Fritz, who served as branch treasurer, Ed Turner, and me. Dr. Thomas then arranged for our group to make a presentation to a meeting of the Detroit Medical Society at the Gotham Hotel in February. The Detroit Medical Society was an association of black doctors. The doctors were very receptive to our idea. They were also looking for a way to honor a recently fallen colleague. On February 18, Dr. Thomas Brewer, who helped organize the NAACP chapter in Columbus, Georgia, was murdered. A white policeman shot him seven times after Dr. Brewer refused to yield to death threats demanding that he stop his advocacy for equal voting rights. Dr. Brewer had many friends and close family in Detroit,

The first Freedom Fund Dinner Committee in 1956. *Left to right:* Joseph Craigen, a member of the Detroit NAACP board; Emory Jackson, editor of the *Birmingham World;* Leon Wallace; Dr. Alfred Thomas, the committee chair.

including two sisters and a brother who was also a doctor. We asked all fifty-nine doctors at the meeting to buy tickets to the Freedom Fund Dinner. They responded in force and gave the campaign an initial momentum that would carry it to success. In addition, Dr. Lionel F. Swan agreed to serve as co-chair of the dinner. At his own expense, he hired two women to call other black doctors and ask them to participate in the event. If a doctor said yes, one of the women would immediately go the doctor's office and complete the transaction.

We enlisted the *Michigan Chronicle* to help with the marketing of the event. Each week leading up to the dinner, the *Chronicle* published the names of everyone who had bought tickets. The recognition was a source of pride for supporters. It also applied subtle pressure on those who had not purchased tickets and whom the community expected to be in attendance. Ultimately, three hundred tickets were sold, virtually all of them to African Americans. Dr. Burton persuaded many of his business acquaintances to subscribe. He even secured a $100 cash contribution from Robert McNamara, a top-level executive at Ford Motor Company who did not want to be recognized because of the possible backlash from white car buyers. McNamara later became Secretary of Defense in the Kennedy administration.

The first Freedom Fund Dinner was held at the Latin Quarter, which was the most elegant banquet facility at the time that accepted black clientele. The evening was a magnificent success and created a great deal of anticipation for next year's event. It also provided impetus to the branch as a whole. In 1957, Damon Keith directed the membership campaign. Under Damon's leadership, branch membership reached 29,000, the highest total any NAACP branch in the country would ever have. Damon also served as a co-chair of the annual dinner and became the first person to reach $10,000 in ticket sales. Each subsequent year, the event raised more money than the year before. The Freedom Fund Dinner almost single-handedly lifted the branch out of its financial straits.

Our fundraising success in Detroit intrigued Martin Luther King. When he became head of the Southern Christian Leadership Conference in 1959 and moved to Atlanta, we began to communicate more often than before. Because we were bound by friendship, Morehouse, and the movement, Martin sought my counsel about raising money, and I freely offered my advice. I understood that Martin would not be able to appear at our Freedom Fund events because the NAACP and the SCLC, in the larger context, were competitors for the civil rights dollar. The private context was very different, however. Whenever I traveled to Atlanta, I visited Martin and his close associate Ralph Abernathy. We met in either Ralph's home or Martin's home and talked at length about fundraising strategies, among other things. It was a very relaxed atmosphere, and each of us felt that we could be ourselves. It was a place of respite from the demands and personas of the struggle. Martin loved a good joke of any sort and was always appreciative of new material. Ralph and I were happy to oblige.

Securing the funds to do the work we needed to do was a continual frustration for all of us in the movement. There was never enough money to fight on the number of fronts we wanted to fight, and we felt disappointed by the disparity between our passionate convictions and our limited resources. The black community in general was not well off, but even so, it could have done better in supporting a cause that meant everything to its future. In particular, the contributions of the black middle class were not commensurate with either its ability to help or the stake it held in our efforts. We in the leadership did not complain about this fact. Rather, we were always seeking for ways to involve more people in the movement. Even though the marches and protests were attracting greater numbers, in reality, a relatively small percentage of blacks were participating, and we wished that more blacks would become active and recognize that there was no honorable way to avoid confronting the enemy.

I was one of the more than 200,000 people in front of the Lincoln Memorial on August 28, 1963, to witness the songs and speeches of the March on Washington. I was not near the stage. I was a soldier in the field gathered with the multitude who had come from all over the country to demonstrate for congressional passage of President John Kennedy's Civil Rights Bill. Martin's "I Have a Dream" speech was the closing and climactic moment of the watershed event. I did not expect to talk to Martin in person in Washington, but we found each other at a private reception later in the evening. Few words were exchanged between us, since it was impossible to articulate the scope and depth of the experience that day. We embraced and shared an unspoken awe of this historic event. In the long and painful struggle, this was a moment of considerable optimism for the civil rights movement. The conscience of the nation was roused. John Kennedy was in the White

1966 Freedom Fund
Dinner participants.
Left to right: Dr. Robert
Weaver, secretary of
HUD; Dick Gregory
(front); Forrest Green;
Dr. James J. McClendon;
Judge Wade McCree.

1966 Freedom Fund
Dinner. *Left to right:*
Dr. Robert C. Weaver,
Beatrice Preston,
Benjamin McFalls.

1970 Freedom Fund
Dinner. *Left to right:*
Retired Chief Justice
Earl Warren, myself,
State Supreme Court
Justice Theodore Souris,
Judge Damon Keith.

At a meeting with federal officials regarding civil rights legislation, Washington D.C., 1963. *Left to right:* Joseph Coles, myself, Damon Keith, Attorney General Robert Kennedy, Richard Marx, State Senator David Holmes, Vice President Lyndon Johnson.

House. His brother Bobby was Attorney General. Federal legislation to end segregation and discrimination was pending. Martin had emerged as a dramatic voice for the struggle. The NAACP, the SCLC, the Urban League, and the Congress of Racial Equality (CORE) were strong and effective organizations. We believed that we had turned the corner, and though the distance to our goals was still significant, it seemed much less daunting than it had just a few years before.

President Kennedy was not initially in favor of the March on Washington. He was concerned that some congressional members who were wavering on the civil rights legislation would react defiantly to being pressured by a mass rally at their doorstep. After Kennedy was unable to dissuade march organizers, however, he lent his support to the event. Kennedy's stance on the march reminded me of a pivotal moment in his campaign for the presidency when he made a remark that was contrary to the aspirations of the civil rights movement. Civil rights leaders in Detroit decided that we needed to intervene and ask the candidate to set the record straight.

During the Democratic presidential primaries in the spring of 1960, Senator Kennedy was asked to comment on the sit-in protesters and freedom riders in the South. Kennedy responded that he supported the protesters insofar as they did not misbehave. Black leaders around the country were indignant at Kennedy's tepid and conditional endorsement of the valiant efforts of civil rights activists in the South working under conditions of great duress and danger. Even before this remark, Kennedy was not doing well with black voters. Although he was liberal-minded and in principle an advocate for the civil rights movement, he was deliberately cautious about stating his unqualified support for the cause and risking further alienation from white Southern Democrats. He needed those white votes to win the presidency, and he compromised his civil rights language to try to keep them in the fold. This compromise offended many in the black community. Leaders such as Jackie Robinson and Adam Clayton Powell spoke out against Kennedy's civil rights position. Some leaders even suggested that Kennedy's Republican opponent, Richard Nixon, might be a better choice in terms of advancing the cause.

After Kennedy's misguided campaign remark, which further damaged his standing with black voters, I met in Detroit with Damon Keith, Joe Coles, Richard Austin, Nicholas Hood, Horace Sheffield, Forrest Green, Jim Wadsworth, and Mildred Jeffrey. We decided that we must find a way to meet with Kennedy and persuade him to abide by his deepest principles and offer unconditional support to the civil rights struggle. Mildred got in touch with Michigan governor G. Mennen Williams, a trusted ally of the movement and a liberal Democratic leader who knew Kennedy personally and could arrange the meeting we wanted. Governor Williams contacted the senator and we were invited to go to Washington and speak directly to Kennedy in his Georgetown home. Unfortunately, I was unable to attend the meeting because of illness. There are very few important appointments in my life that I have missed and deeply regret. This occasion tops the short list.

Damon later reported to me what transpired at the meeting. Mildred Jeffrey, a Michigan delegate to the Democratic National Convention, outlined our argument to Kennedy. However, Kennedy still did not grasp why his civil rights remarks upset the black community. The contingent of Detroit leaders then tried to explain to him why he was losing the respect of black voters. Finally, Governor Williams said to Kennedy, "Look Jack, what they are saying is that if I invite you to dinner in my home, I do not ask you to wash your hands before you come. I assume that you are a responsible human being." Kennedy nodded his approval, and he promised to seize whatever opportunities would emerge in the future to try to correct the bad impressions he had made with black voters by having admonished civil rights protesters to behave during their rightful and peaceful disobedience.

Not long after our meeting, such an opportunity arose, and Kennedy stepped up. He gave a speech in which he extolled the sit-in demonstrators seeking to integrate restaurants and other facilities. The protests, he said, proved that "the American spirit is coming alive again." He commended the demonstrators for their nonviolent actions and said that the social tensions caused by the protests were "part of the price of change."[8] Kennedy firmly allied himself with the movement and its goals of equal justice and said that government needed to get involved to help realize those goals. Kennedy's categorical support for the movement turned the tide with black voters. In the November election, he captured more than 70 percent of the black vote and won the presidency by a narrow margin. The black vote was a decisive factor.

8. Anthony Lewis, "Kennedy Salutes Negroes' Sit-ins," *New York Times*, June 24, 1963.

With a strong ally in the White House, we believed we were on the verge of major breakthroughs. President Kennedy proposed his sweeping Civil Rights Bill on June 11, 1963, the day before Medgar Evers was murdered. The Great March came two and a half months later. The heightened optimism we felt after Washington, however, would soon suffer terrible setbacks. Just two weeks later, the Sixteenth Street Baptist Church in Birmingham was firebombed by the Ku Klux Klan. Four girls burned to death. The FBI, under J. Edgar Hoover, refused to fully investigate the horrific crime. In November, President Kennedy was assassinated, and a terrible pall fell on us all. Moments of past triumph seemed to lose their luster and meaning. The remorseless violence took a toll on my optimism and brought me to a point where I felt overwhelmed. It was painfully evident that the forces of evil had escalated their attacks just when our dreams of justice seemed more attainable. I wondered if it might be impossible to do the job that had to be done, and I despaired that nothing I had accomplished was adequate, particularly when people were losing their lives in the Deep South fighting the enemy on the front line. But I also understood that there was no honorable way to escape the commitment and heartbreak of the civil rights struggle.

I spent fourteen years as the executive secretary of the Detroit NAACP. I took the job in 1950 with the intention of staying three years, but it was soon apparent that the job and the city had other plans for me. Those fourteen years were the most vital and productive years of my life. To realize the challenges of my civil rights work, I had to cultivate expertise in communications, organizational psychology, political strategy and tactics, press relations, and fundraising. The work made me realize that I belonged in Detroit. I came to the city not knowing anyone here, but the network of relationships that grew around me made the city home, and I knew that I could not leave it. The professional and personal ties rooted my life's meaning in this place.

A short time after I came to Detroit, I started to date a young black woman who was a student at Wayne State University. Her name was

Thelma Thorpe. I first met her when she came to my office seeking help from the NAACP after she had been fired from a government job because of her alleged Communist sympathies. Thelma was a non-active member of American Youth for Democracy. The group had come under intense scrutiny from the anti-Communist witch hunt of McCarthyism, and people on the group's membership list were unceremoniously dismissed from their jobs after the government obtained the list. I was very concerned that the constitutional principles of our nation were under attack by ideologues who propagandized that Communists were everywhere and were an internal threat to the nation. So, when Thelma brought her case to my attention, I immediately called two black lawyers—Henry Heading and John Williams—and persuaded them to represent her on a gratis basis, since she could not afford counsel. Thelma lost her case at the local hearing, but her lawyers thought that we should appeal to the next level. I decided to engage a lawyer who had a strong anti-Communist reputation to represent Thelma on appeal. This attorney, Abe Zwerdling, won the case, and the government agreed to rehire Thelma. During the lengthy legal process, I began seeing Thelma. We married in 1951, even before the case finally and favorably concluded.

In retrospect, I think my becoming involved with Thelma and then asking her to become my wife was in part my own statement of defiance against the system of injustice that she was fighting. I also realize that during our marriage, I gave much of my time and my best energies to my work, which was detrimental to our relationship. Thelma and I had three sons, Averell, Brian, and Carl, but after thirteen years of marriage, we were divorced, just as I was departing as leader of the Detroit NAACP.

A few years later, I married Loretta Jenkins. I first met Loretta in circumstances that resembled the way I met Thelma: Loretta came to my NAACP office with four other African American women to file a complaint. All five women were "practical nurses"—nurses who had limited training and who worked under the supervision of registered nurses. The five women told me that the hospital where they were working practiced racial discrimination in its treatment of members of the practical nursing staff. I looked into the matter, but it was never resolved. After Loretta and I were married, she continued to work as a practical nurse.

Loretta and I had one child together, David. I also gained two other children in the marriage to Loretta. Loretta had a son and daughter from her first marriage, Wendell and Angela. The psychologist Erik Erikson has said, "Children confirm parenthood." By this, he meant that the measure of being a parent is how the child comes to feel about you. I loved Angela and Wendell so much that they ultimately claimed me as their father.

In the course of things, the marriage to Loretta fell into great difficulty because of financial issues and other problems, and we were eventually divorced. I felt a deep anguish about this, as I did in my first marriage, because I did not want to be separated from my children. But it was quite evident that Loretta and I could no longer live together. After my second marriage ended, I began to wonder whether I was fit for the commitment of marriage and whether I had all that it takes. I would not redeem these personal doubts until Chacona Winters came into my life.

CHAPTER 4

Detroit Public Schools

It was a difficult decision to leave my position as executive secretary of the Detroit NAACP. I felt that our efforts against discrimination and segregation were getting better results as the civil rights movement gained momentum, and I wanted to continue to push the organization to do more. In addition, I enjoyed a high level of freedom to formulate new initiatives and plan ways to carry them out. However, I was also at a crossroads, both personally and professionally. I had a family to support. My salary at the NAACP was $9,000. We were living paycheck to paycheck without getting ahead. I tried not to dwell on this situation because I felt I was doing meaningful work and being faithful to my calling. But I was thirty-eight years old and I had other obligations. If an opportunity came along that would enable me to continue the fight against racial justice while earning a better living, I was ready to consider it.

In 1963, Michigan became the first state to enshrine a civil rights commission in its constitution. The new state agency was given the responsibility "to investigate alleged discrimination against any person because of religion, race, color or national origin in the enjoyment of civil rights guaranteed by law and by this constitution."[9] The Michigan Civil Rights Commission (MCRC) began its work at the beginning of 1964. It had eight members, each appointed to four-year terms. Governor George Romney insisted that the commission have bipartisan composition and leadership. The first co-chairs were Damon Keith and John Feikens. Damon was very active in the Democratic Party; John was the former head of the Michigan Republican Party.

9. Section 29 of Article 5 of the Michigan Constitution of 1963.

Damon and John asked me to become deputy director of the MCRC. In the course of our work together, John became a stalwart friend of both Damon and mine.

Members of the MCRC, led by William T. Gossett, made a commitment to significantly improve upon my NAACP salary. Gossett was a prominent Detroit attorney and great benefactor of the United Negro College Fund. The salary offer of $14,500 had to be approved by the state senate. Senator James Del Rio, who was one of the key organizers of the 1963 Detroit civil rights march, objected to my proposed salary. Eventually, the matter was resolved, and I joined the MCRC in June of 1964.

The first director of the MCRC was Burt Gordin, who was brought in from Philadelphia. Burt had many years of experience in civil rights work, but to be honest, I believe that he was not more qualified than I to head the office. It was a sign of the times in racial practice that there had to be a white director and a black deputy director. My major responsibilities were in the areas of education and public relations. The work was interesting but not as fulfilling as I had hoped. I did not feel that I was making enough of a difference in the fight for civil rights, and I missed my work as executive secretary of the NAACP. I still participated in some of the branch's programs, but as a matter of principle, I believed it was important that my successor make the job his own without the tension of having the previous leader around. So, I sought to be supportive of the NAACP and still keep a respectful distance while working for the MCRC. After two years with the MCRC, another opportunity arose that presented the kind of challenge I sought.

"Negro Gets a Top City School Job." This was the front-page headline in the *Detroit Free Press* on September 14, 1966. The article reported that I was the first black assistant superintendent in the history of Detroit's school system. I was appointed assistant superintendent for community relations by the Detroit Board of Education. The board acted on the recommendation of Dr. Norman Drachler, who once held the same position and who had been recently promoted to superintendent. Some in the administration questioned whether the board should appoint someone who was not a trained educator, but those voices did not gather support, and I became the highest ranking African American in the system. My duties included establishing effective communications between the schools and the community. I knew that this would be a challenging assignment because public education had become the primary battlefront in the overlapping issues of desegregation, equal opportunity, and black nationalism. In addition, the issue of student rights and demonstrations was becoming increasingly intense.

In 1966, the Detroit school system had the most students it would ever have. The district was the fourth largest in the country. All urban districts were in transition, but none more so than Detroit. The pattern of segregation in Detroit was more pronounced than in any other major northern school district and was increasing at a greater pace than in other cities. Of the nearly 300,000 students in Detroit public schools in 1966, 56 percent were black.[10] The district had twenty-two high school constellations. (A constellation included the elementary and middle schools that fed the high school.) Four constellations were almost entirely white, and five were almost entirely black. The other constellations were losing white students at an alarming rate because of rampant white flight and blockbusting.[11] As a result, the racial makeup of many schools changed dramatically from one year to the next, reflecting the sudden changes in those neighborhoods. This turnover in the student population placed enormous strain on the staff and resources of the affected schools. By 1970 the school system was almost two-thirds black, and the pattern of segregation was even more pronounced. Forty-four schools had fewer than

10. Division of School-Community Relations, "Racial-Ethnic Distribution of Students and Employees in the Detroit Public Schools," October 1970. Walter Reuther Library, Wayne State University.

11. Division of School-Community Relations, chaired by Arthur L. Johnson, "Report of Recommendations of Task Force on Quality Integrated Education in Detroit Schools," September 13, 1967.

twenty black students, and 111 schools had fewer than twenty white students. Projected trends indicated that the district would be nearly all black in twenty years' time.[12]

Against this backdrop of racial segregation, other powerful issues and events had a destabilizing effect on the school system. It was a turbulent time in American society in general and in Detroit in particular. The Vietnam War raged and antiwar protests were in full fever. Martin Luther King and Robert Kennedy were assassinated in 1968. The Detroit riot gripped the city in the summer of 1967. The riot was part of an epidemic of disturbances in American cities stemming from conditions of racism, poverty, and police brutality. Impatience with the painfully slow progress of civil rights efforts spawned a black nationalism movement that captured the interest of many black youth and others in the black community. It was a time when established authority was being challenged. I had spent a good part of my life agitating against the system from without. I was now trying to change the system from within at a time when anyone associated with the system was regarded with great suspicion, especially by activist African American youth, whose passion I instinctively understood even when they looked at me as the enemy.

It was also a time of considerable distrust between the black community and the school system. The system had historically promoted a policy of racial segregation in order to achieve, in its own euphemistic phrasing, "harmonious" schools. To relieve overcrowding in black schools, black students were bused to other black schools instead of nearer white schools. The board altered feeder patterns and school boundaries to maintain predominantly white schools and restrict black attendance. White students going to high school could opt out of a predominantly black school and chose instead to attend a white

12. "Report of Summer Task Force on Desegregation-Integration Alternatives in the City of Detroit School District," chaired by Arthur L. Johnson. Released on September 24, 1971.

school farther away.[13] Because of these discriminatory practices, the black community had good reason to believe that the school system did not have its best interests at heart.

Furthermore, the black community had been shut out of the decision-making process regarding public education. Now, under Superintendent Drachler, the administration was committed to greater community participation in the process. The system was also undergoing a "decentralization" of authority, giving the local schools greater discretion in certain policy and program areas. Nevertheless, these initiatives were hardly sufficient to satisfy militant critics of the system. In June 1967 Reverend Albert Cleage Jr. led a dramatic protest at a public board meeting. Cleage produced a damning report that cited troublesome and accurate statistics about the low achievement and high dropout rates of black students in Detroit. He then placed the blame squarely on the white-controlled school system, which, he said, deliberately inculcated feelings of inferiority in black students to discourage their aspirations and thus support prevailing racist attitudes of the dominant society. "The basic threat to the Afro-American child's pride and self-image," Cleage argued, "is the preponderance of white administrators and teachers in inner city schools."[14] Cleage advocated total black control of black schools. This outlook resonated with many in the African American community, and I understood why, given the growing crisis in the school system. However, I never believed that a quality education for black students depended on the race of their teachers. What mattered was the commitment and ability of teachers and administrators who placed the needs of students at the center of their efforts. I did not believe that one needed to be African American to care about African American students. Moreover, I remained a strong proponent of integration,

13. U.S. District Court Judge Stephen Roth, "Ruling on Issue of Segregation," *Bradley v. Milliken,* September 27, 1971.

14. Quoted in David L. Angus and Jeffrey E. Mirel, "Equality, Curriculum, and the Decline of the Academic Ideal: Detroit, 1930–68," *History of Education Quarterly* 33, no. 2 (1993): 177–207.

which I believed was the best hope of solving Detroit's public education crisis.

One of the important responsibilities of my job was to foster channels that would enable the community to have an effective voice in the system. Our office asked each school to set up a human relations committee to facilitate community input. Each committee consisted of the principal, a number of teachers, student representatives, and parents. Regional committees were also established. In addition, I met regularly with groups of parents concerned about their respective schools. Their complaints often focused on the principal and other administrative staff. This was generally not a racial issue. Rather, it was about leadership style and sensitivity to the community. Parents agitated for more of a say in the selection of administrative personnel and in the way schools were run. I took these complaints to regional superintendents responsible for evaluating school administrators to see how we could change the culture in schools to be more receptive to community issues and concerns.

I was often called to schools to deal with student demands and unrest. The problem of student protests became widespread in Detroit schools between 1968 and 1972. Almost every middle school and high school with a predominantly black student population was affected. In the fall of 1968, students at Mackenzie High walked out and raised the black nationalist flag at the school. At the same time, students at McMichael Middle School demanded to change the name of the school to Malcolm X Middle School. They repeatedly triggered fire alarms to force the evacuation of the building. Protesters also damaged some school property. McMichael students showed up in force at a public school board meeting, and their vociferous outbursts forced the meeting to be adjourned early. The next morning I met with Superintendent Drachler, who wanted my advice on the McMichael situation. My foremost concern, I said, was the students' education. We must not permit the students to destroy their own futures and disrupt their classes. We must bring in the police when necessary to quell disturbances at the school. I then added that

I understood the students' frustration and wanted to earn their trust by initiating a process of constructive change so that the school was more in touch with their cultural identity. Later, I met with student protesters at McMichael and tried to persuade them that their voices were being heard. "When you have won the fight," I told them, "you must recognize the fact." But it was difficult to calm their ardor and sense of urgency, and the situation at McMichael remained tense the entire school year.

In the same school year, a young man named Ron Scott asked for a meeting in my office. Ron was twenty-one years old and a dedicated activist working with tenants in the Jeffries public housing project to improve their living conditions. He organized a rent strike and now was helping a group of Jeffries parents who wanted greater participation in their children's elementary school. Ron brought this group to the meeting and served as their spokesperson. Right away, he pointed to the picture of Malcolm X on my wall and scolded me for failing to comprehend the framework of social revolution. I responded that I read and appreciated a good deal of Malcolm's philosophy. Ron, however, was intent on picking a fight, and he retorted that he considered me a "lackey" of the school system. I interrupted him and exclaimed, "I am nobody's lackey and this meeting is ended!" I asked everyone to leave. The parents apologized for Ron's aggressive comments, but I had to demonstrate that I had the authority and resolve to halt the discussion once my office was disrespected. I knew that Ron was putting me to the test. I was resolute but certainly did not bear any grudge against him for expressing the brash fervor and idealism of youth. And indeed, over the years, Ron and I collaborated on a number of civil rights efforts and eventually became good friends.

These kinds of confrontations with young, militant activists happened frequently during this period. It was a radical change from how those in my generation, when we were younger, related to older and experienced civil rights leaders. We admired those leaders as our mentors and would not have dared to disrespect them. In 1967, I was part of a public meeting regarding the National Urban Coalition, which advocated strong partnerships between business, government, and community groups to promote economic development in the inner city. A young man in the audience stood up and asked me to name the black leaders of the Coalition. I said, "Whitney Young, Roy Wilkins, A. Philip Randolph, and M. Carl Holman." The young man proclaimed, "Well, those are all Toms." I am sure that he felt the same way about me, too.

Many black nationalists regarded those of us who were working for integration as sellouts. We found this deeply insulting, as, of course, it was meant to be. My own views on black nationalism were mixed. I believe in the fundamental principle that an unjust system deserves to be overturned by whatever means necessary if it cannot be changed in any other way. This principle is deeply ingrained in Western democratic thought. However, I subscribe to Dr. Benjamin Mays's philosophy of nonviolent disobedience, which found its fullest expression in his student Martin Luther King. Black nationalists also accused integration advocates of being insecure about the African American identity. I believe that genuine freedom for blacks means that we do not feel the need to live in a neighborhood of white people to experience a sense of self-worth sufficient to motivate and sustain us in our struggle for a successful life. This attitude of self-determination is actually more effective in achieving an integrated society than the approach taken by blacks who try to deny everything black in their striving for assimilation. These blacks are so focused on fitting in that they do not have a clear idea of who they are and what is good and viable in the essential structure of the black community. An integrated society that works to the benefit of all ethnic groups celebrates their respective differences.

Public school students stepped up their protests in 1969 and later. Emotions ran high among students and parents, and teachers and administrators felt besieged and oftentimes afraid. Protesters at many schools insisted that the black nationalist flag be flown on school grounds. At Northeastern, students burned the American flag after the principal refused this demand. At Butzel, students walked out and demanded the removal of the principal, who had fallen ill. A young teacher was stabbed in the protests. At Guest, students and a community group organized a drive to fire the principal because they felt he was slow to institute a more black-oriented curriculum. Unable to cope with the stress, the principal took sick leave. Several administrators and teachers resigned because of the enormous pressure during this time. At some racially mixed schools, heightened tensions resulted in clashes between white and black students. The police became a constant presence at many schools, trying to protect the staff, contain the protests, and keep outsiders from entering the schools and stirring up further trouble.

I tried to balance my sympathies for the concerns of students and parents with my responsibilities to teachers and staff during this time of upheaval. Effecting this balance was sometimes problematic. A case in point was an incident at Webber Middle School in November 1969. Between class periods, a teacher assigned to clear the hall asked a student who was lagging to get to class. An argument ensued, and the student struck the teacher. Later, a parent from the school called me to complain that the teachers' union wanted this student immediately transferred to another school even though the student did not have a record of bad behavior and the student's parents had personally apologized for their child's offense. I went to a meeting at the school about the matter and tried to calm down a group of irate parents who felt that the student deserved a second chance. Since I was the ranking school administrator in the room, I decided that the student should not be transferred. I wanted to convey to parents that the system was sensitive to their concerns. The next morning, the teachers' union picketed outside the central administration building where my office was located. The union asserted that my decision violated its contract, which stipulated clearly the automatic consequences that followed a student hitting a teacher. I realized that I had made a mistake and understood why the contract needed to be written in such strict terms. Shortly thereafter, my hasty decision was reversed.

Student protesters at various schools printed and circulated fliers listing their demands. The lists were strikingly similar from school to school. Students wanted an end to ROTC programs because, in the words of several fliers, "The indoctrination of black youth into the armed forces of America is another genocidal act by the government."[15] Students usually called for the dismissal of the principal, assistant principal, and certain teachers for being unresponsive to their demands. The brunt of these demands had to do with changing the curriculum and culture of the school to recognize the contributions of African Americans. Students wanted mandatory black studies courses and changes in history, civics, literature, and psychology classes. They also wanted school libraries to be restocked with books by black authors. At Mumford High, students asked the principal to change the name of the library to honor Martin Luther King. The principal had become overly defensive because of a kind of siege mentality that afflicted many administrators during this tumultuous time, and he rejected the students' request. I met with him in his office and asked him to set aside his frustration and rethink his decision. I explained to him that he should be encouraged that his students were so interested in learning about issues and perspectives so relevant to their lives. He concurred and assented to the renaming the library.

Students at Central High demanded that the school remove all portraits of white persons from the walls and replace them with pictures of Malcolm X, Marcus Garvey, and other black leaders. At Northern, students wanted the school to be renamed "H. Rap Brown High School." Students at Cooley had a long list of demands, including the removal of police officers and the principal, whom they called an "Uncle Tom and nitwit." When I met with the Cooley protesters at the school library, they locked the doors behind me and insisted that they would not let me leave until I heard all their complaints. I

15. A large sample of student protest fliers is archived in the Detroit Public Schools Community Relations Division collection donated by Freeman Flynn to the Walter Reuther Library at Wayne State University.

did not fear for my safety and listened patiently for several hours. I told the students that changes in the system were both necessary and forthcoming because the school needed to represent the culture and community of its students. I explained that these changes involved a process in which their input must play an important role, and that as long as I had the opportunity to serve in the system, I would make sure their voice was carried to the highest levels. But I also told the students that it was my duty to make sure that they did not rob themselves of an education by disrupting the school to such an extent that classes could not be taught. I sought to persuade them that if they threw away their futures, they were only playing into the hands of the larger enemy they were fighting.

There was no doubt that the curriculum needed to be altered to fairly represent the African American struggle and triumphs—historically, culturally, and intellectually. To accomplish this, the district needed to improve the textbooks and other learning materials used in classrooms. These textbooks, produced by the major publishing houses and invariably written by white authors, were often racially insensitive and neglectful. My office recommended to the superintendent that we should adopt a moratorium on the purchase of new textbooks until the deficits in properly recognizing the African American experience were corrected. Dr. Drachler at first was shocked by this proposal, but after thinking about it for a few days, he called and said that he understood why I felt so strongly. He presented my recommendation to the school board and it was approved unanimously.

Even before I joined the school system, I was deeply concerned with the textbook issue. In 1962, when I was the executive secretary of the Detroit NAACP, we asked the school board to withdraw a book called *History of Our United States* that was being used in seventh- and eighth-grade classes. The book's depiction of slavery was offensive to African Americans. The authors argued that slavery was essential to the South's economy. They never mentioned its inhumanity and even implied that slaves were not interested in being free because they would have lost their economic security when slavery

was abolished. Sadly, this demeaning distortion of history only exemplified the serious problems we faced with traditional textbooks
being used by districts throughout the country.

Within our School Community Relations office, we established a
task force called "Intergroup Relations." The principal staff person
assigned to oversee this committee was Dr. Freeman Flynn. The committee's mission was to provide a detailed analysis of any new textbook the district was considering for classroom use. If the textbook
failed to meet criteria of racial sensitivity, inclusiveness, and historical accuracy, we were authorized to stop its purchase and to work
with the publishers to correct these issues in future editions. The task
force found that stereotyping and discrimination were prevalent in
math, science, history, and civics textbooks. A math book for elementary students featured a problem about "Amos and Andy" shoveling
coal, complete with an illustration of two African American boys. In
several science books, a picture of a clean-cut white Olympic ath-
lete throwing a javelin was contrasted with an Australian aborigine
throwing a spear. Another science book showed an illustration of a
black man and stated, gratuitously, that he loved to dance.

The committee prepared a seven-page analysis of the book *Child
Growth and Development,* published by McGraw Hill. On the cover
of the book was a white boy. The book contained more than 600 illus-
trations that overwhelmingly depicted white children. Black children
were shown when childhood problems were discussed, like emotional
tensions and learning setbacks. A white father was pictured as an
example of nurturing and guiding his son the right way. In contrast,
a black stepfather was shown with his stepson as illustrative of the
disciplinary challenges some families faced.[16] The committee sent its
analysis to McGraw Hill with our unvarnished conclusion about the
book's thrust: "The white child of the white family in the largely white
society is really important; his growth and development deserve our

16. These examples were provided by Freeman Flynn in an interview with Steve
Palackdharry on January 19, 2007.

fullest and best attention in our schools. Minority-group children are much less important and much less worthy of our time and attention; their growth and development are not subjects for general study or concern."[17]

We rejected numerous books, though our decisions caused some controversy in the school system. Several curricula supervisors, while acknowledging the problems in the new books, still felt that the books were an improvement over the previous editions and thus should be used. We, however, were determined to make a stand and correct these persistent problems as soon as possible rather than gradually. Our strategy succeeded. In a relatively short time, our efforts had a profound effect on the publishing industry, which quickly responded after other school districts followed Detroit's lead in demanding multi-ethnic and racially sensitive textbooks. For example, McGraw Hill used our analysis of *Child Growth and Development* to made significant changes to the book. The new edition met our criteria for acceptance by the district. Afterward, I received a letter from Alexander Burke, the general manager of the textbook division at McGraw Hill. He thanked us for our review process: "You have served as a catalyst for the publishing industry and for education, and I hope you will be increasingly pleased with the impact that your efforts are having."[18]

The textbook issue was a moment of triumph for us. We were able to work with a historically recalcitrant institution—namely, the publishing industry—and persuade them to do the right thing for African American children and our community. The issue of segregation in the school system was a different matter entirely. This was an uphill struggle against powerful political forces and the full gravity of racist attitudes. We embarked on this struggle knowing that the very

17. Quoted in Freeman Flynn and Max Rosenberg, "One Textbook, One Publisher, One School," *Quest* magazine, Detroit Public Schools Staff Journal, Autumn 1971.

18. Quoted in Freeman Flynn and Max Rosenberg, "One Textbook, One Publisher, One School," *Quest* magazine, Detroit Public Schools Staff Journal, Autumn 1971.

prospect of equal educational opportunities for black children in Detroit was at stake and that the failure to achieve our aims would be terribly detrimental to our community for many generations to come.

There was a great consensus among the top-level school administrators that a desegregation plan needed to be implemented. In April 1970 the board approved a plan, by a vote of four to two, to reassign about 9,000 white and black high school students. The limited desegregation effort involved eleven of the twenty-two high schools. The plan immediately stirred heated opposition from white residents in the affected neighborhoods. They formed a citizens' action group and started a drive to recall all four white board members who supported it. The group also persuaded state lawmakers in Lansing to enact legislation that would prohibit the board from executing the plan and compel the school system to assign students to the nearest school. Governor William Milliken signed the bill into law three months after the plan was first announced by the board. One month later, the four board members were recalled—the first time any board member had been recalled in the 128-year history of the Detroit school system.

While the white community was outraged, there was no real push from the black community for desegregation. A survey at the time of black parents revealed that while 80 percent preferred integrated schools, most were against busing their children to achieve integration.[19] Consequently, desegregation was a relatively low priority in the black community. When black parents were asked to rate seventeen factors that contributed to a good education for their children, an integrated school ranked twelfth. I strongly disagreed with this sentiment, which I believed was rooted in the community's understanding that the white power structure was fiercely resistant to integration and had always frustrated any attempts to make it happen. The community was resigned to this fact, but also defiant. It con-

19. Market Opinion Research, "Quality of Education Study in the Black Community of the City of Detroit," December 1971. The survey was commissioned by New Detroit, Inc.

cluded: Since it is almost futile to push for integration, then empower us to manage our own schools. "Black control of black schools" was the rallying cry.

I thought this approach was a step backward and was not in the best interests of African American children, who, I believed, would pay a terrible price for this separatism. I believe that American society is best served by an integrated school system that fully embraces the rich and natural diversity of the American people. Thurgood Marshall and the other architects of *Brown v. Board of Education* had it right when they argued that the only way to ensure equal educational opportunity for African American children is to put them in the same classes as white children. This does not mean in theory that black children cannot be educated in schools that are racially segregated. Nor does it mean that a black child must be seated next to a white child in class to achieve academically. Rather, the need for integration is a pragmatic matter in a society where an ingrained pattern of segregation and discrimination inherently affords white children much greater educational opportunities and encouragement than black children. The fundamental problem is racism, defined as power accompanied by prejudice resulting in oppression. Ultimately, the solution is the elimination of racism. In the meantime, legal remedies are required to reduce the oppression.

In the midst of the controversy over the initial school desegregation plan, I began discussions with representatives of the Detroit NAACP about seeking a remedy in court to force the issue. Also present at these meetings was Aubrey McCutcheon, who was chief negotiator and, like myself, both black and a deputy superintendent for the district. The branch was working with an NAACP attorney named Louis Lucas from Memphis, Tennessee. Lucas was an expert on the issue, but Aubrey and I disagreed with his approach of suing only the Detroit school system on behalf of select students. We believed that the State of Michigan must also be held responsible for the segregated conditions in the district. Superintendent Drachler and others in the administration also strongly believed that it would be unfair and ineffective to sue only the Detroit Board of Education. So, Aubrey and I arranged a meeting in New York with Nathaniel Jones, the NAACP general counsel, and others at the national office. They decided to support our argument, and on August 18, 1970, the NAACP filed suit in U.S. District Court in Detroit challenging the state law that barred the district from implementing its desegregation plan. Our community relations office then served as liaison and consultant to the NAACP attorneys. Even though the school board was one of the defendants, it was no secret that the school administration wanted the NAACP to win.

The case was known as *Bradley v. Milliken,* and it would ultimately become one of the most important school desegregation cases in American history. Bradley was the name of a black family in the city who agreed to be one of the plaintiffs in the suit. Judge Stephen Roth was randomly assigned to hear the case. Roth was a Democrat who had been appointed to the federal bench by President Kennedy in 1962. He had a reputation as a judicial conservative who carefully examined the evidence through the hard lens of precedent. We were hopeful that Judge Roth would be guided by the spirit and rationality of *Brown v. Board of Education* (1954), in which the Supreme Court recognized that school segregation has a harmful psychological effect on black children and that society is legally and morally obligated to mitigate segregation to protect the rights of all children. We were also hopeful that Judge Roth would be open to an argument we had begun to prepare addressing school segregation in the broader metropolitan area.

The trial began in April of 1971. Both sides agreed that the pattern of segregation in the school system was in large measure a product of how segregated the city itself was. Attorneys for the defendants contended that housing segregation entirely explained the segregated school system. Our side argued that the district had historically and intentionally played a part in creating the segregated school system. We also presented evidence of how local, state, and federal agencies had promoted housing and school segregation through numerous discriminatory practices and policies. As a result, Detroit had become the most segregated metropolitan area in the nation, and the situation was only worsening because of accelerated white flight. It was apparent that these trends undermined any school desegregation plan that was confined within the boundaries of the city. There were simply not enough white students remaining in the Detroit system to create an adequate racial balance that could be realistically termed "integration."

In the summer of 1971, as the trial proceeded, I chaired a task force charged with setting forth fundamental reasons to desegregate the schools and various plans that would achieve it. We based our report on the best available sociological research.[20] This research indicated that the prevailing difference in academic performance between white and black students in Detroit and nationwide was related to economic status and had very little to do with race. Once the variance in economic status was controlled, the racial difference in scholastic achievement disappeared.[21] In addition, studies consistently showed that black children in integrated schools had higher academic aspirations and test scores than black children in segregated schools. For this positive integration effect to occur, the school had to have a majority white, middle-class student population. Again, the economic status of the students was the salient factor. Black students, who in general are disproportionately poor, clearly benefit from being in a school culture where white middle-class values are the norm. Our push for desegregation in public education was as much about economics as about race. Attorneys for the defendants in the court case accepted the findings that socioeconomic standing determines educational success far more than race. In fact, they argued that this was why racial desegregation should not be the goal

20. "Report of Summer Task Force on Desegregation-Integration Alternatives in the City of Detroit School District," chaired by Arthur L. Johnson. Released on September 24, 1971.

21. S. C. Rankin, "A Study of the Relationships among Economic Status, Race and Achievement for Detroit Public Elementary Schools," June 1971. Walter Reuther Library, Wayne State University.

in the effort to provide equal educational opportunities for black students. Our point, however, was that in American society, race and economic status are inextricably linked because of severe and persistent discrimination. Racial desegregation is necessarily economic desegregation. Accordingly, the aim of our task force was to come up with a long-term plan that achieved a consistent racial mix in Detroit schools of about 60 percent white to 40 percent black. This plan included nearby suburbs in Wayne, Oakland, and Macomb counties.

In 1971, there were almost one million students attending public schools in the metro Detroit area. About one in five was black. Of these black students, 85 percent lived in Detroit, even though only 30 percent of all the students in the metro area were enrolled in the city. The suburban districts were virtually all white. Oakland County was 96 percent white. Macomb County was 98 percent white. Wayne County, excluding Detroit, was 94 percent white.[22] Given these stark circumstances and the rate of white flight from the city, the only viable desegregation options had to be metropolitan in scope.

Judge Roth ultimately reached the same conclusion. He issued his ruling six months after the trial started and instructed the State Board of Education to come up with a metropolitan plan that would involve large-scale busing. Predictably, the ruling provoked a firestorm of protests from white residents in the suburbs. Suburban politicians pledged to fight desegregation to the end and to take their cause to Washington D.C. In March 1972, President Richard Nixon, in a nationally televised address, called on Congress to enact a moratorium on school busing. The Justice Department then sought to get involved in the Detroit case but was rebuffed by Judge Roth. Four months later, Judge Roth ordered the implementation of a desegregation plan involving the Detroit district, fifty-two suburban districts, and almost 800,000 students. This plan would never take effect, however. The case

22. "Report of Summer Task Force on Desegregation-Integration Alternatives in the City of Detroit School District," chaired by Arthur L. Johnson. Released on September 24, 1971.

was appealed to the Supreme Court, which issued its ruling in July 1974, some three years after *Bradley v. Milliken* first began. In a five to four decision, the Supreme Court struck down the metropolitanwide plan. The Court acknowledged that the pattern of school segregation in the city violated the constitutional rights of black students, who were entitled to equal educational opportunities. However, the Court also emphasized the principle of "local control of local districts" and thus ordered a Detroit-only solution to the problem.

I was outraged by the Supreme Court's decision in *Bradley v. Milliken*. The decision recognized that black children in Detroit were suffering an injustice that was fundamentally wrong but then prescribed a remedy that everyone knew was utterly meaningless. In effect, the Court fashioned a ragged political compromise that effectively ended school desegregation efforts in the United States. At the time of the ruling, two-thirds of all black students in the country attended schools that were more than 80 percent black.[23] If cross-district solutions to the problem of segregation were not permitted, then solutions were simply not possible. In his dissenting opinion, Justice Thurgood Marshall pointedly observed:

> Our Nation, I fear, will be ill served by the Court's refusal to remedy separate and unequal education, for unless our children begin to learn together, there is little hope that our people will ever learn to live together . . . Desegregation is not and was never expected to be an easy task . . . In the short run, it may seem to be the easier course to allow our great metropolitan areas to be divided up each into two cities one white, the other black but it is a course, I predict, our people will ultimately regret.[24]

Eventually, in the winter of 1976, Detroit implemented a modest plan that involved about 20,000 students. Even this limited effort frightened and angered the remaining white parents with school-

23. "Wrong without Remedy," *New York Times* editorial, July 28, 1974.
24. *Milliken v. Bradley,* 418 U.S. 717 (1974), dissenting opinion by Thurgood Marshall.

children, who now hastened their efforts to leave. In a ten-year span, beginning with the Detroit riot in 1967 and continuing through the desegregation efforts, three-fourths of the white families fled the city.[25] By 1990, Detroit schools were more than 90 percent black. Almost half of these children lived in poverty—an unconscionable situation in the richest country in the world, though the national conscience remained indifferent to their plight. Black children in the city could not help but internalize the lesson that American society did not care about them. The academic performance of Detroit students declined even further, and the dropout rate exceeded 50 percent. By every important measure, the school system had disintegrated.

Thurgood Marshall's dissent in *Bradley v. Milliken* was quite prescient, though one important prediction has not borne out. The American people do not "regret" the great racial divide that characterizes so many metropolitan areas and that consigns black children to unequal opportunities and compromised dreams. Dominant society remains very comfortable with the deep divide that is now more entrenched than ever.

If the city's black children attended schools that were mostly white, there is no way that American society and leadership would have allowed the schools and educational culture to deteriorate as they have in Detroit and other urban districts that are predominantly black. The absence of a white constituency means the absence of genuine political concern in the corridors of power. Experience has taught me an unfortunate truth: racism runs deep in the bloodstream of white America. I have said this publicly many times, and some commentators have accused me of being extreme in my judgment for failing to recognize how much American society has changed. However, the ingrained racial inequities in public education continue to illustrate this persistent truth about racism in America in stark and tragic terms.

25. Jeffrey Mirel, *The Rise and Fall of an Urban School System: Detroit, 1907–81* (Ann Arbor: University of Michigan Press, 1993).

CHAPTER 5

Two Tragedies, 1967–1968

The Riot and New Detroit

After the 1967 Detroit riot erupted, a top white leader in the city re-putedly said that maybe the white leadership had been talking to the wrong black leaders in the city. By this comment, the white leader meant that since recognized black leaders were unable to forewarn public and corporate officials of the imminent disaster, these black leaders must have been out of touch with the pulse of the black community. The misguided criticism stung black leaders, who responded that they had been speaking out for a long time about the tension building in the black community over the issues of discrimination, segregation, and police brutality. It was white leadership, we argued, who did not listen and who did not understand the depth of despair black people felt. This was no time, however, to debate past failures in communication. The city was on fire.

The riot, or the "rebellion," as many people prefer to call it, began early Sunday morning on July 23, 1967, after vice police raided an after-hours club on 12th Street and Clairmount. More than eighty African Americans were in the club celebrating the return home of two Vietnam War veterans. The police decided to arrest all of them and called for backup. An angry crowd gathered outside the club as the patrons were being loaded into police vehicles. As the vehicles pulled away, the crowd pelted them with bottles and rocks. Then, some in the crowd smashed the windows of a clothing store next to the club. The vandalism and looting spread quickly through the Virginia Park neighborhood, then to other parts of the city. Soon the arson began. On Monday alone, almost 500 fires were burning. Firefighters from as far as eighty miles away were called to the city. At the scene of many fires, snipers shot at the firefighters and their vehicles. The riot lasted five days and was one of the worst in American history. Forty-three people were killed; thirty-three of them were black. More than 7,000 were arrested. More than 2,500 stores were looted or burned. It was a tragic experience that came close to destroying this city.

Not long after the riot began, Hubert Locke called me at home. Locke was the administrative assistant to the police commissioner. He said that disturbances had developed on the west side on 12th Street and on the east side on Mack Avenue and that it could be the start of a major riot unless the situation were contained. Locke asked me to attend an early-morning meeting with other black leaders at Grace Episcopal Church on the corner of Virginia Park and 12th streets. At the meeting, the leaders paired off, and each team was given a bullhorn to take to the streets and appeal to people to return to their homes. I was paired with the young congressman John Conyers, who was serving his first term as representative from the 14th district, of which Virginia Park was a part. We agreed to take my car and that I would drive while he spoke with the bullhorn through his rolled-down window. We proceeded on 12th Street toward the epicenter of the upheaval until the crowd was so thick that we could no longer move the car. John and I got out and he climbed onto the hood of the car.

I will never forget the din and fury that swirled around us: the discordant sound of yelling; laughter, cursing; trashcans hurled through store windows; and the commotion as people grabbed whatever merchandise they could. It was frightening to witness firsthand the breakdown of law and order, and to worry that the mayhem might suddenly engulf us. John shouted through his bullhorn to the crowd, "Stay cool, we're with you! But, please! This is not the way to do things!" The crowd reacted defiantly and taunted us with shouts of "Uncle Tom" and accusations that we were agents of the police and the establishment. John's attempts to reason with the crowd only seemed to provoke them further. Someone threw a bottle that barely missed us. I climbed onto the car hood and spoke directly into John's ear to be heard above the din. "Let's get the hell out of here," I said. "We cannot do anything

Standing on the hood of my car with me, Representative John Conyers speaks to the crowd at 12th and Clairmount streets in Detroit during the 1967 riot on Sunday, July 23. (Photo by Jerry Hostetler, courtesy of the *Detroit News*)

more. And I'd like to take my car if I can." A news photographer captured this moment, and the picture appeared in newspapers around the country the next day. As John got back into the passenger's seat, he told a reporter standing nearby, "You try to talk to those people and they'll knock you into the middle of next year."

I backed the car out and was able to maneuver through the crowd and escape by turning on Hazelwood. I thought about the lesson I had just learned in the crucible of 12th Street. No one controls a riot with reason. The chaos had a mind and momentum of its own. Ultimately, I was convinced, a riot has to be forcibly brought under control. Later that day, I drove to other areas in the city. The upheaval on 12th Street had set in motion a cascade of events that shocked not only the city's white leadership but many black leaders too, including me. I felt utterly disheartened watching the plumes of dark smoke rise across the city. On Woodward Avenue near Orchestra Hall, I saw a man carrying on his back a large television console he had stolen. He was burdened by the weight but seemed pleased with his take as others with more portable goods moved past him. They were capitalizing on the disorder to get things they might not otherwise acquire. I don't know if this man had ever committed a crime before this occasion. But most everyone in the streets seemed unburdened by conscience in this mass contagion of looting and destructive behavior.

I went back home and received a call from Damon Keith. He said, "Arthur, it occurs to me that there are no black community leaders providing any counsel to the governor, the mayor, and the chief of police on what to do to bring an end to this crisis—and to bring an end to it without a large number of killings." Damon suggested that we drive down to the command post at police headquarters. I agreed and he picked me up, and we headed downtown. Governor George Romney, Mayor Jerome Cavanagh, and Chief Ray Girardin were gathered in the chief's office, and they immediately invited us to participate in their discussions. We would stay until dawn.

Shortly before midnight, the mayor called United States Attorney General Ramsey Clark at home and told him that the city was in the throes of a very dangerous situation. The whole nation was now looking at the terrible images of the riot and awaiting the city's plan to restore order. The critical question for all concerned was: Should federal troops be called in? An affirmative answer expressed the judgment that conditions were out of control and that law and order had broken down. Though this judgment seemed straightforward, as is usually the case, there were political and legal considerations that complicated matters. President Lyndon Johnson was a Democrat. So was Mayor Cavanagh. Governor Romney was a Republican of national stature and the leading contender for the Republican nomination in the upcoming 1968 presidential race. At this point in history, it was assumed that President Johnson would be his party's nominee, and so, to secure federal troops, Governor Romney would have to ask his political rival to intervene in his jurisdiction and admit that the combined forces of the Detroit police and Michigan National Guard were insufficient to quell the riot. In addition, according to federal law, the governor would have to declare that there was an "insurrection" occurring in the city. Romney was concerned that this declaration would make it difficult for business owners and homeowners whose property was damaged to collect from insurance companies.

In a small conference room down the hall from the chief's office, a group of black community leaders was also debating the issue of bringing in federal troops. There was considerable opposition to using federal troops because their weapons would be pointed most often at African Americans, and the black community had historical reasons to be concerned about an overreaction by the troops. For this reason, Congressman Conyers was against the request. But there was also the recognition that if the rioting continued unabated for many days, the city would be so devastated that it might never recover. Charles Diggs, representative for the 13th district, emphasized this point and argued for federal intervention.

At about 2:30 a.m., the governor said it was time to decide and that he favored asking for federal troops. He turned to the mayor, who agreed. Next, he turned to the police chief, who concurred with the mayor. Then, to our utter surprise, the governor asked Damon and me for our opinions. Damon and I understood that we had no official authority to vote in this matter, but we were grateful to Governor Romney and Mayor Cavanagh for respecting and acknowledging our interests in this critical decision. Damon said yes. I also said yes. My answer was firm and unhesitating. Though I worried about how many blacks might be killed in this conflict, I was even more apprehensive about our ability as a community to end this tragedy before many innocent lives were lost and much of the city was destroyed. Damon and I stressed to the governor, the mayor, and the police chief how important it was to protect the rights of civilians when the city was occupied by armed forces. They agreed, and we trusted them to emphasize this point with the military authorities.

After our unanimous vote, the governor phoned Attorney General Clark to ask for federal troops to enter Detroit and restore order. Clark promptly alerted Stanley Resor, the secretary of the army, to begin preparations. He then briefed the president. At 3:40 a.m., Clark called the governor and said that troops could be in the city by late morning. As it turned out, however, because the commander of the Michigan National Guard argued that state and local forces could bring the situation under control, federal militia and troops did not move into the city until after midnight on Monday. Almost 13,000 soldiers were deployed. By Thursday morning, order in the city was almost restored. A welcome rain fell on the city and further helped to calm the streets. The next day, federal forces began their withdrawal.

That same Friday, I participated in a press conference with the governor, the mayor and Cyrus Vance, who served as White House liaison during this crisis. The officials spoke about continuing efforts to secure the city and to bring food, supplies, and medical attention to residents. I was asked to speak on behalf of the community. I thanked all those trying to help the city cope and recover. "We are witnessing today," I began, "one of the most eloquent expressions of the human spirit in spite of the tragedy and ashes." Many people are giving their best, I said, but, when the ashes settle, we will find that so much more will be required of all us to get at the root causes of this catastrophe.

In many respects, the riot was both shocking and predictable. Predictable because the causes of the riot were the same issues that the black community had wanted addressed for a long time: persistent police brutality and harassment; housing segregation and overcrowding, exacerbated by urban renewal targeting black neighborhoods; job discrimination, unemployment and poverty. For five days in the long, hot summer of 1967, these pent-up frustrations of intractable racism convulsed the city.

The riot opened deep wounds and left permanent scars on the city. Its psychological and physical toll would have grievous consequences. A corrosive pessimism about Detroit's future became the prevailing attitude about the city in the regional and national psyche. The exodus of whites from the city accelerated. Most of the businesses destroyed by looting and arson did not come back, and once-vital commercial areas were left moribund. The city suffered dramatic declines in jobs, corporate investment, tax revenue, and property values. The slope of Detroit's economic downturn became even steeper.

Just days after the riot ended, the New Detroit Committee was born. It was the nation's first urban coalition of political, corporate, and community leaders dedicated to examining and changing the underlying conditions that provoked the riot. The committee had thirty-nine members who came together at the request of the governor and mayor. Joseph Hudson Jr., head of Hudson's department stores, agreed to lead the committee. At the first meeting, on August 10 in the McGregor Memorial Building at Wayne State University, he told the business leaders that they were expected to personally participate in New Detroit and not assign one of their associates in their stead. The city's crisis, he said, demanded the highest level of ongoing attention and responsibility. Seated next to me at this meeting was Henry Ford II. All of us pledged our commitment to make New Detroit more than just a name.

I believe that New Detroit was an important development in the city. It has made a difference in improving Detroit, though admittedly, not the dramatic gains we have hoped for. New Detroit has brought to the table as equal participants white and black leaders in the city and metro Detroit. The open and honest dialogue has been beneficial. Grassroots community leaders have enjoyed unprecedented access to corporate and government decision-makers, and this has helped community organizations secure support for their programs. New Detroit has also provided significant funding to community groups working to address issues of racial justice, youth training, and economic empowerment.

Speaking to Henry Ford II at Cobo Hall in Detroit in 1973.

Twenty-eight of the thirty-nine members of the New Detroit Committee formed in 1967 after the riot. (Photo courtesy of New Detroit)

New Detroit has done its best under the adverse conditions of Detroit's depressed economy and the metropolitan area's stubborn segregation. It is imperative, under these conditions, that we come to a better understanding of the resources required to achieve long-term goals of revitalizing Detroit. However, for this to happen, there must be a fundamental change in our nation's priorities and policies to address the conditions of racial injustice and persistent poverty that afflict and isolate the city.

Martin's Assassination

On the evening of April 4, 1968, I attended a meeting of civil rights advocates at Cobo Hall. It was the same venue where Martin Luther King first delivered his "I Have a Dream" speech during the Great March in the summer of 1963. Martin weighed heavily on my mind that evening.

I left the meeting with a good friend, Dr. Charles Morton, who gave me a ride home. Like Martin and me, Charles was a graduate of Morehouse College. He, too, knew Martin well. We began to talk about our concerns for Martin's safety and about whether Martin was making a mistake by becoming so heavily involved in the peace movement. Martin's outspoken opposition to the Vietnam War had made him vulnerable to a great deal of criticism from various political groups and the media. Even many of his friends and other black leaders were at odds with Martin over his decision to link his civil rights activism and his antiwar stance. They believed that this connection did not serve the civil rights movement well and carried strategic liabilities. For one thing, it risked alienating the Johnson administration. The administration had pushed through landmark civil rights legislation and was implementing "Great Society" programs meant to address poverty and racial injustice. Martin responded to his critics in a famous speech on April 4, 1967—exactly one year before this fateful night when Charles and I sat in his car discussing this controversy. Martin said then:

Cowardice asks the question, "Is it safe?" Expediency asks the question, "Is it politic?" And Vanity comes along and asks the question, "Is it popular?" But Conscience asks the question, "Is it right?" And there comes a time when one must take a position that is neither safe, nor politic, nor popular, but he must do it because Conscience tells him it is right.[26]

Charles and I talked for about half an hour while parked in my driveway. When I walked into the house, my children—David, Angela, and Wendell—were very upset and in tears. They asked me, "Don't you know what happened?" I said, "No." My children then said, "Daddy, they killed Dr. King." I broke down and cried. It was the first time my children saw me weep. It was a moment of utter despair and disbelief. It was also a moment of sheer terror in the realization that a great and vital life could be extinguished so abruptly by the enemy.

I watched the television coverage that night and spoke to many friends by phone. All of us felt a sudden void at the core of our world that seemed to throw the very meaning of our struggle into question. But as we collected ourselves, we knew that we could not let an assassin's bullet impede the ideals for which Martin stood and gave his life. That my tearful children were the ones to inform me of Martin's death brought this home even more keenly.

In our grief over Martin's death, we came to discover that we were each a part of his legacy, and there was consolation in our spiritual inheritance. This inheritance strengthened our resolve to do what Martin had asked of us. It also compelled us to measure our efforts against the courage of conviction that Martin embodied. Martin never held back in the struggle he waged. He gave his life in the line of duty for the cause of freedom and human dignity. The finest tribute we could pay Martin was to stay on the battlefield and carry the fight forward.

Ever since he stepped to the forefront of the civil rights movement, Martin lived with the growing premonition that his life would be cut

---

26. Martin Luther King, "Why I Am Opposed to the War in Vietnam" (speech delivered on April 4, 1967, at the Riverside Church in New York City).

short. In his final speech, delivered the night before he was assassinated in Memphis, the premonition was overwhelming. Martin spoke prophetically:

> I would like to live a long life. Longevity has its place. But I'm not concerned about that now. I just want to do God's will. And He's allowed me to go up to the mountain. And I've looked over. And I've seen the Promised Land. I may not get there with you. But I want you to know tonight, that we, as a people, will get to the Promised Land. And I'm happy tonight. I'm not worried about anything. I'm not fearing any man. Mine eyes have seen the glory of the coming of the Lord.[27]

Amen!

---

27. Martin Luther King, "I've Been to the Mountain Top" (speech delivered on April 3, 1968, at the Mason Temple in Memphis, Tennessee).

CHAPTER 6

Wayne State University

When I retired from Wayne State University in 1995, the university held a ceremony to honor my twenty-three years of service. The president of Wayne at the time, David Adamany, spoke to the audience of friends and associates gathered on campus in Detroit. He said something that touched me deeply: "Arthur has been the conscience of the university."

Ten years later, I attended a speech by the distinguished historian Lerone Bennett at a lecture series the university created in my name to address issues that were my life's work. Lerone was a schoolmate at Morehouse College, and he spoke on the eve of Martin Luther King Day. Before he spoke, Wayne president Irvin Reid began the event by talking about my years at the university: "One can easily say that the modern history of Wayne State University is Arthur Johnson, if you think about the urban perspective that the university has taken on over the years."

I cite these two comments by university presidents with some reluctance, since I have always viewed my work as an end in itself. But the comments serve to spell out what motivated my role at Wayne State. I wanted to be the voice of the university in matters of equal opportunity, fairness, and diversity. I also wanted the university to be more sensitive and responsive to its urban environment and its mission to serve the city.

My association with Wayne State began in 1965 when I joined the faculty as a part-time sociology instructor. I taught courses in race relations and urban sociology. I got to know many of the administrators at Wayne, including George Gullen, who was vice president of university relations. In 1972, Gullen became president of the university,

Wayne State president David Adamany congratulates me on my retirement
from the university in 1995. Lynne Schaefer, vice president of administration
and finance, stands behind us. (Photo courtesy of Wayne State University)

and he asked me to take over the job that he vacated. I accepted his
offer and left my position as a deputy superintendent of the Detroit
Public Schools. I relished the new challenges.

Wayne State is a major institution in the nation's collegiate system.
Its enrollment places it in the top thirty of the largest universities in
the country. Wayne is the only urban research university in Michigan.
Because it is an urban university, many people mistakenly assume
that the student body at Wayne is mostly African American. There is
a significantly higher percentage of African Americans at Wayne than
in the general population as a whole, but the university enjoys great

diversity in its student makeup. Wayne State's stature and diversity attracted me to the job in university relations. At the same time, I knew that Wayne—and all other major institutions under white leadership—needed improvement in areas of racial equality.

Though my appointment as vice president of university relations was significant, it was also in keeping with the racial pattern of administrative opportunities in higher education at the time. My executive position was significant because eight different administrative units reported to my office, including alumni affairs, development, equal opportunity, neighborhood relations, and the public radio station WDET. My appointment, however, came at a time when African Americans were beginning to break through on the university relations side of the administration rather than on the more prestigious and intellectually esteemed academic side. When I joined Wayne State, there was not a single high-ranking black in the academic leadership. This deficit was consistent with the institutionalized practices of racism in the general academic community. These practices tended to reinforce the idea of the intellectual inferiority of African Americans. Indeed, in my early years at Wayne, some in the administration seemed surprised by my readiness and interest in academic affairs.

I had just started the job when President Gullen called me with an urgent request. He asked me to look into a protest of black students who were upset that there were no African Americans in the Hilberry Theatre, which is part of Wayne's theater department. The Hilberry has a national reputation for excellence and is the only graduate theater company in the country staffed by promising artists selected through a rigorous audition process. Before I met with the protesters, President Gullen told me that he would authorize whatever changes I believed were needed to address the absence of African Americans at Hilberry. I listened at length to the students' concerns and then suggested establishing a program to recognize African American experiences and contributions in theater. The program was soon implemented, and it brought prominent black actors to the campus as visiting lecturers. Performers such as James Earl

James Earl Jones speaks with me at my home on Renfrew Street in Detroit in June 1972, while my son Wendell and my second wife, Loretta, listen.

Jones, Ossie Davis, and Ruby Dee spoke at Hilberry and other venues on campus about their approach to the craft and the challenges of the profession. In addition to this program, the university made a commitment to review and improve the training of black student artists at Wayne and to increase their numbers.

The changes in the theater department enhanced its prestige and at the same time addressed legitimate concerns about racial diversity and discrimination. I have long maintained that racial diversity enriches the educational experience of students and teachers. Diversity is a goal that all academic programs should strive to achieve, not because it serves a political purpose, but because it has inherent and important educational value. It broadens students' perspectives. It teaches appreciation and respect of cultural differences. It better prepares students for work and citizenship in a multiethnic society.

In an urban environment, the multiethnic character of American culture is manifest. It is particularly important that a university in this setting honor the respective concerns of the diverse student groups that make up its enrollment. I strongly believe that this effort must be an essential part of the educational mission of an urban university. At Wayne, our office implemented programs in remembrance of the Holocaust, the Armenian genocide, and Martin Luther King. We helped established programs to serve the Native American, Hispanic, and gay and lesbian communities. I founded the Phylon Society at Wayne State to focus attention on the concerns of African American faculty and staff, and to pay homage to my intellectual mentor, W. E. B. DuBois. DuBois had started the scholarly journal *Phylon* when he was chair of the sociology department at Atlanta University.

I wanted to make sure that Wayne State's Martin Luther King memorial program would be first-rate and attract not only students and staff but also the community at large. As the most prominent institution of higher learning in Detroit, Wayne was in a unique position to create an important memorial event to honor Martin, for whom Detroit was a like a second home. At the heart of the program, my office organized a large luncheon that featured a distinguished civil rights speaker. The keynote speakers at the first few luncheons were former Morehouse teachers and classmates of Martin and mine. Professor Robert Brisbane was the first speaker. Dr. Brisbane founded the political science department at Morehouse, was a prominent author and scholar, and trained and mentored many civil rights leaders. The King memorial program soon became a signature event for the university and a must-attend event for many community and corporate leaders in Detroit. One year, the National Bank of Detroit was holding a board meeting the morning of the event and adjourned the meeting early to make sure all the board members could attend the luncheon. I was also particularly proud that the King program consistently attracted an integrated audience.

My efforts to enhance diversity and end discrimination at the university were both programmatic and policy-related. One of my first policy assignments at Wayne was to examine the salaries for women and minorities. Our office found clear evidence of systemic discrimination in employee salaries based on factors of race and gender. I took the findings to President Gullen and urged him to act on the matter. I argued that the compensation deficits for blacks and women implied to everyone concerned that minority staff persons were not as valuable to the university as white males. The president agreed that this egregious situation needed to be corrected. The anti-discrimination initiative was met with resistance by some supervisors responsible for personnel and salaries in their departments. For example, in the public information office, a young woman named Nancy Cunningham was making significantly less than others in the office who had the same job classification. I told a university personnel officer that in the interest of fairness, she deserved equal pay. The officer became very upset, and from the way he spoke, I understood that his resistance stemmed from the fact that he did not really believe in what he was being told to do. We arranged a meeting in my office. I explained to him that the pattern of salary iniquity at the university was the result of years of discrimination. He was following a tradition that had to change. Later, an appropriate adjustment was made in Nancy's salary.

My office of university relations also closely examined the pattern of compensation increases given to faculty, staff, and administrators at Wayne. We discovered that black employees on average received raises that were 3 percent less than those of their white counterparts. I wrote President David Adamany that nothing in my experience at Wayne demonstrated a pattern of racial discrimination as much as this finding. Adamany responded that the figures, if accurate, were alarming. However, because the racial discrepancy was so alarming and yet had not been previously raised as an issue, he was concerned that the finding could be based on a miscalculation. Ultimately, Adamany was persuaded that we were right, and he ordered that the necessary compensation remedies be made promptly.

The discriminatory patterns of salaries and pay increases were ingrained in the institution and operated by dint of unquestioned and long-standing practices. White supervisors did not conspire to create and enforce these patterns. Individual supervisors made decisions on staff compensation based on historical precedent and traditional judgments. The cumulative effect of all these decisions maintained the patterns of racial discrimination. The system functioned in such an automatic way that iniquities were not discussed. This is the pernicious nature of institutional racism.

I was appreciative of President Adamany's support of my efforts to fight institutional racism at Wayne State. Adamany, however, was a very unpopular president among staff and students at Wayne, although there was a begrudging respect for his visionary ambitions for the university. He was driven to make Wayne one of the top research universities in the nation, and he succeeded in doing so. The prestigious Carnegie Foundation designated Wayne State a "Research 1" institution in 1994. Under Adamany's leadership, the university embarked on the largest building project in its history and added three new colleges. Undeniably, Wayne State grew in national stature and academic standing because of David Adamany's initiatives.

Adamany had replaced Thomas Bonner as president of the university, and Bonner had replaced George Gullen, who had hired me. All three administrations that I served had difficulties with the university faculty, staff, and culture. Gullen was conscientious and straightforward in his relationship with the university and the community. He was deeply committed to Wayne's urban mission and diversity programs. He helped elevate Wayne State's medical school to premier stature, and under his leadership, it became the largest single-campus medical school in the country. Gullen, however, did not possess the type of academic background and qualifications that many faculty and staff members believed should characterize the president of the university. Before joining Wayne State, Gullen was a vice president of the American Motors Corporation. Much of his career experience had been in the private sector. When Gullen retired as Wayne's president in 1978, there was already a distinct tension in the university culture caused, in large measure, by the faculty's desire to have a strong academician as the university's leader.

This concern influenced the board of governors in its selection of Tom Bonner. Bonner was a distinguished medical historian who had served as president of the University of New Hampshire. Though Bonner's academic credentials satisfied the faculty, his leadership style soon alienated many at the university. At a time when Wayne was experiencing the most serious fiscal crisis in its history, resulting in layoffs and tuition increases, Bonner brought in an unprecedented number of public relations consultants to recommend changes to the university's organization and image. This expenditure stirred resentment on campus. One of the changes instituted by Bonner affected my position at Wayne. My title was changed from vice president of university relations to vice president of community relations. In the lexicon of university culture, this change amounted to a downgrading of my position. Perhaps realizing this, Bonner arranged a reception for me, in an apparent attempt to make me feel better about the situation.

Upon the advice of the consultants, Bonner hired an executive assistant named Patti Knox. She was a former vice chairman of the Michigan Democratic Party. Knox did a number of things that were an affront to my office at the university. She also made some petty and insulting remarks about my wife Chacona and me. I told Knox that I would not tolerate her actions, and I arranged a meeting with Bonner to discuss the matter. In my twenty-three years at Wayne, this was the only time I went to the president to lodge a complaint against a colleague. Bonner listened and then replied, "Well, Arthur, you will have to push back." I left the meeting irritated at Bonner's lack of sensitivity.

My problem with Bonner's leadership, in some respects, was indicative of the growing dissatisfaction on campus with the Bonner

Wayne State University president Tom Bonner *(left)* presented an honorary degree to Mayor Coleman Young in 1979 while I *(right)* was a vice president at the university. (Photo courtesy of Wayne State University)

presidency. The extensive and expensive use of outside consultants was only one of many issues raised by Bonner's detractors. Concerned that his tenure as president was in jeopardy, Bonner invited me to lunch one day to ask me to assess the mood at the university and to advise him about what to do. I told him that I remembered his words when I asked for his intervention in an important matter to me, and that I was now returning those same words to him: "You will have to push back." Faced with mounting pressure, Bonner resigned after four years in office.

My relationship with David Adamany was mixed. It began on a disappointing note. When I first came to the university, President Gullen asked me to serve on the executive council. The council met weekly and was responsible for preparing materials for the board of governors and making recommendations about important policy issues. The council consisted of vice presidents and other leading executive officers at Wayne. When Adamany became president, I was the only African American on the council. However, Adamany decided to drop me from the council and did not speak to me about the matter. I did not raise an objection and I let the matter go, since I realized it was the president's prerogative to choose the council members. Later, two board members, Max Pincus and Murray Jackson, one black and one white, approached me individually and expressed concern that I was not a part of the council and that Adamany would not receive the benefit of my advice. I replied, "If David can tolerate my absence, I can take it." Despite my comment, Max and Murray pursued the issue, and a short time later, I was reinstated to the council.

In the course of Adamany's tenure, my access to the president was as good as anyone else's in the administration. My advisory role with him grew over the years. Though Adamany's demeanor was often adversarial, I understood that he wanted people of strong conviction and confidence around him. I admired his ability to comprehend big issues in exacting detail. He knew the university organization very well. He asked each department to prepare reports on its structure, staff, and projects, and he read those reports carefully. Others at Wayne would often ask my advice about how to successfully persuade Adamany about an important consideration. I told them that it was imperative to know more about the subject than he did, to be prepared to answer tough questions, and to not be intimidated by his assertiveness. Adamany had little patience for those who failed to meet these expectations. He also liked to maintain power by reminding others of the strict limits of their authority and the broad scope of his own. These reminders often took the form of written notes expressing displeasure with the recipient's actions. Each time I received such a note from Adamany, I would put it away for two weeks and then go in and speak to him about the matter from a fresh and reasoned perspective. Since I disciplined myself not to be reactive, my discourse with Adamany was both constructive and productive, and I was able to advance the causes that were important to me and the institution I served. I earned Adamany's respect, and he eventually appointed me as a senior vice president.

From the beginning, I supported Adamany's ambitious plans to push Wayne State into becoming one of the nation's leading research and urban universities. I also cautioned him that he had too much on his agenda and suggested that his plans would enjoy greater backing if he were less contentious. I wanted Adamany's efforts to succeed both because I was very sensitive about how the university was judged academically and because I understood that Detroit must be home to a great university if the city were to be revitalized and regain its national eminence. So, although many at Wayne were glad to see Adamany step down as president in 1997, I maintain that the university and the city are better because of his leadership.

There were a number of faculty and student protests during the Adamany years. I steered clear of most of them, since they were not related to my responsibilities in the community relations office. However, one student protest in 1989 required my attention and counsel. On April 12, about 250 African American students occupied the student services center and demanded that the university institute an Africana studies program dedicated to the study of the history and culture of people of African descent. The students argued that this program was essential for several reasons: Detroit was predominantly African American; Wayne State had a high percentage of black students; and the university needed to acknowledge and address the fact that slavery forcibly disconnected people of African descent from their heritage and history. While I agreed with the student demands, I did not approve of some of their tactics. Students issued an ultimatum to the president and gave him only two days to meet their terms. I met with some of the student leaders during the protest and told them candidly that this ultimatum was a mistake. There is an African proverb, I explained, that you never back your opponent into a corner. It causes your adversary to circle the wagons at a time when resolving the issue in your favor requires diplomacy. The students backed away from their two-day ultimatum and then staged their protest as a "study-in." They continued to occupy the student center but also attended their classes and entered into negotiations with the administration.

In the administration, I was part of the ad hoc group strategizing about how to deal with the protest. There was considerable disagreement and confusion about what to do. Because of my past experiences, I understood the dynamics of the situation in a way that my colleagues did not. I made it clear that I intended to be the voice of the students on this issue. I also argued that no forceful action should be taken to evict the students and that it was imperative that no student should be harmed or punished in the situation. After almost two weeks of the study-in, a peaceful resolution was reached between the administration and the protesters. A new Africana studies department was created, and the university pledged funds for additional faculty and resources to make the department viable.

Of all my efforts at Wayne State, perhaps the one of which I am most proud is the Detroit Festival of the Arts. Wayne enjoys a unique place relative to other universities in the country. No other urban campus in the nation is located in such close proximity to almost all of the leading cultural institutions in its city. I believed that Wayne's location provided an opportunity for us to spearhead the creation of a cultural celebration event that would rival the very best in the country. The university administration was generally supportive of the concept, though a prominent member of the faculty objected because of his highfalutin notions of art. The nearby museums and cultural institutions were receptive to the idea of a festival, with the notable exception of the Detroit Institute of Arts. The director of the DIA, Sam Sachs, made it known that he did not want the festival on his grounds. I went to see Sam and persuaded him that his concerns about the festival being "an arts fair" were unfounded and that I intended to convene a distinguished jury to judge the arts and crafts showcased at the festival. The first Detroit Festival of the Arts was in 1986 and was a spectacular success. In the following years, the event grew into one of the premier annual events in the city, attracting more than half a million people over the three-day celebration of the visual, performing, and literary arts. The festival drew significant participation from suburban residents, and the crowds were very integrated. For this to happen in the most segregated metropolitan area in the nation was an important accomplishment. I strongly believe in the power of the arts to build bridges across divided communities.

I retired from Wayne State in 1995 when I was seventy years old. I came to love the university, though Morehouse will always occupy a special place in my heart because of the way it shaped my character and convictions. There are many similarities between Wayne State and Morehouse in how the universities have risen to the challenges they face. Wayne does not get the credit it deserves as an academic institution because it is situated in Detroit, a predominantly black city. Morehouse is overlooked as one of the great academic institutions in the country because it is a historically black college. Both Wayne and Morehouse have been committed to providing a good education to many promising students whose options were limited by their financial means or by hardships that affected their previous academic record. Wayne deserves high marks for its special attention to the needs and interests of minority students. A nationwide study by a Harvard University team found that African American students at

Wayne rated their campus experience more favorably than black students at other major universities. This is a testament to the fact that Wayne is doing well in fulfilling its mission as an urban university.

I left Wayne State feeling good about the work I had done and its impact on the university. I can truly say that I gave the university my best effort and that I stayed true to my core convictions in my endeavors. I can also say that I never fell into the jaded administrative trap of seeing students as numbers rather than as individuals. For much of my time as a vice president at Wayne, I also taught a class in race relations. I enjoyed teaching and felt as though my students found the course engaging and enlightening. But like any instructor, I wondered if I was making a difference with my students. This question was answered for me in one of my last semesters teaching. After the final exam, the students in my course asked if I could wait before the class was dismissed. They presented me with a silver cup and applauded my efforts that semester. It was one of my best and most memorable moments at the university.

I always tried to keep my office open to students and to serve them in the same spirit that I was served by the faculty and staff at Morehouse. I remember a new student who walked into my office and was quite flustered because she could not find the building where students go to register. I put her in my car and drove her there. On another occasion, a student came to my office and was distraught because all her furniture had been removed from where she had been living and was sitting by the curb. She needed to pay a mover to take her things to another place where she could stay, but she had no money to pay the mover. I had $100 in my wallet and I gave it to her. I wanted to help, and I could not see any other way of helping her deal with this urgent problem. I don't mean to say that everyone should respond this way or that one should make this kind of giving a habit. But under the circumstances, I felt it was the right thing to do and hoped that this bit of compassion might also help this student remain in school. I have learned that a small act of kindness can sometimes make a big difference in another's faith that things will get better.

1961 Detroit NAACP Awards Night in the Latin Quarter. *Left to right:* Clementine McClain, Betty Canty, Sylvia Lee, myself.

A party hosted by the Detroit NAACP in honor of Sammy Davis Jr. at the home of Ruth and Dr. Howard McNeal in Bloomfield Hills in 1963. *Left to right:* myself speaking, Governor John Swainson, Dr. McNeal, Davis.

At the same event in 1963, I share a laugh with Dr. McNeal. Over my left shoulder, Rosa Parks is smiling.

Left to right: Democratic presidential candidate Hubert Humphrey, Vernon Jordan, myself. Detroit, 1968.

The five partners in my only serious business venture, called Urban Era Associates, in Detroit, 1974. Our firm sought to advise corporations about urban and race issues. *Left to right:* Mitch Tendler, Colin Cromwell, Hubert Locke, myself, Bert Levy.

After a Detroit NAACP event in 1973 where Langston Hughes was the featured speaker. *Left to right:* myself, Dr. Juanita Collier, Langston Hughes, Joya Person, Artis Lane.

Receiving an honorary doctorate degree from the University of Detroit–Mercy president Maureen Fay in 1996.

Backstage after Lena Horne's show "The Lady and Her Music" at the Nederlander Theater on Broadway in 1981. *Left to right:* myself; Lena Horne; Joseph Winters Sr., my father-in-law.

Left to right: my granddaughters Olivia, Alexandra, and Rachel with their parents, Bruce Sewell and Angela Johnson Sewell; my wife, Chacona; myself; my grandson Brian Jr. with his parents, Brian Johnson Sr. and Jeri Johnson.

My family at a community tribute in my honor for the benefit of the College Bound Kids Learning Center on November 6, 2007. *Top row standing, left to right:* James Johnson, my brother; Wendell Johnson Sr., my son; Rita Johnson, my daughter-in-law; Angela Johnson Sewell, my daughter. *Next row standing:* Brian Johnson Sr., my son; Karen Johnson, my sister-in-law; Olivia Sewell, my granddaughter. *Next row standing:* Alexandra Sewell, my granddaughter; Jeri Johnson, my daughter-in-law; Rachel Sewell, my granddaughter. *Standing behind and on side:* Winifred Johnson Harrison, my sister; Erika Dillard, my granddaughter; Sheryl Reid, my niece; Elizabeth Johnson Reid, my sister; Shirley Johnson Ellis, my sister. *Seated:* Chacona Winters Johnson, my wife; myself; and Mable M. Winters, my mother-in-law. (Photo by Marcus Patton)

CHAPTER 7

President of Detroit NAACP

I served as president of the Detroit NAACP from 1987 to 1993. It had been more than two decades since I had a leadership role in the organization. Much had changed in this time regarding the perception of the NAACP. When I departed as executive secretary in 1964, the NAACP was one of the leading civil rights organizations in the nation. Now, when I was elected president, many African Americans, especially the younger generation, were questioning the role and contemporary relevance of the NAACP. Some of this questioning stemmed from a lack of knowledge about the organization and its efforts. Some of it reflected the growth and aspirations of the black middle class. And some of the criticism was clearly necessary to the health and advancement of the organization. Critics wondered if the NAACP was still capable of effectively addressing issues of discrimination and segregation.

In 1987, Detroit was almost 75 percent African American. Coleman Young was in his fourth term as mayor. Young was the first African American to serve as mayor of one of the nation's top ten cities. I worked hard for his election and remained a strong supporter during his twenty-year tenure. I was a member of Young's "kitchen cabinet." This group, composed of trusted friends inside and outside the administration, met regularly in the mayor's residence every month on a Saturday afternoon for a few hours. Besides the mayor and myself, the other participants in these meetings were: Fred Martin, the mayor's chief of staff; Charlie Williams, director of the Detroit Water and Sewerage Department; Ron Hewitt, the mayor's executive assistant; Reverend Charles Butler of New Calvary Baptist Church, where the mayor attended; Damon Keith; Malcolm Dade; and Martin Taylor.

The mayor put every item of importance to the city on the table, and the discussion was always open and freewheeling, in content and language. He kept the group fully involved, and he set no limits on comments or questions.

The group sought to advise the mayor as he tried to deal with the enormous problems Detroit faced from white flight, the deteriorating public school system, and crime; and the loss of jobs, businesses, industries, and the tax base. Despite its state of perpetual crisis, Young was determined to not let the city die from all the social and economic ills that plagued it. He fought for the city with everything he had and was never afraid to speak his mind. He pointed to racism whenever he saw it, and for this he was excoriated by white suburbanites and the media as a divisive figure.

Many critics of Mayor Young accused him of "playing the race card" when he argued that racism was the most significant factor in the problems afflicting the city. Like many of the unfair charges leveled against the mayor, this dismissive accusation incensed him. Young's temper was legendary, and he was prone to aggressive and profane responses when he felt his dignity had been challenged. Unfortunately, these outbursts sometimes got the best of him.

On one such occasion, the mayor had just finished a press conference when a reporter yelled out a question about the salary increases given to city department heads. The reporter asked Young how much of a raise was given to Joyce Garrett, who worked for the mayor's office and who was also the city's "unofficial first lady." The Mayor became indignant, snarled at the reporter, and exclaimed, "None of your goddamn business!" The television cameras captured Young's outburst, and it was replayed many times on the local news.

Viewing the coverage, I became concerned that the mayor, in attempting to fend off an insult to his dignity, had reacted in an undignified manner. I called each member of a small group of black friends whom Young trusted and to whom he would listen. All of us kept our arms around the mayor—sharing in his triumphs; encouraging him through the frustrations of the office; and supporting him through the agony of being constantly investigated by federal authorities for no other reason than the fact that he was a powerful and defiant black political leader. Those same authorities habitually leaked misleading details of their investigations to reporters in order to humiliate and harass the mayor. Young believed, and justifiably so, that the federal authorities were conspiring with many members of the media to bring down his administration. That was one of the reasons that he often reacted so angrily to reporters' aggressive queries.[28] I called Damon Keith, Forrest Green, James Wadsworth, Richard Austin, and Joe Coles and told each of them it was imperative that we meet with the mayor as soon as possible. All agreed. I then called the mayor and asked him to sit down with us. A few days later, we gathered in a private room at the Book Cadillac Hotel.

I opened the meeting by summarizing the mayor's confrontation with the reporters and the news coverage of the incident. I told the mayor that we all felt his ugly reaction was harmful to the effectiveness of his office because it conveyed weakness in the lack of self-control. I ended my opening remarks by reminding the mayor of a classic quote from Euripides: "Those whom the gods wish to destroy they first make mad." Other members of the group then underscored the negative repercussions to the mayor's leadership and image by allowing himself to be baited by his detractors.

After our comments, the mayor expressed with deep feeling his appreciation for the group's friendship and loyal support. Then, looking directly at me, he said, "Arthur, I am the most powerful black leader in the state, and I cannot stop these sons of bitches from attacking my family. They have done everything they could to hurt me." The mayor's voice then broke—something I had not seen before in all my years of friendship with him. The task of managing Detroit under dire circumstances was hard enough. But to have to cope with the stress of relentless attacks on his integrity was almost too much, even for someone as strong and resolute as Coleman Young.

28. Young and Wheeler, *Hard Stuff.* See esp. chapter 10.

The election of Coleman Young marked the ascendance of black political power in Detroit, not only in the mayor's office, but also in the city council and city agencies. However, this political power did not, by any means, spell the inevitable end of racist practices by certain institutions operating within the city. These practices directly diminished the quality of life and standard of living for black residents in the city. Two offending institutions in particular were the focus of much of my efforts as president of the NAACP: the banking industry and the insurance industry. Our efforts against the discriminatory practices of these industries were part of a branch campaign launched in 1988 called "Project Freedom."

In June 1988, the *Detroit Free Press* ran a series of articles called "The Race for Money." The investigative series documented the discriminatory practices of the major banks in metropolitan Detroit in declining mortgages and loans to black Detroiters. The banks were also guilty of redlining, a practice in which banks refuse or limit mortgages and loans within areas of the city that have significant black populations. The *Free Press* series showed that black Detroiters were much less likely to qualify for a home mortgage than suburban whites in the same income bracket. Even within the city, prospective homeowners in predominantly white neighborhoods were far more likely to receive a mortgage than blacks of comparable income who wanted to buy homes in a black or mixed neighborhood.

Home ownership is the bedrock of stable and vital neighborhoods. The failure of banks to extend mortgages to qualified blacks not only deprived them of a fair share of the American dream but also had the long-term effect of contributing to the deterioration of neighborhoods and the accelerated flight of the black middle class. The unfair lending practices of the major banks also made it difficult for blacks to secure business, home improvement, and auto loans. In effect, the banks were punishing blacks who wanted to make Detroit their home and participate in the revitalization of the city.

The *Free Press* series provoked outrage toward the banking establishment among Detroit residents and leaders. The banks adamantly denied practicing discrimination and disputed the findings in the newspaper articles, despite overwhelming evidence to the contrary. We had all known anecdotally that the banks were historically guilty of redlining and racist lending practices. When I was executive secretary of the NAACP, we fought the same issue and made some headway, but the banks were stubbornly resistant to change. After the *Free Press* articles brought the issue to the forefront of public consciousness, I seized the opportunity to organize black leadership in the city to compel the banks to abide by the fair lending laws. Mayor Young was also very outspoken about the issue, and indeed, wanted to take over in leading the fight against the banks. I went to speak to the mayor and told him that the effort was in good hands. This was a job that the NAACP should do, I said to him, and you should let us do it. After all, I continued, if you get in middle of this and appear to be the one in control, it will only encourage opposition from some quarters where such opposition might not otherwise come. The mayor agreed, and I continued my efforts to rally the community around the issue.

As a result, the Ad Hoc Coalition for Fair Banking Practices was founded to monitor the lending practices of banks and urge them to comply with anti-discrimination and fair-housing laws. The advocacy group had about 140 members and included representatives from community organizations, unions, churches, and civic agencies. The coalition was chaired by Bernard Parker, head of an important grassroots organization in the city, and me. We arranged meetings with the leaders of seven of Detroit's commercial banks and two savings and loan associations. Our presentation emphasized three principal points:

1. The mortgage and home improvement lending practices of the banks were harming blacks, Detroit neighborhoods, and the city as a whole.

2. Detroit banks were not participating in major development projects at a level commensurate with their resources and obligations to the city under the law.

3. The remedies we were seeking would fundamentally improve relations between Detroit banks and the city of Detroit and its residents.

We pressed the banks to submit proposals detailing how they would change their practices. Only one bank, the National Bank of Detroit (NBD), declined to submit a formal plan in writing. I held private discussions with Tom Jeffs, a vice chairman at NBD, and Al Glancy, corporate chair of New Detroit and chairman and CEO of Michigan Consolidated Gas Company. Jeffs promised me that if our group did not demonstrate against the bank and force the issue, he would work behind the scenes to make sure that NBD would do more than the other banks. I presented his promise to the coalition steering committee that I chaired. Several members of the committee still wanted to demonstrate against NBD to force the bank to produce a written agreement like the other banks. I argued that I trusted Jeffs's word, but if the committee issued a call for demonstrations against NBD, we had to be absolutely committed to staying on the picket line for as long as it took to win the fight. I asked them, "Are you prepared to be there the whole time?" The NBD issue caused heated and legitimate debate, and I struggled to keep the coalition together. Eventually, the committee decided not to protest against NBD. If the vote had gone the other way, I would have joined the picket line. Ultimately, NBD honored its promise to effect more favorable lending practices in the city. I was grateful for the role Jeffs and Glancy played in those efforts.

After months of negotiation, the Ad Hoc Coalition secured $2.7 billion in financial commitments over a three-year period from the banks. The coalition later became a permanent organization called the Detroit Alliance for Fair Banking. The alliance successfully negotiated with the banks to provide billions of dollars in loans toward homeownership opportunities for low-income residents, neighborhood revitalization, and small businesses.

Sixteen months after the Ad Hoc Coalition began, I testified about the issue of fair banking practices before a subcommittee of the

Senate Banking Committee in Washington D.C. I told the assembly: "The city of Detroit has been hurt badly, and unnecessarily so, by the greed, callous and racist attitudes of the many who have contributed to the disinvestment patterns of this modern day tragedy. Here, state and federal government bear a large part of the blame for the problems afflicting not only Detroit, but virtually every major urban center in the nation."[29] I recommended three changes in government policy:

1. Implement stricter standards of compliance for banks in meeting their community reinvestment obligations.

2. Require the collection and periodic analysis of data regarding the lending practices of local banks to minorities and the poor.

3. Provide greater financial assistance and guarantees to facilitate growth and development in our core cities.

These recommendations were only partially adopted, and consistent enforcement of the fair lending laws remains a national issue. Responding to pressure from our group, Detroit banks began to move away from their discriminatory practices. Nonetheless, those practices continued. A 1993 federal study showed that many Detroit banks made it extremely difficult for African Americans to obtain mortgages for homes in city neighborhoods that were more than 25 percent black.[30] In 2004, Old Kent Bank settled a lawsuit brought by the Justice Department after persistent complaints about the bank's redlining practices. In a five-year period ending in 2000, Old Kent

29. Testimony of Arthur L. Johnson before the Subcommittee on Consumer and Regulatory Affairs of the Senate Banking Committee, Washington D.C., October 29, 1989.
30. Jonathan Brown and Charles Bennington, *A Study of Racial Discrimination by Banks and Mortgage Companies in the United States* (GIS Action for Economic and Social Justice, 1993, http://public-gis.org/reports/redindex.html).

made more than 15,000 loans to small businesses in metro Detroit. Only 335, or 2.2 percent, were made to small businesses located in mostly black neighborhoods. In addition, Old Kent opened its first branch in the city only after the Justice Department began investigating the bank.[31] Getting the financial institutions to treat Detroiters equally continues to be an uphill struggle, and until the banks show a firm commitment to fair lending practices and the city at large, efforts to revitalize Detroit's neighborhoods and commercial areas will be hampered.

The other grievous instance of institutionalized redlining that we decided the NAACP must attack was in the insurance industry. The difference in auto insurance premiums between city and suburban residents was outrageous. The largest auto insurance provider in the city was the Auto Club Insurance Association, or AAA. It insured more than 40 percent of Detroit car owners, since several major auto insurance agencies refused to underwrite in the city for anything less than extortionate rates. The rates AAA offered Detroiters were relatively better but still excessive and blatantly discriminatory. The company had established twenty different insurance-rate zones covering the metro Detroit area. The zone with the highest rate charged premiums that were more than twice that of the zone with the lowest rate. The high-rate zones invariably fell in Detroit, while white suburban areas enjoyed the lowest rates, with the maximum rate disparity occurring between the city and suburbs. Within the city, residents in predominantly white areas were charged significantly less than residents in black areas. These racial discrepancies in auto premiums were for base rates. Premiums increased for drivers who committed traffic infractions or were involved in accidents. Since the increase was based on the initial base rate, black drivers paid much more of a surcharge and thus were being penalized far more for similar problems.

31. United States Department of Justice, "Detroit Bank Charged with Discriminatory 'Redlining' Lending—Bank Pays $3.2 Million to Settle First Ever Discriminatory Commercial Lending Lawsuit" (press release, May 19, 2004).

Redlining by the insurance industry meant that those who were least able to afford high premiums were charged the most. City residents on average had a significantly lower standard of living than their suburban counterparts and a disproportionately high percentage of their income was going to pay for car insurance. In addition, many Detroiters were unable to afford even a used car to get around in because the premiums were prohibitively high. The high insurance rates provided another reason for residents to want to leave the city. The rates also further damaged the image of the city by unduly signaling to everyone that it was a dangerous and unattractive place.

We tried several strategies to get the insurance companies to lower their rates in the city. We asked Butch Hollowell, a young attorney on our board, to chair a fact-finding committee. In addition, we commissioned a foremost expert on insurance rates to analyze the situation in metro Detroit. In 1988, Hollowell and I met with Herman Coleman, commissioner of the state insurance agency. Coleman told us the agency lacked sufficient staff to review the differential rates the insurance companies charged throughout Michigan. He also said that, in his opinion, there was no way to determine when rates were "excessive" or "unfairly discriminatory." In effect, insurance companies were free to charge whatever rates they wanted and not worry about government oversight.

We also tried to negotiate with AAA officials. Those negotiations broke down after eighteen months when AAA said that it would be willing to eliminate its discriminatory rate structure only if the NAACP supported its efforts to secure state legislation that would limit the rights of victims of car accidents to sue for injury. We refused this deal, and on my recommendation, the NAACP decided to sue AAA in federal court for violating state and federal anti-discrimination laws. The class-action case began in 1990, and I knew that it would be a protracted and expensive legal battle. Indeed, of all the anti-discrimination legal initiatives undertaken by the branch, this was the most costly. More than $100,000 was spent to cover legal, research, and administrative expenses. The issue, however, was so important to the citizens of Detroit and the future of the city that the money and energy invested by the branch were worth it. The legal battle was still going on in 1993 when I decided not to seek reelection as president of the NAACP after having served three consecutive terms. This was a very difficult decision and ultimately was driven by my being promoted to senior vice president at Wayne State University. The demands of this executive post made it hard for me to devote the attention that I believed the NAACP presidency deserved. After I left office, my successor ended the legal action against AAA.

Without a legal or legislative remedy, Detroiters continued to be gouged by the discriminatory practices of the auto insurance industry. In 2006, Detroiters paid higher premiums than residents of any other city or town in America. The average annual premium for a Detroit resident was $5,894—more than six times the national average and almost three times more than the average for the rest of Michigan. Because of these exorbitant and discriminatory premiums, Detroit was the costliest city in the nation in which to own a car,[32] which is a bitter irony for a place known as the "Motor City."

I disagreed with the decision of the new NAACP administration not to vigorously pursue the case against AAA, but there was little I could do about it. After I announced my intention not to seek reelection as president, a power struggle ensued for control of the branch. I met with Ernest Lofton, a leader in the United Auto Workers (UAW) and head of a NAACP member group called the "Freedom Caucus." I urged Lofton to respect the need for NAACP independence from interest groups. I argued that if the NAACP were to remain relevant in the struggle of African Americans, it could not be perceived as an appendage of the UAW or any particular labor, political, or religious organization. The NAACP must be faithful to the civil rights aspirations we hold in common. History bears good witness to our striving together based on shared principles that transcend parochial differences, I argued. But Lofton did not agree with my perspective, and he

32. *Runzheimer International's Mobility Report,* Winter 2007.

was determined that the Freedom Caucus would push its candidate, Wendell Anthony.

Ultimately, after an impassioned campaign, Anthony was elected president. Anthony had no history of significant involvement with the branch but was anxious to lead the organization. He quickly moved to consolidate power and to purge the branch of individuals opposed to his way of doing things and with ties to the "old guard." A deep schism developed in the community between those who had built the NAACP into an effective civil rights organization and the Anthony administration. I was acutely disappointed with this turn of events. The branch no longer represented the historic vision that made it a leader in the civil rights struggle. As a result, its very relevance in the community came into question.

I no longer have much contact with the branch, and under the Anthony administration, branch history has been rewritten to diminish or even expunge my contributions to the Freedom Fund Dinner and various NAACP initiatives to fight racial injustice. Under my leadership as president, the branch began the "Buy Detroit" campaign in 1989, chaired by Horace Sheffield Sr.[33] The annual campaign urged Detroiters and suburban residents to shop, dine, and conduct business in Detroit as much as possible to help revitalize the economic life of the city. Major department and grocery stores had fled the city, and even Detroiters had grown accustomed to frequenting suburban malls, stores, and restaurants to spend their consumer dollars. The aim of Buy Detroit was to enhance commercial activity in the city and, in so doing, expand job and business opportunities for African Americans and others in Detroit. During the holiday shopping season, the Buy Detroit campaign issued a Retail Shop and Service Guide featuring businesses in city. It also organized promotional events and special discounts to entice shoppers to come downtown. The campaign proved to be a success, each year drawing more participants and sponsors, and was eventually renamed "Shop Detroit."

---

33. See appendix E.

The Anthony administration asserts that it initiated Buy Detroit despite a well-documented historical record that proves otherwise.[34] It claims credit for settling the lawsuit against AAA for the benefit of Detroit residents—even though the terms of the settlement have not been made public and Detroiters continue to be gouged by outrageous premiums. The Anthony administration also claims to have dramatically increased the branch's membership roll. However, this increase actually stems from a new accounting procedure in which lifetime memberships are added to the annual membership subscriptions to produce the total. During my tenure, we did not include lifetime members as part of the tally we gave to the national organization, though in retrospect, we should have in order to present a deeper picture of the branch's strength.

Over the years, I have tried to be modest about my efforts and accomplishments at the NAACP, both as executive secretary and as president. It was always the work that mattered, and never the credit. However, I vigorously oppose the rewriting of history to serve expedient and political ends, and this is why I have taken some time in this chapter to help set the record straight about branch history. It pains me today to be out of touch with an organization that I loved and to which I devoted my best energies and a great part of my life. I can only hope that a new generation of leadership will come forth and reinvigorate the NAACP with the passion and courage required to continue the fight for racial justice.

34. A biography of Wendell Anthony states: "Under Anthony's leadership, the Detroit branch of the NAACP began an important 'Buy in Detroit' campaign to promote economic activity within the city. He also played a crucial role in negotiating a settlement with the state's largest insurer, the American Automobile Association, over an NAACP suit that charged bias in its setting of insurance rates for Detroiters" ("Wendell Anthony," www.answers.com/topic/wendell-anthony).

CHAPTER 8

Friendship with Damon

Damon Keith and I became close friends shortly after I arrived in Detroit in 1950 to lead the NAACP branch. Our friendship, as I write today, is in its sixth decade. It not only spans a veritable lifetime, it is the defining friendship of my lifetime. There has never been a time in our friendship when we were not there for each other. We have been brothers in the struggle for racial justice. We have shared an extraordinary range of experiences that so many years together inevitably bring: the triumphs and setbacks, the joys and heartaches. As a result, there is a deep and implicit understanding between us. We not only understand how the other is feeling; we understand the myriad reasons why.

Damon has attained the status of a legal legend. A number of his decisions as a federal judge are regarded as among the most important in the history of American jurisprudence. Damon has been a stalwart advocate of the rights of all individuals to equal opportunity and justice under the law. He has shown remarkable courage in standing up to institutions and interests whose actions and policies violated constitutional principles. In the process, he has helped move the nation a little closer to its own ideals. One of his early rulings was so significant that it will always be known as the "Keith decision." The ruling went against the Nixon White House and paved the way for the Watergate investigation that ultimately forced the president to resign in disgrace. Damon later rendered landmark decisions related to desegregation, anti-discrimination efforts, affirmative action, and other civil rights issues.

The principles of compassion, conscience, and fairness expressed in Damon's opinions are embodied in who he is as a person. He has

NAACP membership committee meeting at the Elmwood Supper Club, Windsor, Canada, 1956. *Left to right:* Dr. Rachel Keith, Damon Keith, Thelma Thorpe Johnson, myself, Joe Coles, Ruth Coles, Mamie Green, Forrest Green.

"Soul Food Luncheon" in the chambers of Judge Damon Keith, 2003. *Left to right:* Governor Jennifer Granholm; Charles Chambers, president of Lawrence Technological Institute; Judge Keith; myself. (Photo by Monica Morgan)

never forgotten from whence he came and those who helped and inspired him along the way. As a result, he is motivated by a deep sense of responsibility to help others. At a time when federal judges were not hiring African American law clerks, Damon stepped up and provided opportunities for many promising black attorneys. He hired more black law clerks in the twentieth century than all other federal judges combined.[35] His clerks have enjoyed uncommon success. They have become judges, law professors—among them Lani Guinier at Harvard—and eminent attorneys. One of his clerks, Jennifer Granholm, became two-time governor of Michigan. Damon swore her in both times. All of his clerks consider themselves members of the Keith judicial family and extensions of their mentor's conscience. Damon considers this legacy even more important than his historic judicial record.

The friendship between Damon and me emerged and grew through shared endeavor, enjoyment of each other's company, and the core convictions that we hold in common. We share a sense of basic fairness that operates in all our relationships and motivates our commitment to a more just society. We believe that the black experience should lead to a sense of responsibility to make America a nation of freedom for everyone. We expect African Americans to stand up in difficult times and face the risks inherent in the struggle for racial justice. We believe that it is incumbent upon blacks who have "made it" to do whatever they can to help other African Americans. This obligation, we hold, is part of what it means to be black in America. We don't think that blacks are better than white Americans, but we certainly believe that we are just as good in every respect and can hold our own on a level playing field. In this regard, my friend Professor Charles Willie once said to an assembly of mostly African Americans, "You in this audience, don't you ever believe that you are

35. This fact was provided by the Duke University professor of law James Coleman, who is himself a former clerk of Judge Keith, in an interview with Steve Palackdharry in April 2001.

Damon Keith *(right)* and myself at a United Community Services meeting in Detroit in 1984.

twice as smart as white people. I have seen what the opposite belief has done to white people."

In our civil rights work, Damon and I always asked ourselves if we had the courage to do what was required. We felt we couldn't live with ourselves if we had compromised when we should have not. Sometimes we found it difficult to understand what we should do, but we also knew that it was vital to cultivate relationships with mentors who could advise us on the best course of action. Among our mentors, Joe Coles was our foremost counselor. We followed our mentors' advice and were better able to serve our community as a result.

We also came to understand that different members of our community were not prepared to assume the risks involved in the battle against racism. Some had too much fear. Some felt they had specific contributions to make and were not comfortable with other forms of protest. One of the great moments in the civil rights movement occurred on Easter in 1939 when the great African American singer Marian Anderson sang at the Lincoln Memorial before a crowd of 75,000 and millions of radio listeners. The concert was arranged by Eleanor Roosevelt and the NAACP after Anderson was denied the opportunity to perform at Constitution Hall by its owners, the Daughters of the American Revolution, because of her skin color. Anderson reluctantly agreed to sing at the Lincoln Memorial because she preferred to avoid being out front on the civil rights struggle. She did not consider herself a "fighter," she said, but her powerful voice stirred the nation's conscience that Easter Sunday when she sang "My Country 'Tis of Thee." Almost twenty-five years later, Martin Luther King gave his "I Have A Dream" speech at the Lincoln Memorial. He spoke of the great day in the future "when all God's children will be able to sing with new meaning, 'My country 'tis of thee, sweet land of liberty, of thee I sing.'"

When Damon and I are with a group of people and he begins to talk about our civil rights work together, he sometimes likes to joke that we were able to build a great friendship because our approaches complement each other. Damon, he insists, is the "street fighter," whereas I am the "gentleman." This characterization gets a good laugh because it is hard to view Damon, especially at this latter stage in his life, as a "street fighter." He is not only a towering figure in the law but a gentleman who exudes a certain warmth and charisma. This hardly seems like the disposition of a "street fighter." In reality, we are both a combination of "street fighter" and "gentleman." These days I serve on the board of a number of cultural and corporate organizations. In these contexts, I sometimes couch my tough criticisms diplomatically. Indeed, a fellow board member once said of me, "To keep people listening, Arthur throws his bricks covered in velvet." I strongly believe that we owe it to our cause to be wise in choosing words and tone. Language is as important as any other instrument for change, if not more so.

When Damon talks about being a "street fighter," he is referring, in part, to his struggle to attain a powerful position within the system. After he graduated from Howard Law School in 1949, he returned to Detroit and was working as a janitor when he got word that he had passed the bar on his second try. Harsh discrimination made it very difficult for black attorneys to make a living in the profession, but Damon built a viable practice through sheer determination. He also did significant work for the NAACP and the Democratic Party and developed important contacts in the community and political sector. In 1964 he partnered with four other African American lawyers to create the firm of Keith, Conyers, Anderson, Brown, and Wahls. The firm soon became one of the most influential minority law firms in the nation.

In 1966 a judicial opening became available on the U.S. District Court for Eastern Michigan because of the pending departure of Judge Wade McCree. McCree had been elevated by President Johnson to serve on the Court of Appeals for the Sixth Circuit. In the political environment of the time, it was understood that McCree's replacement on the district court would also be African American. Because the position was a federal judgeship, the appointment would be made by President Johnson based on the recommendation of Michigan's Democratic senator Philip Hart.

Both Damon and I were friends with the senator. Hart was so widely respected that he was known as the "conscience of the senate." The senator had high regard for Damon's legal mind and sense of integrity, and he informed Damon privately that he would be recommending him to the president. However, a complication soon arose about who was the best African American candidate for the position. The controversy would draw many black community leaders into the conflict.

The complication occurred when the word began to circulate that Damon was the leading candidate for the judgeship. Otis Smith began to lobby behind the scenes for the appointment himself, believing that he was better qualified. Otis was the first African American to serve on the Michigan Supreme Court. He was appointed to the state court by the governor in 1961 but lost in his election bid in 1966. Damon served as Otis's campaign manager and worked hard to rally support for Otis in the black community. He drove Otis to campaign stops and black churches all over town. Damon also held a private fundraising event in his home. Ultimately, despite Damon's best efforts, the black vote in Detroit was not enough to offset the balloting in other parts of the state.

Among his many talents, Damon's campaign skills were renowned. He had a keen mind for campaign strategy and organizing and worked tirelessly to meet goals that exceeded what many people thought possible. He chaired the membership campaign of the Detroit NAACP and brought the membership roll to its highest total in history. His leadership helped make the Freedom Fund Dinner the premier NAACP fundraising event in the nation. In 1955, he served as campaign manager for Wade McCree, who was vying for the Wayne County Circuit Court. Political experts at the time had predicted that an African American could not win a countywide election for judge. However, McCree was elected, and Damon played a key role in proving the experts wrong. Now that McCree was leaving the Eastern District Court, Damon expected his support. McCree, however, decided to endorse Otis Smith.

I tried to give Damon all the support that I could and, at the same time, maintain the integrity of my relationships with Otis and Wade. Wade and I were members of a group of thirteen men that got together several times a year for dinner. The group included both white and black community leaders. We talked about the problems in the city and possible solutions. I decided not to ask Wade about his endorsement choice because I worried that it could cause tension between us, and this tension could hurt the group's dynamics. In any case, we were dealing with the prospects of two men—Otis and Damon—both of whom were eminently worthy of appointment.

Otis gathered support among white political leadership in the city and state. He won the backing of a number of black leaders, though the consensus among black leaders clearly favored Damon. As the contest between Damon and Otis became public, the Detroit newspapers weighed in on the issue. Both the *Free Press* and the *News* wrote editorials favoring Smith as the better choice. The *News* pointed to the fact that Damon had taken the bar more than once. This was a trying time for Damon, but he was confident that he was up to the job and would excel if given the opportunity.

The conflict over the appointment put Senator Hart in a very delicate situation. He knew all the principals in this dispute very well and certainly did not want to offend any of them. He asked me my opinion, and I told him that Damon would be a good judge because he is a good man. I also stressed with him that Damon was eminently qualified for the position and that his first preference to recommend Damon was on the mark. Still, the senator was facing mounting political pressure, particularly as Smith picked up increasing support from white institutions and leadership.

A group of black leaders and I understood that the outcome of the contest between Damon and Otis was something that needed to be settled in the black community. We decided to meet and make sure that this decision was not ceded to white leadership and white institutions placing pressure on Senator Hart. The group included Joe Coles, Dr. D. T. Burton, Forrest Green, August Calloway, Dr. Lionel Swan, and Franklin Brown. We met in a conference room at Burton Mercy Hospital, where Dr. Burton was chief administrator.

The group looked at the controversy as an opportunity for black leadership to change the way political appointments for blacks were traditionally made. There was a prevailing belief in the African American community that when a black person was selected for a high honor in the system, the individual chosen was typically not the one that black leadership would have selected but rather someone who was more compatible with the interests and sensibilities of white leadership. As a result, from the perspective of the black community, blacks who moved up in the system often faced some suspicions, fairly or unfairly, about whether they were going to do the right thing and whether they were going to be strong enough to say what needed to be said to the powers that be. I suffered such nagging suspicions myself when I was promoted at the board of education and at Wayne State University. Both Wade McCree and Otis Smith had to deal with such suspicions in their respective judicial appointments.

The group of black leaders understood that the controversy over Damon's possible appointment to the district court had nothing to do with his worthiness but stemmed from the attitude that an African American candidate for the bench ought to suit white judgments about whether that candidate was acceptable. We decided that we needed to break this pattern of white people selecting which black person would be crowned. All of us knew that Damon was ready in all respects to assume his place on the district court. We also knew that he would always stand on principle and never be intimidated by power.

We explained these issues to Senator Hart, and he was brave enough to affirm our reasoning. He said he was determined to stand by Damon and recommend that President Johnson appoint him. From a historical viewpoint, this was a landmark moment for black leadership and the black community. We had succeeded in our efforts to relay to the white power structure that it could not continue to dictate which blacks will be honored for what post. We had established that our voice must play a critical role in these decisions.

Even as it advocated for Damon, the group of black leaders was very concerned about offending Otis Smith. We all admired him—as a person and for his illustrious record in public service and the private sector. Because of my friendship with Otis, the group asked me to sit down with him and explain our perspective and why we all believed it was Damon's turn. I met with Otis and told him that our efforts on Damon's behalf were not intended as a fight against him and that we certainly were not implying that he was not worthy of the appointment. "You are fully prepared for this post," I said, "and we know it. But we simply think it is Damon's turn to be recognized, and we ask you to understand that." Otis eventually accepted our argument, with some reluctance and disappointment. After losing his election bid for the State Supreme Court, he anxiously desired the lifetime appointment to the federal judiciary. It was also evident that the public controversy over the appointment had taken a toll on him. Not long after our talk, Otis withdrew his name from consideration for the position.

When Damon became a judge, our relationship entered a different phase. His duties to the office meant he was no longer free to do the advocacy work for the civil rights struggle that he had done in the past. He also operated under a different set of time constraints and responsibilities. However, Damon made a concerted effort to keep his friendships intact and as strong as ever. In many respects, Damon and I grew even closer as our professional lives diverged.

Damon's wife, the late Dr. Rachel Keith, was the ideal partner for him. They complemented each other perfectly and raised a family of three daughters—Cecile, Debbie, and Gilda. Rachel was also a remarkable individual and trailblazing civil rights figure. She was the only African American woman in her class at the Boston University School of Medicine. In 1949, the year she graduated, she was featured in the *Boston Globe* for accomplishing the highest score in history on a medical school exam. Dr. Keith interned at Detroit Receiving Hospital at a time when black physicians were regularly denied opportunities at major hospitals because of discrimination. Later, she entered into private practice, where she was highly sought after because of her expertise and dedication. She also devoted considerable time to treating the poor and uninsured, and she served on the boards of numerous community, medical, and cultural organizations.

Rachel was my primary physician for thirty-five years. She saw me through some of the difficult times of my life. She was there for me after the deaths of three of my sons. She advised and comforted me after my diagnosis of Parkinson's disease. I trusted her knowledge and friendship implicitly.

Rachel died suddenly in January of 2007. Damon was in Washington D.C. swearing in new members of the black Congressional Caucus when Rachel collapsed. He rushed back to Detroit, and when he arrived, a small group of friends met him in his chambers. These included Bill Pickard, Alex Parrish, Judge Eric Clay, and Judge John Feikens. Chacona and I were also there. As two couples, the Johnsons and the Keiths, we had enjoyed almost thirty years of close friendship.

Damon was my best man when Chacona and I got married in 1980. It was my third marriage. Before the ceremony, Damon joked with me, "Arthur, this is your last time at bat." I laughed and replied, "I think so, too." The ceremony was set for four in the afternoon but threatened to be delayed because my pastor was running late. I turned to Damon and asked for his help. He searched among the eighty friends at the wedding, found Reverend Nicholas Hood and Reverend James Wadsworth, and asked them to step in. The two pastors decided how to divide the ministerial duties and then conducted the ceremony together.

During our wedding vows, when the pastor asked me, "Do you promise to share all your worldly goods?" Damon was at my side and laughed. I then laughed with him. Damon knew that I didn't have any money and possessed few assets of tangible value. On the long road he and I had traveled together to that moment of shared laugher, it had always been this way. Some twenty-five years earlier, when I was executive secretary of the NAACP and Damon was chair of the Freedom Fund Dinner, I went to see him to talk about the event. After we finished our discussion, he asked me if I had a nice suit to wear to the elegant affair. I replied, "No." He said that he had accounts at Hudson's and Hughes & Hatcher and insisted that I go to one of them, find the suit that looked best on me, and have it tailored. I took him up on his gracious offer. I felt relieved to be smartly dressed for an event that I had helped create and at which all the leaders in the black community were gathered. Damon anticipated this and knew it was important for me to feel at ease that evening. He is the type of friend who wants for his friends what he wants for himself.

After the wedding, I told Damon that when I proposed to Chacona, I explained in all honesty my financial situation to her. "I have no money," I told her, "and I don't know when I will have any, but if you stick with me, in the end you will not be left in distress."

Over the years of our marriage, our finances improved because of both of our efforts and financial opportunities facilitated by two good friends, Bill Pickard and Al Glancy. We have been able to enjoy many of the finer things in life, including travel. Rachel and Damon joined us on a number of trips. In 1982, the four of us and another couple, Abe and Anna Venable, went on a Caribbean cruise together. On the voyage, the captain explained some of the impressive things about the beaches on Martinique, including the fact that it had topless bathing. Damon and I looked at each with the same unspoken thought—well, we should let the ladies take the sightseeing tour while we stretch our legs and stroll along the beach. The mischievous feeling was somewhat reminiscent of our bachelor days in Detroit, when we would visit the lively nightclubs in Paradise Valley. In this case, now thirty years later, our wives knew exactly what we were up to and agreed to play along with it. Indeed, Chacona accompanied us on our outing.

On the beach, Damon and I were taking in the sights, replete with running commentary, when Chacona pointed out that we were missing the most beautiful woman in this spectacular setting. The woman was topless, standing in the crystal blue water, talking to some young men. I had my camera in hand, and Damon asked me, "Why don't you take a picture?" I was reluctant to do so. We had moved close enough to the woman and her companions to hear that they were speaking French, and I was concerned because I didn't know what they were saying about our presence. I also felt that people are entitled to be asked before you snap their photograph. I did not speak French, and even if she understood English, my motives were too transparent and embarrassing to broach the question. Well, the next thing I knew, Damon was in the water with this woman and they were talking. I took several pictures of him conversing with this stunning woman and obviously basking in the moment.

Later Chacona and I decided that we would help Damon preserve the pleasure of meeting this beautiful woman on the beach. So, for a Christmas present, we gave him several enlarged pictures of the encounter.

Damon and I related this story to a group of close friends gathered at his home. We were reminiscing about the past, marriage, and our friendship. I told the group, "The point of this story is that in special circumstances, Damon speaks French fluently." I then asked Damon where the pictures were. He said that they were under lock and key in his chambers. He had put them there, he said, because he did not want Rachel to see them. We all laughed, knowing that Rachel herself would have found Damon's innocuous adventure quite amusing. Still, we also understood that his safeguarding the images thus was part of his protective nature. He would never risk offending his bride.

Damon's chambers in Detroit are a walking museum. The walls are lined with photographs documenting the people he has met in his long and preeminent career as a lawyer, "street fighter," and federal judge. There are pictures of him with Thurgood Marshall, Joe Coles, Martin Luther King, American presidents, international statesmen, famous entertainers and athletes, his law clerks, and many others. All of these images will one day become a part of his archival collection housed at Wayne State University. However, there is a set of images that, I strongly suspect, future researchers will never see. They remain vivid in my memory because of what they show about my closest friend: his zest for life, his sense of adventure, his charisma, and his loyalty. And ultimately, his impeccable integrity—all attest brightly to the character of this very special individual.

CHAPTER 9

Death of Three Sons

My first marriage, to Thelma Thorpe, gave me three sons: Averell, Brian, and Carl. Averell was born in 1952, Brian in 1955, and Carl in 1957. A fourth son was born in my second marriage: David, in 1966. My second wife had two children from a previous marriage, Wendell and Angela, whom I claim as my own. I loved all six of my children with the kind of passion that my grandmother loved me. She was my role model of what parental love should be: unconditional, understanding, and sheltering. My grandmother's love saved me from my stepfather's mistreatment and gave me the confidence to strive and succeed in the racist South. I wanted to offer my children a comparable gift. Black parents have a special responsibility to prepare their children for a world in which racism is still prevalent and to instill a sense of self that racism cannot corrode. I believe that I fulfilled this responsibility to my children. Sometimes, however, tragic forces enter the lives of our children against which we as parents are utterly helpless.

Of the four sons born to me, three died before the age of thirty. Two committed suicide. The other died of a sudden and vicious illness. Before these tragedies, I had not realized how much my day-to-day sense of well-being was anchored in the lives of all of my children. It is said that the death of one's child is one of the most traumatic events any adult can experience. Losing three of my children in six years nearly destroyed me.

My oldest son, Averell, took his life on September 11, 1980. Just twelve days earlier, I had married Chacona, my third wife. The wedding was unquestionably the happiest day of my life. After my second marriage had ended, I reconciled myself to living alone, and I was not sure that I wanted to make this level of commitment again. Chacona changed my attitude. Everything seemed right about our marriage. My emotional and spiritual connection with Chacona was so strong that I felt it must be a gift from God. This gift arrived relatively late in life. I was fifty-five years old when we married. Chacona was about half my age at the time. She was well educated, having received a bachelor's degree in business administration from Saint Augustine's College and a master's degree in public administration from The Ohio State University. She was also stunning. I celebrated our love with an almost youthful enthusiasm, and I looked toward the future with renewed optimism.

The extreme contrast between great happiness and profound despair happened in a very short period. The experience of grief always throws the future into question, but the death of a child intensifies a sense of hopelessness, because a child is the very embodiment of the future. The loss of a child feels like the loss of the most promising part of oneself. It is spiritually devastating. No other crisis in my life threatened my will to live and my faith in God's goodness the way the death of each of my sons affected me.

Averell was twenty-seven when he took his own life. Five years earlier, he began to show symptoms of mental illness. I remember quite well the moment when I realized that something was terribly wrong. He called me and asked if we could have a beer together because he wanted to talk about some problems related to his work at a bank. When we met, he talked feverishly about his female supervisor and how she was out to hurt him. As I listened and inquired, it became increasingly evident to me that his story did not make sense. I had never heard him speak this way before, and I became worried that my son might be mentally ill. The next day, I took Averell to see a prominent psychiatrist in the area, and he diagnosed my son as schizophrenic.

With medication, Averell was somewhat able to control the effects of his illness for periods, but the disharmony between his mind and his environment was always there. I remember taking him to a performance of the Detroit Symphony Orchestra. He loved concerts, but he could no longer synchronize his mind with the music, and he

Averell with his younger
brother Brian in 1957.

Left to right: my son
Averell, my sister Shirley,
my son Carl, my son
Brian. Detroit, June 1978.

My wedding to Chacona (Winters) on August 30, 1980. Left to right: myself, Reverend James Wadsworth, Chacona, and Toni Martin, the maid of honor.

My son David *(left)* at the same wedding reception. David was nearly fourteen years old at the time.

applauded at inappropriate times. He just couldn't help himself, although a part of him knew better. He was formally trained in music. In his late teens he even started a rhythm and blues group modeled after the band Earth, Wind & Fire. His younger brothers, Brian and Carl, were the other members. They did not have formal training, but they looked up to Averell and were anxious to learn from him.

Averell was frustrated by his inability to manage the dark emotions staining his thoughts. He was very self-aware, and he educated himself about the disease afflicting him. He was in and out of the hospital. One evening I visited him at the psychiatric ward of Henry Ford Hospital. We went out to dinner, and when we returned he asked me earnestly, "Dad, what is wrong with me?" This was the most painful question that anyone had ever asked me. My son was reaching out from a place of great loneliness and sadness, and I tried to reassure him. I desperately wanted him to know that he was never alone, but I could feel a forest of darkness in him that my love could not illuminate. It was the most helpless feeling in the world.

Later, I spoke to Averell's psychiatrist at the hospital. I implored him, "Please tell me anything I can do. What can I do to help my son?" The doctor's response was cold and clinical, "What do you mean what can *you* do?" I said that I didn't know what I meant, and I left thinking that I would not ask this question aloud again. Its sentiment was not like me. In my own work, I sought to take on the powerful forces of racial injustice, and my efforts had some efficacy in bringing about changes for the better. But in the matter of my son, I was completely at a loss.

Even in the throes of his mental illness, Averell was always respectful and loving. When he was a boy, he asked me many times to legally change his name to "Arthur Johnson Jr." to affirm the fact that he was my oldest son. The last time he made this request, he was twelve years old. I explained to him how proud I was of him and how important it was to me that he should have his own identity. He understood and agreed. This never changed how close he felt to me and how deeply sensitive he was to my feelings about him.

A month before his death, Averell called me from a halfway house where he was staying after being released from the hospital. He asked me to come see him as soon as I could. Twenty minutes later, I met him on the steps of the Considine Recreation Center on Woodward Avenue, and we went for an evening walk in the city. At one point he stopped, turned to me, and said, "Dad, have you ever been in a position where you had no place to go and nothing to do?" The desperation in his words broke me up and I began to cry. It was the first time I had ever cried in front of him about his struggle with schizophrenia. I had cried many times about his struggle in private, but I had always tried to hide my distress and keep the faith in his presence. This night, however, I could not hold back the tears. My son put his arms around me and said, "Oh dad, this is the bomb." He was relieved that we could share this moment of heartbreaking understanding.

On the day he died, Averell came to see me at my office at Wayne State at 9:30 in the morning. He was neatly dressed and groomed and told me that he had a job interview that day. I said that was wonderful, and I offered him some money to buy a few things he needed. Averell was a person of modest material wants and he never accepted more money from me than what he needed. We talked for half an hour about his future and other things. He seemed eerily reconciled and calm. I thought this was because he had made a decision to move his life forward. After Averell left, my son David came to my office for career day. David was still with me when I received a call from my son Carl that afternoon. He said that Averell had shot himself and was dead. My mind began to ring with a kind of deafening silence. Everything after that felt like a blur.

Averell had shot himself in his mother's home. The body was lying near the top of the stairs leading to the second floor. I went to the house, but I didn't want to see him. Finally, I forced myself to look at the body, but not closely. I just could not bring myself to do that.

My mind obsessively went over everything that Averell said and did in the last few weeks of his life. In retrospect, there seemed to be so many signs. I tormented myself wondering how I could have missed them. I had interpreted them as meaning he was putting his life in order so that he could start anew. I had an uneasy suspicion that something else might be at work, but I suspended those feelings in my hopeful yearning that his future was coming together. Perhaps we can never completely rid ourselves of the guilt that we should have known and been able to intervene. The deep wound in our conscience heals with time but always remains tender. And should the wound be violently reopened, our vulnerability is even more acute—though we would not have thought that possible.

Two and a half years after Averell ended his own life, David made the same bitter choice. David was only seventeen years old. He hanged himself in the basement of our home while Chacona and I were out. I remember the foreboding feeling as we entered the house. David's dog TJ did not greet us at the door as usual. I called out for my son in the tense stillness. My heart was already hammering into my head as I descended the stairs to look for him. Chacona followed me. At that moment near the bottom of the steps when I saw his suspended body, I felt as though a switch were thrown in my brain, overloading all its circuits with torrential memory. They say that in a near-death experience your entire life flashes before your eyes. The death of a child is near death for the parent.

I cried out, "Oh David. You didn't let *this* do you in." What I meant by "this" were all the painful experiences he had endured in his young life. They reeled in my mind like a film moving at light's speed. I remembered a scene when he was about ten years old. It was a very cold winter morning with heavy snow. School was closed and David was home. At that time, home was an almost insufferable place. My marriage to his mother had virtually disintegrated, and a kind of sickness had set in that can deform your personality and make you at times unrecognizable to yourself. On this bitter day, I could not remain in the house and was determined to attend a meeting downtown. However, my car was not running, and when I asked David's mother to use her car, she refused. So I started walking to the bus stop four blocks away. David was distressed about this, and he ran after me. When he caught up with me, he pleaded, "Dad, don't go. You don't know when the bus is coming. You'll freeze out here." He was a child, and yet he wanted to protect me from the storm.

I remembered coming home after work one evening. David was outside playing with other kids on the block. I tried to enter the house, but my wife had locked it from the inside and would not let me in. I asked David to go to the back door, crawl through the milk chute, and then open the door. He was small enough to do so. His mother tried to prevent him from crawling in, but he still made it into the house. However, she forbid him to unlock the door. I became so angry that I kicked the door in while she was talking on the phone. This was the most violent thing David had ever seen me do. His mother grabbed a knife and threatened to stab me. Just then, Angela and her friend Judy came to the front door. David had the presence of mind to unlock the door and let them in. After a tense standoff, Angela, with help from Judy and David, was able to remove the knife from her mother's hand.

Angela, David, and I left the house together. I left knowing that I would not live there again. In the tumult of that moment, there was a sense of relief to be leaving this daily conflict, but the prevailing feeling was one of sadness. I worried about how the children would cope—particularly David, since he was still a child. He had been forced already to experience so much pain and turmoil during his formative years. Angela had an apartment of her own, and she invited David and me to stay with her for as long we needed. As we settled in that night, I thanked Angela for her graciousness and then gently said to David, "You are going to school tomorrow morning and I am going to work."

The ending of the marriage brought many more experiences that were equally as hard on David. He was also confused and torn. Eventually, he decided that he wanted to live with Chacona and me. We arranged for him to see a therapist regularly because of all he had been through and because his concentration was lacking at school. About a month before his death, David's therapist suggested that his sessions be cut back from once a week to twice a month. We all agreed that David was doing better. Two weeks later, however, he said something very disturbing at the dinner table. He blurted out to us, "I know how people hang themselves." I rebuked him for talking about such subjects and abruptly changed the conversation. He was a teenager, and teenagers are prone to drama, especially when a romantic relationship is going poorly. David's girlfriend had recently informed him she wanted to cool things between them and that they should begin to date other people. After his suicide, David's therapist told us that this was the likely trigger for David's action. He could not cope with another female rejection.

In the few seconds it took me to reach David's body, my entire world was thrown into a vortex of despair and disbelief. When reality is unbearable, the mind tries to detach itself from the senses. I was beside myself. I began to scream in a voice that was seemingly not my own. It issued from a place of abysmal darkness. I remember saying, "David, not you. Not again, God. Not again."

A recurring question spun in my mind: How could you do this to me, David? The question seemed almost selfish. It had no rightful place in the horror of the moment—though I would learn later that it is a question "survivors" often ask themselves when the tragedy occurs and for a long time thereafter. I sometimes think that if suicide victims only understood beforehand how much pain and despair their acts would cause loved ones, they might have chosen to live. And yet, I am certain that David knew in his heart how much I loved him. He must have known that I would be utterly devastated. Or perhaps his troubled mind could not connect the two.

I grasped his legs and tried to lift his body to relieve the pressure on his neck. My screams had caused the upstairs neighbors in our two-family flat to come running into the basement. At the same time, Chacona returned with a knife and climbed on a chair and cut the tether. My son had hanged himself with his dog's leash. TJ had not come to the door to greet us because he had stayed with David's lifeless body.

I would not let go of David. I was out of my mind with grief and unresponsive to anyone's request of me. I wondered if I had failed him despite all my efforts to help him grow up with aspirations for a fulfilling life. I thought about how overwhelming his despair must have been for him to take his own life, and I could not stand the thought that he had felt so much pain. I felt sick with guilt that I was not there for him in his moment of greatest need. If only I had not gone to the NAACP meeting that evening. I cradled him as if only the two of us were left, in the eye of the storm. The voices around me seemed from another world. The police had arrived, and they were demanding that I release my son. They wanted to handcuff me for my own good and take me upstairs so the body could be examined. Chacona was pleading with them not to do that to me. Finally, I let go.

Chacona called my doctor, Rachel Keith, and she and Damon rushed over. Rachel gave me a powerful sedative that began to calm me down. Damon wrapped his arms around me, and we cried. He did not say much. He consoled me with his tears, and I felt strengthened by our mutual vulnerability. To be held and comforted by a good friend is so important at a time like this. You feel utterly stranded, as if you've missed the last flight home and you'll never make it back. You feel estranged not only from the world, but from God.

Rachel called my pastor at Tabernacle Missionary Baptist, Reverend Frederick Sampson, and he came right away. I embraced him and cried out, "I haven't lost my faith." I do not know if my exclamation at that moment expressed what I truly felt or was an attempt to persuade myself and defy fate. The question asked by Jesus on the cross resounded in my mind: "God, why hast Thou forsaken me?" I wondered why I did not warrant better treatment from God.

David died in April, after Easter had passed. Studies show that April has the highest suicide rate of any month of the year.[36] Some

---

36. Daniel Romer, Patrick Jamieson, Nancy J. Holtschlag, Hermon Mebrathu, and Kathleen Hall Jamieson, *Suicide and the Media* (Philadelphia: Annenberg Public Policy Center of the University of Pennsylvania, 2003).

believe this is because the coming of spring raises hopes of personal renewal that may make life's disappointments seem even worse. In the days after David's death, I searched for answers and thought about what I could have done differently to save his life. If only I had heeded the warning signs that had somehow eluded me, a part of me thought. Another part of me was more forgiving, and this part was reinforced by close friends and my wife. Had Chacona not been by my side at every moment, I don't know if I would have been able to stay on my feet and stop looking for answers that could never be found. I was also encouraged by the outpouring of affection from David's friends. I was glad to know that he had created a strong circle of companionship. His friends kept in close touch with Chacona and me for quite some time after David was gone. We shared a bond, and I was appreciative of how much they cherished the memory of my son.

David's death was a constant presence in the house, but I felt that moving would be like abandoning him. The psychological pulling and tearing of being in the house took a toll on me. Still, I thought I should be strong enough to hold it together until the pain subsided. My daughter Angela summed up this trait of mine by telling me, "You are always toughing it out, Daddy." I think that I learned this level of perseverance by watching how my grandmother coped with adversity, though I am sure that she herself would have advised me not to continue to dwell here. Chacona, Rachel Keith, and Angela coaxed me for a year to move to another place. I finally agreed, but it was a heart-wrenching decision.

The year after David's suicide was perhaps the most difficult of my life. I could not work up to the level of my own expectations. I had always received the highest evaluations from my superiors, wherever I worked. But this year, my immediate supervisor at Wayne State, Michael Luck, wrote an evaluation stating that my productivity had fallen off. He added that perhaps the tragedy of losing my son had caused this decline. I was offended that he would make such a comment in an offhand way. It only added insult to injury.

Just when I felt hopeful of reaching emotional equilibrium after these two suicides, my son Carl suddenly became ill with acute abdominal pain. The doctor at the hospital said his pancreas was so inflamed that it appeared he had suffered a hard blow to that area. I never learned what actually caused the inflammation. The doctor informed me that Carl's illness was life-threatening, and I prayed for his recovery.

Of all my children, I had the most difficulty building a strong relationship with Carl. He was the youngest son of my first marriage, and he never came to terms with our divorce. He was inclined to hold me accountable for the family coming apart, and he tended to resent me for that. Nevertheless, he was a kind and gentle person and was particularly attentive to the little things that made others happy. I always wished that he would take better care of himself. He became overweight and I was concerned about his health.

Carl was admitted to the hospital on a Monday evening and he passed away on Saturday morning of the same week. I was with him late Friday night. Doctors did not expect his condition to change much in the near future, and so I kept a speaking engagement early Saturday morning. It ended ahead of schedule, and I went immediately to the hospital. When I approached his room, I was met by our family physician, Dr. Lionel Swan. He said that Carl's kidneys had failed. Carl died in 1986, three years after David and six years after Averell. He was twenty-nine.

I was sixty years old when Carl died, an age when you feel mortality in your marrow and spiritual questions have even greater significance. In my darkest hours of grief, I never doubted that God existed. However, I felt forsaken and was caused to wonder about the purpose of faith.

The process of recovery was very slow. Sleep did not come without difficulty, and my dreams were always troubled. During the day, I often felt like a ghost of who I once was. I was not only haunted by my sons' deaths, I worried constantly about my surviving children—Brian, Angela, and Wendell. All grieved in their own way for the loss of their brothers. I told my wife and my friends that I felt as though there was a bottomless pool of tears in my chest and I was weeping within. I was unsure whether I would do anything of value again.

I have learned a great deal about suicide, searching for reasons and truth that would not come. There is no painless readjustment, no stifling of feelings of guilt—it is all bad. But over time, with the help of Chacona and my friends, I gradually felt whole again. I was able to remember my sons' innocence and joy without becoming lost in the tragedy. I found the strength to speak to other parents whose children had committed suicide. I tried to assure them that the agony of remembrance would get better, and the day would arrive when the loss of loved ones would not be the first thought in the morning or the last before going to sleep at night. In the course of my healing, I experienced the meaning of the Christian paradox that God is closest to those whose suffering is greatest. I could feel His infinite mercy easing my anguish. After all the complications of struggle and sorrow, I felt my faith anchored in a simple truth: God is love.

I sometimes find it hard to believe that I have arrived at this point. But I am firmly reconciled with my belief in God's love and mercy, despite all the pain I have suffered. I understand, without any disillusionment, that faith cannot protect us from tragedy and injustice. Faith serves to help us survive these crises and to sustain our hopes when circumstances dictate that hope should be lost. My faith has helped renew my sense of purpose and my dedication to the struggle for civil rights. I do not ask God for answers about why my sons are dead. I know that such answers are not forthcoming. Instead, I call on my faith to help me realize my life's calling. As my pastor Reverend Sampson liked to say: "Life is not a mystery to be solved; it is a mystery to be lived."

The tragedy of losing three sons is permanently etched in all my emotions. It has deepened my ability to love and my appreciation of life's gifts. It has made me more open and vulnerable to the suffering of others. I am easily affected by news events, stories, and music where pain and tragedy are presented. The loss of my sons taught me more about love, compassion, and beauty than I ever knew before. It taught me about the art of living, and, ultimately, that art *is* life. In the same year that Carl died, the first Detroit Festival of the Arts came alive. I worked through some of my grief in bringing this event to fruition. As I walked through the festival, I was moved by its vibrant success and how it quickened the pulse of the cultural and university district. I thought: This is my gift to the city of Detroit, a city that I love deeply despite all its heartbreaking struggles and setbacks. Or perhaps the heartbreak has only deepened my love. I also thought: I offer this gift in honor of my sons. May their memory live on in this celebration of life and the indomitable creative energy of the human spirit.

CHAPTER 10

Searching for the Good Life

I realize that it is somewhat presumptuous to offer advice on "searching for the good life." It assumes that I have somehow arrived at this destination and have something to say about lessons learned along the way. At this point in our journey together, I hope the reader will forgive my bit of presumption and find some meaning in my advice, derived not only from experience but also from those who have influenced and guided me.

In writing about the "good life," I hasten to say that I am not referring to material and financial wealth. I am not referring to fame or celebrity status, or living a long life, either, even though that, too, is a wonderful blessing. I do not intend to talk about the role of technology in enriching and extending our lives. Ultimately, I believe, a good and fulfilling life is rooted in relationships, core principles, and a deep sense of purpose.

Music and Wholeness

I have been a regular concertgoer at the Detroit Symphony since I arrived in the city in 1950. My love of music derives from my grandmother and her love of the great Negro spirituals and hymns. My grandmother was an uneducated domestic servant for most of her life. She was the greatest influence during my youth, and the formative lessons she taught me are the cornerstone of who I am. Her passion for the music of the black church instilled in me our musical heritage and inspired me to appreciate other music as well. Because of her gift, I not only possess music as an essential interest, but music has the power to possess me. It transports me to another place, beyond the strictures of the world left behind. In this vital place, as the poet T. S. Eliot wrote, "You are the music, while the music lasts."[37]

Although my grandmother did not follow classical music, I developed the habit at an early age of listening to the national radio broadcasts of the *Ford Sunday Evening Hour* featuring the Detroit Symphony Orchestra. This music came to me from another world, but I found it strangely compelling and listened intently. I could hardly have suspected that I would one day be so deeply involved with this renowned orchestra.

My interest in this *other* music was reinforced by attending performances of our glee club at Parker High in Birmingham, Alabama. I also remember an English teacher self-consciously playing on the piano Chopin's *Polonaise* for a student program in the school auditorium. From a technical standpoint, I am not sure how good that performance was, but the sound was dazzling to me. Two years later, at age sixteen, I went alone to a recital by the great Marian Anderson at the Birmingham Civic Auditorium. Although confined with other African Americans to the segregated balcony, I listened to the music with heart and mind. It was an unforgettable experience.

At Morehouse College in Atlanta, I attended my first orchestra concert. It was performed by the Atlanta University Center Orchestra under the direction of Morehouse professor Kemper Harreld, regarded then as the dean of black American musicians. Professor Harreld organized the orchestra, which was made up of students from black colleges in Atlanta. His enthusiasm, expertise, and commitment encouraged me to take his course at Morehouse in music appreciation. I began to understand the intricacy of classical music. As I educated myself further about the music, my appreciation deepened.

For many years, attending the symphony in Detroit was often an uneasy experience for me. I had dedicated my life to fighting against discrimination and segregation, but inside the performance hall I was one of the few black faces. I often asked myself how I should deal with

---

37. T. S. Eliot, *Four Quartets* (1943; New York: Harcourt Trade, 1968).

The pianist André Watts, myself, and my wife, Chacona, at Orchestra Hall in Detroit in 1987.

this situation. Should I boycott the symphony in protest? Should I deprive myself of the joy of hearing this great music performed in order to make a political statement? To whom does this music belong? Those who stage its performance? The listener immersed in the timeless moment? Or something more universal, beyond the particular distinctions? Before the music began and after the music ended, these questions often nagged me. During the music I was hardly conscious of myself at all, and thus of all the issues that separate us, including race. Music is deeply spiritual to me.

I answered the questions by deciding to stay and fight rather than disengage. I also held fast to the premise that none of us—performers, listeners, administrators, or donors—none of us own the music that we hear. I know the greatness of Mahler's *Resurrection,* the works of Beethoven, Brahms, Bach, and others. The music is a gift to the world, and it is color-blind. I, too, stake my claim. I want the world to know that you may deny my place in the orchestra, but you cannot deny my listening.

In 1988, the issue of racial discrimination in the classical music field made headlines across the country. The controversy originated in Detroit and sparked debate within all major American orchestras and their boards of directors.[38] I was serving on the board of the Detroit Symphony Orchestra (DSO) at the time, as I still do.

That year, two black state legislators in Michigan, Morris Hood and David Holmes, held up state funding for the DSO to voice their objection concerning the lack of African American musicians in the orchestra. Hood and Holmes chaired appropriations committees in the Michigan house and senate, respectively. Both were from Detroit. For fourteen years, they had been pressuring the DSO to hire more black musicians, and yet, of the ninety-eight musicians in the DSO in 1988, only one was African American. The DSO was deep in debt, and about a fifth of its annual operating budget came from the state. Without state funding, its very viability was at stake.

The lack of black orchestral musicians was typical of major American orchestras. Indeed, the Detroit Symphony, one of the top orchestras in the country, was one of the few to have a black player at all. The classical music realm was still a white institution. The musicians, patrons, sponsors, administrators, and musical repertoire—all were overwhelmingly white. This was the way things always had been, and many people took it for granted that this was the way things would always be.

White members of the DSO board were upset with the political intrusion into the financial operations and artistic decisions of the orchestra, which at that time was lead by Günther Herbig. These board members argued that the hiring of DSO musicians was already determined through blind auditions and that affirmative action had no

---

38. Isabel Wilkerson, "Discordant Notes in Detroit: Music and Affirmative Action," *New York Times,* March 5, 1989.

place in the selection process. They viewed the Detroit Symphony as an institution set apart from the struggle of the city and its people.

I disagreed. I told the board that the DSO had left the legislature no choice but to intervene because of our lack of initiative to change a situation that needed to be changed. "Had we done our job as board members," I said, "we would not be held hostage by the legislature." I asked them to put themselves in my position, coming to the symphony week after week and seeing, for many years, no black faces on stage—and now just a single black musician on stage. In a city that was 80 percent African American, it was unconscionable that the orchestra bearing its name should defend this extraordinary deficit. I argued that if the DSO were to survive and remain a relevant cultural institution, we had to make a greater effort to both reflect and engage the community outside the performance hall.

Under pressure from the legislature, the DSO hired another black musician by promoting a musician who had regularly played with the orchestra as a substitute. Subsequently, the DSO would add a third African American musician. Although the DSO still has a long way to go in this effort, it is now one of the leaders in the classical musical world in efforts to further diversity. The DSO began a fellowship program to enhance the career development of black orchestral musicians. The Detroit Symphony has been a key supporter of the Sphinx Organization, founded in 1996 by Aaron Dworkin. Sphinx is based in Detroit and is nationally acclaimed for its successful initiatives to train and promote young black and Hispanic musicians in classical music. These programs promise to significantly increase the number of talented and accomplished black musicians, and this should ultimately help increase the diversity in orchestras across the country.

After the crisis in 1988, the DSO has made a stronger commitment to the city. It teamed with the city to launch the Orchestra Place Development Project in 1996. The enterprise has revitalized an important stretch of midtown Detroit. The DSO enhanced its educational program to reach many more schoolchildren. The DSO also collaborated with the Detroit Board of Education to construct the

Detroit School for the Arts adjacent to Orchestra Hall. Eugene Miller, chairman and CEO of Comerica Bank, played a key role in helping to create this "magnet" public high school for aspiring young artists, which opened in 2005. These and other projects have made the Detroit Symphony the leader in urban outreach and development among all orchestras in the nation. In the process, it is no coincidence that the DSO has become one of the few orchestras experiencing increased revenues and attendance.

As a DSO board member, I have advocated not only for greater opportunities for black musicians and greater participation in the community but also for the recognition of outstanding and yet neglected works by African American composers. The Detroit Symphony responded and has taken the lead in presenting these works to the public. In 1991, under the direction of its music director and conductor Neemi Jarvi, the DSO embarked on an ambitious recording project that included the music of African American composers. The works of Duke Ellington, William Grant Still, and William Dawson have been recorded by the DSO under the Chandos label.

The DSO has become one of the leaders in providing opportunities for black conductors at the associate and resident level, including Paul Freeman, Leslie Dunner, and Thomas Wilkins. The symphony has also featured many African American guest conductors. There was a time when talented African American conductors had to leave the country to pursue their craft. Everett Lee and Dean Dixon were told that American orchestras and audiences would not tolerate a black man standing above and leading an all-white orchestra. Lee and Dixon went to Europe, and each earned acclaim as guest conductors for various European orchestras, but American orchestras were reluctant for a long time to give them the chance they deserved.

In 1981, the DSO became the first orchestra to offer "Classical Roots" concerts as part of its annual program and subscription series. The concerts feature the work of African American composers, conductors, musicians, and vocalists, and in the early years were organized by the community and held at local churches. Then, in 2000, to broaden the base of the classical roots experience, increase the audience, expand the knowledge and recognition of African Americans in classical music, and generate revenue, we added a fundraising event to the concerts called the Classical Roots Celebration. This annual affair, which includes a reception, dinner, and afterglow in addition to the concert, has become one of the DSO's most important and high-profile fundraising events. The celebration helps support the African American Composer Program, the African American Fellowship Program, and other DSO programs.

As part of its Classical Roots concerts, the DSO has commissioned and performed works by Adolphus Hailstork and Hannibal Lokumbe. Many of the Classical Roots works, inspired by the black gospel tradition, include a chorus. This part has been frequently performed by the Brazeal Dennard Chorale, based in Detroit and regarded as one of the foremost choirs in the country.

One year, as part of its Classical Roots concerts, the Detroit Symphony performed Undine Smith Moore's *Scenes from the Life of a Martyr*, based on the life of Martin Luther King. Moore was known as the "dean of black women composers," and *Scenes from the Life of a Martyr* was nominated for the Pulitzer Prize in 1981.

The DSO's performance was the first time I had heard this large orchestral work with chorus. On the stage were African American voices and additional African American musicians, lead by the guest conductor Isaiah Jackson. Orchestra Hall was sold out that night, and the audience was mostly black. When the performance concluded, the audience rose in extended applause. I turned to my wife and said that this was the first time I had heard a work performed by any orchestra that had for me the exalting power of Beethoven's *Ninth* and also spoke the language of my cultural heritage. The music that possessed me had ended, and I still belonged to its gathering.

If not for my love of music, I believe, I would not have lived this long. After the deaths of three of my sons, I was almost inconsolable. Music offered a place of refuge and solace. It did not relieve my grief, it seemed to understand my grief, and this understanding deepened the meaning of the music. In my darkest suffering, my experience of the music was even more poignant. Lost in the music, I was not lost at all.

The grief has subsided over the years, but the poignancy in the music remains. The music remembers and understands me well. The music also remembers and understands when I was well. The advance of Parkinson's has taken a toll on my memory, mobility, and energy. The connections of memory and thought—which form the tapestry of consciousness—fray and sometimes fall apart. I have come to accept this toll in a stoical way, and I strive to continue my life's work as best I can, without dwelling on the creeping erosion of my faculties.

I first began to experience symptoms in 1999, when I was seventy-four years old. I did not immediately connect the symptoms with Parkinson's, since I did not suffer the tremors in hands or feet that often characterize the disease. Though my hand was steady, I found, however, that I could not control my penmanship as before. I could not keep my writing on a straight line, and I could not maintain a consistent size in words and letters. I also had problems coordinating my feet, and my steps became labored. Finally, I felt a general weakness, stiffness, and instability in my body.

I was examined at great length by my personal physician, Dr. Rachel Keith, and she said that I needed to see a neurologist since my symptoms indicated the possibility of Parkinson's or another neurological problem. Before I left her office, I told her, "Now Rachel, if the diagnosis is serious and the disease progresses rapidly, I do not want to end up in your hands. I do not want you to come to my hospital room to take care of me." Rachel completely understood my concerns. She was much more to me than my doctor. She was a dear friend, and I wanted to spare her the worry of dealing with the medical details of my possibly deteriorating condition. So, I was ready to be transferred into the care of other doctors.

The first neurologist I saw did not diagnose Parkinson's. He attributed my physical and cognitive symptoms to the normal aging process. He also said that, in his opinion, because my handwriting was still better than his, I did not have the disease.

There are no definitive diagnostic tests for Parkinson's. It is a neu-rodegenerative disease that affects the brain and spinal cord. This microscopic cell damage cannot be detected, even by the most so-phisticated brain scans and imagery. There are cardinal symptoms that typify the disease, but the combination and intensity of symp-toms varies from person to person. How the disease progresses also differs significantly from person to person. Thus, the expertise of the neurologist—in taking a comprehensive history and making subtle judgments based on detailed observations over time—is crucial in reaching an accurate diagnosis. Accordingly, I sought the opinions of two other specialists.

Chacona went with me on the day a neurologist informed me that I indeed have Parkinson's. The doctor recommended a course of treatment and explained that the disease was not a death sentence though there is no cure and that I must be prepared for the worsen-ing of symptoms. However, with medication and attentive care, the doctor said, I could likely manage the disease and be productive for many years.

When we arrived home, Chacona asked me, "Are you afraid?" It was an unusual question, because she had never seen me express fear, despite the adversity and challenges I had experienced. Chacona, in knowing me so well, understood that I consider fear to be a humiliating experience.

I answered Chacona's question, "No, I am not afraid." My response was earnest and was not intended just to ease her worries about my state of mind. Whatever fear I might have felt because of the diag-nosis was outweighed by many other things in my life. I had the love and support of my wife, my children and grandchildren, and many friends. I had learned early in life, mainly from my grandmother, to always take the good with the not so good, and to ride out hard times. And finally, I was not one to let adversity get the best of me.

I have continued, as much as I possibly can, to serve on boards, attend community functions, visit regularly with friends and family, and travel. I credit my remaining active to three things: the dedication of my doctors, my compliance with their regimen, and my continuing sense of purpose and belonging. I feel fortunate that the Parkinson's has not advanced more quickly than it has.

As the disease worsens, music means even more to me. Every note and chord belongs, and each has its invariable and inevitable place in the pattern. When my mind dwells in the music, it feels whole again.

The City

The American poet Theodore Roethke wrote, "I believe the spiritual to be more desperate in the center of the chaos, which is Detroit."[39] Roethke did not intend this comment as an insult to the city. Rather, his comment recognizes the historical prominence of Detroit and how the striving of this great city ultimately signifies the soul and destiny of a nation and its entire people.

Detroit was the center of the American Industrial Revolution, the Great Migration, the development of the middle class, and suburbanization. White flight to the suburbs made Detroit the most racially divided metropolitan area in the country, and in the process Detroit became a focal point for the great social issue of our time: racial justice. Coleman Young wrote that during his tenure as mayor, "Detroit [was] the blackest, most segregated, most isolated, most restructured, most abandoned, most disenfranchised, most detested, and possibly the most feared city in America."[40] Racism was the key cause of the struggles the city suffered and continues to suffer, and those struggles have been exploited by those who scorn the city to rationalize their racism.

So much disdain has been heaped on Detroit and Coleman Young. When Young was mayor, one could not distinguish between this disdain for the city and for its leader. The mayor stood for the city, in

39. Theodore Roethke, *Straw for the Fire: From the Notebooks of Theodore Roethke, 1943–63* (New York: Doubleday, 1972), 167.
40. Young and Wheeler, *Hard Stuff*, 325.

many different ways. And in some respect, he still does. As Lonnie Wheeler wrote in his introduction to Young's autobiography, Young's story is a "metaphor that illuminates the black and urban predicament with one incandescent life."[41] Young's stubborn will to overcome the forces of racism, poverty, and fear are emblematic of Detroit's perseverance and spirit. Indeed, for many, including myself, his triumph represents abiding hope for the city he loved.

Local and national media outlets have exploited Detroit's struggles to propagate an egregious image of the city as the epitome of America's urban ills. One of the worst examples of this unfair coverage occurred in November 1990 when the ABC network magazine show *Primetime Live* produced a segment called "Detroit's Agony." The segment portrayed the city as a wasteland of crime, decay, and economic ruin. It also featured an interview with Mayor Young angrily cursing the ABC reporter Judd Rose. Before the segment was scheduled to air, I was asked to be part of a delegation put together by Wendell Anthony. We went to New York and met with executives at ABC News to tell them that the program was an inaccurate and gratuitous insult to a city of about a million residents, and that we were not going to stay silent and let the network vilify Detroit and its mayor. The news executives did not defend the program. They listened attentively and said they appreciated our sharing our criticisms and concerns. Nevertheless, the program aired, with only minor mentions of the hopeful and vital aspects of the city.

I believe that these aspects will continue to gather and grow. My faith in Detroit is part of my faith as a whole. Through personal tragedy, I have experienced the Christian paradox that God is closest to those in deepest despair. Detroit has suffered grievously for a long time. The city's African American population has borne the worst of this suffering. In many ways, the struggle of Detroit is the struggle of black America. Despite all the setbacks, I still foresee a dramatic change in the life and look of the city. And in Detroit's remaking, we

41. Young and Wheeler, *Hard Stuff*, x.

shall come closer to witnessing the "city on the hill" than ever before. Only then shall the striving of African Americans for equal justice be fulfilled.

Although Detroit has suffered a dramatic population loss, recent developments are cause for encouragement. Since I came to the city in 1950, Detroit has lost more than half of its population, and its racial demographics have been reversed. In 1950, Detroit had 1.8 million residents and was about 85 percent white. According to 2006 census estimates, the city has fewer than 900,000 people and is about 85 percent black. In the course of this unprecedented white flight, even stately and historic neighborhoods—like Boston Edison, Palmer Woods, Sherwood Forest, and Rosedale Park—endured the effects of abandonment. These neighborhoods have stabilized now, and their property values have climbed. In addition, downtown Detroit is attracting young professionals who are drawn to the city's diversity, cultural institutions and opportunities, and sports and entertainment venues. Two-thirds of these young residents moved downtown from the suburbs, and their increasing presence is bringing a new energy and excitement to the city.[42] There is reason for hope in Detroit despite the general neglect of America's urban plight by policymakers and the public.

America does not show much concern for its cities anymore. The balance of attention has shifted to the predominantly white and affluent suburbs. Many people seem to feel that the city is an anachronism. The life of the city is disconnected from their everyday concerns, and the dying of the city not does disturb their conscience and their belief in the greatness of their country.

This narrow-minded perspective not only lacks compassion but is simply wrong. (If indeed one can separate compassion and truth, which I do not believe is possible.) History has shown that the

---

42. Downtown Detroit Residential Market Study prepared by Katherine Beebe & Associates for the Lower Woodward Housing Fund, an initiative created by Detroit Renaissance, Inc., September 2006.

measure of a nation is the state of its cities. When its cities fail, the nation follows. As the renowned sociologist Jane Jacobs wrote, "Societies and civilizations in which the cities stagnate don't develop and flourish further. They deteriorate."[43]

For too long, through malignant indifference, we have let racism, poverty, hunger, and violence poison our society and the American ideal of equal opportunity. Though all of us understand that a quality education is the precondition of the American ideal, we lack the will and commitment to do what is necessary to fix our schools in the inner city. Our failure consigns already disadvantaged children to an inferior education and robs them of a better future. We cannot hope to be a better nation without addressing the problems of our cities and restoring their vitality.

Other nations care about their cities much more than we do. They understand that the city is more than a place of residence, commerce, and culture. There is something mystical about the city—in the way it connects us to forces much larger than ourselves. Lewis Mumford wrote about this in his outstanding work on urban history:

> The final mission of the city is to further man's conscious participation in the cosmic and the historic process. Through its own complex and enduring structure, the city vastly augments man's ability to interpret these processes and take an active, formative part in them, so that every phase of the drama it stages shall have, to the highest degree possible, the illumination of consciousness, the stamp of purpose, the color of love. That magnification of all the dimensions of life, through emotional communion, rational communication, technological mastery, and above all, dramatic representation, has been the supreme office of the city in history. And it remains the chief reason for the city's continued existence.[44]

I do not relate well to people who have not found the city's special place and function in their lives. With all its scars, warts, and signs of desperate struggle, I claim Detroit as my city, and as much so, I claim

---

43. Jacobs, *Cities and the Wealth of Nations,* 232.
44. Mumford, *The City in History,* 576.

all cities. I celebrate their beauty in the midst of dysfunction and disorder. It has been said, "Cities are the priesthood of the arts." Artists gravitate to cities to express themselves in works that reflect who we are to ourselves. Cities nurture our best aspirations as a people and a nation; and for the good of us, or perhaps in spite of us, cities survive with a life of their own.

I have loved the city in the way that Langston Hughes sang of Harlem. I know and I can hear and feel the pulse of the city's awakening. I love its bustling energy and sleepy ways; its variety, music, color, and laughter; its thousands of voices speaking at the same time in different languages. The drumbeat of work, play, and worship. And when I am quiet and listening, I can hear the unmistakable whispers of joy and sadness, life and death. I feel safe in the wonderment of all of this. And I know that I am not alone.

Racism in the Bloodstream

There is no mystery about being black in America. There are no subtleties in its stark reality. Being black carries a mark of racial oppression that is fixed at birth and continues to the grave. Such is the practice of racism in one of the most color-conscious nations in the world.

In 1903, W. E. B. DuBois declared in his groundbreaking work *The Souls of Black Folk,* "The problem of the Twentieth Century is the problem of the color line."[45] Because of racism, DuBois said, the black individual always feels an inner conflict between two separate identities: being black and being American:

> It is a peculiar sensation, this double-consciousness, this sense of always looking at one's self through the eyes of others, of measuring one's soul by the tape of a world that looks on in amused contempt and pity. One ever feels his two-ness—an American, a Negro; two souls, two thoughts, two unreconciled strivings; two warring ideals in one dark body.[46]

45. DuBois, *The Souls of Black Folk,* from chapter 2.
46. DuBois, *The Souls of Black Folk,* from chapter 1.

Today, more than a century after DuBois wrote these words, being black in America is still to know the truth of his psychological insight. African Americans still struggle to reconcile the identities of "African" and "American," because America refuses to recognize their hopes and humanity as integral to society. Racism remains a rampant and virulent force in our national life. Incidents of racial violence in the North and South, the trends of increasing racial segregation, the unyielding patterns of racial discrimination, the racist comments by numerous public figures—all attest to the unmistakable undercurrent of racism in the American mainstream.

These racial conditions have created the reality of two Americas: one white, the other black. The black person lives every day with an acute awareness of his or her blackness. However well educated, highly placed, rich, successful, or attractive one may be, he or she is always the "other." The awareness stems from seeing and hearing all too often the intentional and unconscious expressions of racism. Being black is living with the knowledge that although you may be better qualified than your white supervisor, there is little hope of remedying the unfairness. It is understanding that the chances of getting the best jobs are against you. It is seeing yourself, after all the years of civil rights struggle, still not treated fairly in education, employment, income, insurance, banking, housing, health care, and participation in American democracy. It is being over-represented in the harsh realities of poverty, crime, and prison. It is knowing that in your lifetime the barriers of race will not be lifted.

Being black in America is not being fairly appreciated for your artistic and creative contributions to the nation's culture. It is also resilient joy, as Langston Hughes described in verse, in spite of the sadness and pain. It is optimism in the face of long suffering and denial. It is belief in America.

Being black in Detroit is seeing your city severely damaged by economic disinvestment, primarily because your city is predominantly black. It is living with a chronic and staggering rate of unemployment, especially among young blacks. It is failing to utilize black economic resources to support black needs and interests in the city. It is hearing your city ridiculed by the media and suburbanites. It is listening to whites express their views about the social pathology afflicting the African American community without acknowledging the root factors of racism and poverty. It is being defensive about your position and community because too many people believe the city is not worth the effort and commitment to save it.

One-third of whites believe that racism is not a problem in America today.[47] Among politically conservative whites, that percentage is undoubtedly higher. This group not only denies that racism against blacks exists today, it contends that blacks are guilty of "reverse racism" when they advocate that institutions must create and reserve opportunities for blacks to redress persistent racial discrimination and oppression. The exclusion of whites from the particular opportunities set aside for blacks, the right wing argues, is a form of "racism." This argument adds insult to unconscionable injury. In order to serve an ideological agenda, it trivializes the human toll of more than two centuries of racial oppression. This is both morally repugnant and intellectually dishonest.

African Americans cannot be fairly charged as racists. *Webster's Third International Dictionary* defines *racism* as "the assumption that psycho-cultural traits and capacities are determined by biological race and that races differ decisively from one another, which is usually coupled with a belief in the inherent superiority of a particular race and its right to domination over others." Blacks do not profess belief in a doctrine of racial superiority by which they seek to dominate white people. The words used by black protests against white domination may be strident and confrontational, but such utterances are not racist. Rather, they are expressions of deep resentment against white oppressors. It is not racist for African

---

47. Poll results from interviews conducted December 5–7, 2006, by Opinion Research Corp.

Americans to appeal to a black community consciousness when seeking the economic and political support of other blacks. Blacks are not asserting the supremacy of this social consciousness—a consciousness that stems from shared culture and a common history of oppression, suffering, and perseverance. They are only recognizing how integral and important this consciousness is to the black identity.

A corollary to the accusation of "reverse racism" is the charge of "playing the race card." This phrase has also been popularized by opponents of affirmative action. It was designed to nullify legitimate black claims against the system. I believe that the term *race card* is part of the euphemistic language of a racist mentality. It seeks to stigmatize any complaint of racial discrimination and deny the application of principles of fairness to redress past injustices. The fact that some African Americans have picked up the term and use it against other blacks is regrettable. But this does not lessen its hypocrisy or excuse its affront.

The problem of the "color line" in America is so deeply rooted and intractable that I frequently ask myself, What have I learned from my more than fifty years of constant participation in the struggle that may help others who continue the fight for racial justice? Based on my experiences, ten truths and realities stand out:

1. Racism runs in the bloodstream of white America. I have found this to be true in the schoolhouse and the courthouse, in the corporate boardroom, in law enforcement, in health care, in the distorted portrayal of African Americans in the media, and finally, in the patterns of unequal treatment of African Americans that persist at all levels of our society. This is not to say that all white Americans are racists or harbor racist attitudes. Many white Americans understand the reality of racism and are committed to the fight against it. However, many whites deny that reality and, in so doing, are complicit in racist conditions and conduct because they refuse to stand up against them.

2. The simple and persistent truth at the center of racism is that the continued oppression and debasement of African Americans is caused by the determination of white Americans to maintain their power and advantage based on skin color alone. The racists would have us believe that black skin color makes African Americans less human, less intelligent, less moral, less respectful of the work ethic, and even less peaceful than white Americans.

3. Racism continues to function as America's most intractable social problem. For black Americans, the "game" has been fixed and was fixed from the very beginning. In the American political economy, the rules of fairness do not apply to blacks.

4. The great majority of white Americans and even some African Americans wait for a situation in which there is too much trauma, too much blood, and too much of an assault on our moral conscience before they recognize and respond to the cruelties of racism. They need to see pain and violence before accepting the demand that something be done. Only when the suffering of victims is unbearable do they see the need for justice and corrective action.

5. The most costly and tragic failure of our community and government structure, at all levels, is not alleviating the tremendous burden of racial oppression and unequal opportunity placed on black children. It is not possible to measure the current and long-term negative effects of the underfunding of our urban public schools. The urgent educational needs of disadvantaged black children are sharply defined and evident for all to see. No aspect of the race problem touches me more deeply and with as much pain as America's broken promise to its inner-city children.

6. Diversity initiatives and affirmative action programs, proven effective in helping to correct racial inequities, will be rejected by the

white majority. Across the country, diversity and affirmative action efforts, particularly in higher education, have come under assault in the courts, state legislatures, and political referendums. Each successful challenge emboldens opponents of affirmative action in their grand scheme to eliminate diversity and affirmative action policies everywhere.

7. The racist power structure seeks out certain African Americans to do its bidding and confuse the issues of racism. Sadly, some of the principal leaders of the anti-affirmative action crusade are black conservatives—men like Ward Connerly and Justice Clarence Thomas. Both Connerly and Thomas richly benefited from affirmative action programs and then promptly turned their backs on their own community. Even worse, they have the gall to term their efforts against the black community as "civil rights initiatives"—an act of unforgivable sacrilege that dishonors all the sacrifices of the brave men and women who came before them and made possible their own opportunities for achievement. Connerly and Thomas represent a small but disturbing number of successful blacks who lack a clear sense of history, community, and identity and who have chosen to follow the racists' prescription for black success in America to satisfy their expedient and personal ambitions.

8. In spite of conspicuous and celebrated achievements by African Americans at all levels of our society, the American media continues to focus on the extremes of violence and dysfunction in black life. This focus shapes and reinforces the negative image that whites have of blacks and, to some extent, that black Americans have of themselves. This negative image can be readily exploited to scapegoat blacks or to justify feelings of anger, hatred, and revenge directed at blacks, particularly black males. Examples abound, and the media never seems to learn from its terrible mistakes. In Boston in 1989, after Charles Stuart killed his pregnant wife, he blamed a black man for the murder, and the accusation struck a chord with the media, police, and

white community. Because of the prevalent negative stereotyping of black men, the public and authorities were predisposed to think that a black man must have committed the horrific crime. Police stopped and interrogated black men at random in black neighborhoods and eventually arrested an innocent black man. Five years later in South Carolina, when Susan Smith drowned her two young sons, she, too, claimed that a black man was the killer. Once again, the media, public, and authorities immediately believed the unlikely story. The negative stereotyping of the black male reinforces the perception that he is inclined to be a danger to society and is unredeemable if he has committed a criminal act. When eleven-year-old Nathaniel Abraham shot and killed another boy in Michigan, the prosecutor elected to try him as an adult even though Nathaniel had the mental capacity of a seven-year-old. Nathaniel is the youngest person ever tried as an adult in the United States.

9. No past gains in the struggle for racial justice are fixed and settled. Thus, we cannot afford any complacency about the progress we have made.

10. No past defeats should diminish our aspirations and efforts to fight discrimination, segregation, and bigotry. Setbacks and sacrifices are inherent in the struggle. Some progress—however slight, indefinite, and subject to reversal—is the basis upon which hope for the future is built.

In my darkest days of dealing with the issue of racial justice, when it seemed that the struggle was hopeless, I would dream that the entire white community was like a mob.

Even in my dream, however, there were always white figures standing above the mob, saying bravely, "But this is not right. It is not fair or just." Often, the consoling voices were those of white friends. Sometimes the voices were of the very well known, like Eleanor Roosevelt, John and Bobby Kennedy, Lyndon Johnson, Jimmy Carter and Bill Clinton, Judge Waties Waring, Justices William Brennan and Hugo Black. I remembered those voices, and others like them, and felt grateful that I could hear them along with those of Frederick Douglass, Harriet Tubman, W. E. B. DuBois, Benjamin Mays, Ralph Bunche, Thurgood Marshall, Rosa Parks, Fannie Lou Hammer, Nelson Mandela, Damon Keith, Malcolm X, Paul Robeson, Leon Higginbotham, Martin Luther King Jr., and others. These courageous voices, both white and black, made the difference for me between fending off despair and the death of hope.

I pray that you will always not only hear those voices of freedom, you will also raise your own voice as well, and do what justice and right demand.

The Good Life

My discussion here about "the good life" is essentially spiritual. By this, I do not mean a particular religion. Rather, I am referring to the striving for higher ideals. All spiritual matters resonate with mortality—not only our own, but of loved ones we have lost along the way. T. S. Eliot wrote:

> We die with the dying:
> See, they depart, and we go with them.
> We are born with the dead:
> See, they return, and bring us with them.[48]

In the tragic deaths of three of my sons, I felt as though I had died with them. In time, they returned anew in memory and changed me in the process. They put me in touch with what really matters in life, and I hold their legacy with passion.

I have reached an age where many of my close friends are no longer here. They too abide in memory, where again, relationships change and become more *spiritual,* and are never lost. They, too, figure in the counsel I offer the reader.

---

48. T. S. Eliot, *Four Quartets* (1943; New York: Harcourt, 1968).

The five keys to living the good life, I believe, are:

> Love
> Doing more than required
> Honoring others
> Purpose
> Faith

Love. This is the simplest, most noble, and most essential element of a good life. Sigmund Freud spoke of the necessity of love in these words: "In the last resort we must begin to love in order that we may not fall ill, and must fall ill if, in consequence of frustration, we cannot love."[49]

Love was the most powerful source of Martin Luther King's energy and leadership. Allison Davis, the great social anthropologist, described King's sense of mission: "King believed that men can save themselves from their own mutual hatreds, for they have the capacity to turn hatred into its opposite—mercy and love of mankind. He taught his followers to renounce hatred, to learn to deal with the enemy as fellow human beings, to give up the desire for personal revenge and to forgive injuries once and for all."[50]

Love and mercy are the highest expressions of the presence of God in human beings. William Blake echoes this thought in his poem "The Divine Image":

> For Mercy Pity Peace and Love,
> Is God our father dear:
> And Mercy Pity Peace and Love,
> Is Man his child and care.
> For Mercy has a human heart
> Pity, a human face:
> And Love, the human form divine,
> And Peace, the human dress.[51]

49. Sigmund Freud, *Collected Papers*, vol. 4 (New York: Basic Books, 1959), 42.
50. Davis, *Leadership, Love, and Aggression*.
51. William Blake, "The Divine Image," *Songs of Innocence and Experience*.

Doing more than what is required. Each of us should strive for excellence and to make a difference in the work we do. Simply meeting the standard expectations for the task at hand is not enough. It cheats not only those with whom the work is shared, but also ourselves. Doing more than what is required is seen in a variety of human experiences:

The orchestra conductor's commitment to finding new secrets in the music he has performed many times before

The doctor giving the best possible care to a dying patient

The assembly line worker for whom the best quality vehicle is yet to be built

The donor for whom giving more represents a sense of duty

The teacher who will not give up on the student for whom the light of learning is not yet turned on

The disabled person who recognizes no human barriers to achievement

Doing more than what is required is the continuing belief in new discovery. It is marking every phase of one's work with high aspirations and "ego integrity"—a term used by the psychologist Erik Erikson to describe an individual's accumulated confidence and ability to bring order and meaning to his or her experiences and endeavors. This is exemplified by Tiger Woods, Oprah Winfrey, and Bill Cosby. Doing more than what is required in our studies, our work, and performances must be a standard of the good life.

Finding the value of one's life as a means of respecting and honoring the lives of others. This is best illustrated with a true story. I remember a television interview with the African American actor

Charles Dutton after he had been nominated for a Tony Award for a role on Broadway. Dutton had led a troubled life as a young man and served thirteen years in prison for serious crimes, including a manslaughter conviction when he was seventeen years old. In the interview, Dutton maintained that he had acted in self-defense when he stabbed the man to death in a fight. He was then asked if he had ever felt any remorse for the life that he had taken. He answered that he did not experience remorse until his successful performance on Broadway, some eighteen years after he had killed the man. In his success, Dutton discovered for the first time the value and meaning of his own life. Only then did he come face to face with the intrinsic worth of the life he had taken. And only then did his conscience ache, and he wept in agony.

Purpose. Nelson Mandela, Martin Luther King, and Rosa Parks each brought precious meaning to the ideal that we find ourselves through giving ourselves to a larger cause. A man or woman who has not found this truth is one who has yet to find the right job, the right work, and the right challenge. King said, "I submit to you that if a man hasn't discovered something he will die for, he isn't fit to live."[52] On the night before his assassination, King felt a deep premonition of danger, but proclaimed in victory, "I've been to the mountaintop. . . . And I've looked over. And I've seen the Promised Land."[53]

We hear this truth again passionately stated by Mandela in the trial leading to his imprisonment in 1964. Mandela spoke of his dedication to the rights and freedom of his people, saying that this struggle was his life. He concluded, "I have cherished the ideal of a democratic and free society in which all persons live together in harmony and with equal opportunities. It is an ideal which I hope to live for and to achieve. But if needs be, it is an ideal for which I am prepared to

52. Martin Luther King Jr., speech delivered on June 23, 1963, in Detroit, Michigan.
53. Martin Luther King Jr., "I've Been to the Mountain Top" (speech delivered on April 3, 1968, at the Mason Temple in Memphis, Tennessee).

die."[54] This is the ultimate statement of commitment where nothing is saved of individual interest except for the right and the opportunity to keep struggling. What life-giving and sustaining forces within Mandela enabled him, after twenty-seven years of wrongful incarceration, to walk out of prison a whole man, still gracious, dignified, free of bitterness and hate, and able to lead his country to victory? This is human triumph at its most sublime. It is the most and the best that we can give and get. It is everything that the good life embraces.

Faith. Scripture defines faith as "the substance of things hoped for, the evidence of things not seen."[55] Faith is the acceptance of life on its own terms, understanding that life is not always fair and gentle, and that, in the reality of things, life is both life and death. This is perhaps the most difficult of the challenges that confront us in the eternal search for the good life. But it is also the most forgiving and rewarding. Without such faith, we shall surely perish.

The Reverend Harry Wright, retired pastor of the Cornerstone Baptist Church in Brooklyn, New York, described an experience at the Grand Canyon. He said that his son, standing by his side, looked down in the deep and mysterious gorge of the Grand Canyon, turned to him, and said: "Daddy, something happened here!" No questions, no profound speculation, no answers to the mystery—just a simple and confident response to the grandeur and silent majesty of what he had witnessed. "Something happened here." Just as something grand and mysterious happened at Focus Hope, a landmark community and civil rights organization in Detroit.

I believe that these five principles leading to a good life are worthy of trust and emulation. To arrive at a place where all these principles work in concert is a triumph that is at once profoundly human and spiritual.

54. Nelson Mandela's opening statement in his trial before the Pretoria Supreme Court, April 20, 1964.
55. Hebrews 11:1.

Eulogies: Work, Love, Gratitude, and Remembrance

One of my longtime friends, Dores McCree, approached me at the conclusion of a memorial service for one of our friends and said, "Arthur, you have become our community's unofficial eulogist, and I want you to offer a eulogy at my service." Later, Dores and I met again at a memorial service for one of our friends and she repeated her request.

I was moved to go through my personal files and collect copies of all the memorial tributes I have been privileged to offer. I was surprised at the number of such tributes I had given over the years. I began to feel that Dores was directing my attention to something of special value in the relationships that inspired these tributes.

I found in my files thirty-six of these eulogies, not including several eulogies I had delivered but for which I did not have the written text. As I read all of these pieces together, I felt humbled and uplifted at the same time. I realized that in focusing my thoughts on what is good and laudatory in the lives of these friends, I was rediscovering the ties that bind us as friends and companions.

Therefore, in memory of many friends who have passed on, I am including here the full text of these tributes.

BOB BAKER 1918–1996

I have come to this farewell tribute to Bob Baker with a deep sense of appreciation for what this good man stood for and shared in his life: dedication to the education of our children; a strong belief in equity and social justice; the courage and conscience to found the organization of school administrators and supervisors, and to lead the teachers' federation; an unswerving commitment to achievement that has been the mark of this distinguished family; and finally, I cite with appreciation the rich romance that has embraced Bob and Connie for the past fifty-four years.

In a special way, it is this wonderful romance that has captured and kept my attention. Bob and Connie became one heart and soul, and to love one was to love them both. They have been the kind of partners who bring honor and beauty to marriage. It is what Chacona and I have cherished above all about our good neighbors and friends.

Against the body blows of illness, which threatened Bob's life in recent years, Connie fought with all of her extraordinary strength to keep Bob from harm's way. And Bob lived with serious illness for so long because of his partner's loving care and constant attention. Only God would bring this struggle for life to a peaceful end; and he would have to consult with Connie first.

With all the good works that Bob Baker has left to his credit, and for which we gratefully celebrate his life, I want to praise him for having the good sense to marry Connie when the both of them were young so they could have the long life together that has been their richest blessing.

I say to you, Connie, and to all in the family assembled here today: this is what God has given in his mercy, love, and generosity. Let us then be thankful and rejoice. It is perfect.

ALBERT BHARUCHA-REID   1930–1985

When I received the news of the tragic death of Albert Bharucha-Reid, I experienced some of the terrible pain I felt barely two years ago with the similarly tragic death of my young son. Al called at that time from Atlanta to offer caring words of comfort. He was emotional. I knew he cared, and his caring, along with that of my family and other friends, has helped me to survive. We talked occasionally in the following months, and I think we were always in touch with our feelings.

I am very proud of Al's scholarly work. I got the measure of his outstanding achievements by reading the record, because like many of us, I did not know anything about probability theory in mathematics. But in my searching, I came early to the realization that Al, as some of our students like to say, was "heavy." At the center of his immense creative energy, his restless and inquiring mind, was a gentle, sensitive, and warmly considerate person. A top scientist! Yes! But a remarkable human being first, who brought to his work and his relations with colleagues a sturdy and deep regard for human values. He therefore saw the university as an institution of the highest human purpose, aspirations, and passions.

One liked the reserve, quiet dignity, and scholarly demeanor of Al, because he wore those qualities gracefully.

He was in all respects an original but one who kept in touch with the common cause of all who suffer oppression, neglect, and alienation. When we think about the special character of this man, the scope and enduring value of his work, and his love of us, we must know that we are the receivers and the bearers of a rich inheritance in which there is just cause for celebration in spite of our awful pain and sadness today. It is this thought above all that I want to leave with you who were Al's closest colleagues, to his sister, brother, and other relatives, and to his sons and their mother, Rodabe.

GERALDINE BLEDSOE 1900–1991

When Judge Ford offered me the privilege and honor of speaking briefly at these final rites for her mother, I accepted readily because I knew whether publicly or privately or both, I would thank God for giving us—all of us—Geraldine Bledsoe for all of these years. Here truly was a great lady whose life and service were marked first by love and devotion, intelligence, and an unswerving commitment to justice, fair play, and equal opportunity for all.

Her footprints are indelibly marked on the path of the civil rights movement in America, and the story our city cannot be fully told without citing the contributions of Geraldine Bledsoe. She was always there, standing for the right causes at the right time, and she knew that the standing was not worth anything if it was not against the forces of intimidation, oppression, and defeat. No racist bully frightened her, and no unworthy challenger wore her down. This was a true warrior with a great lady's grace and compassion. To all her sterling qualities, she added the stamp of love, love in the deepest, Christian, and noblest sense. She did not half love any one who was fortunate enough to come within her circle, and you were richly blessed to be there.

In this farewell tribute to this dear friend, I want to share with you a personal experience from our journey together. In the late fall of 1986, at the last minute, I was persuaded by a group of friends that I should become a candidate for the presidency of the Detroit branch NAACP. I did not want this, and Chacona wanted it less. On the day of the election, the weather was terrible with icy rain and sleet. As I paced the halls of the Northwest Activities Center where the voting was taking place, I looked through the glass doors, and there struggling up the steps with her walker, puffing and almost breathless, was Geraldine Bledsoe coming to vote for me.

I asked myself at that moment, Am I truly worthy of this? And tonight I answer that, in grateful memory of Geraldine Bledsoe, for the rest of my days I shall work to be so worthy.

Thank you, my friend.

JUDGE ARTHUR M. BOWMAN 1915–1988

Of all the good men and women I have known who have served the bench and the legal profession, no one has honored both the purpose and commands of the law more faithfully than Arthur M. Bowman. A man of strong character, gentle manners, and a fervent commitment to our shared goals of community, he made his mark on his times as much by the cherished values that guided him as by the worthy triumphs of his distinguished career. He was an uncommon man, dedicated to the common good.

He understood and felt the pain of America's terrible burden of racial injustice, and throughout his professional career, he found meaningful and constructive ways to express his conscience. With his loving wife, Thelma, at his side, Arthur Bowman was a consistent and loyal supporter of the NAACP. He was a life member. In the NAACP, through his early advocacy of legal services for the poor, and other worthy causes, he fashioned a legacy of social responsibility that his children and all other members of his family can possess with genuine pride.

I owe Arthur Bowman a debt that I could never repay, but if lasting respect and a grateful remembrance will count at all, I shall feel somewhat relieved. The source of my debt is such that I share it reluctantly and with a tinge of embarrassment. It was the result of my failure several years ago to pay some overdue traffic violation fines. When I went to the proper office to pay my fines, I was promptly arrested and subsequently taken to Judge Bowman's court. As I walked into the courtroom, I was directed by the police officer to be seated in an area reserved for persons under arrest. But Judge Bowman spoke promptly to the officer, saying, "Don't seat that man there; that's Dr. Johnson." Humbly and with an acute sense of shame, I said, "Thank you, Your Honor." I shall never forget that moment, and the fact that Judge Arthur Bowman used the authority that was his to preserve for me a measure of personal dignity.

Thank you again, Your Honor.

ARTHUR BROWN 1922–1997

I want to thank Claire for giving me the privilege of speaking at this memorial tribute to her husband and my very dear friend, Arthur Brown. Simply and gratefully, I would like to celebrate the splendid life and achievements of Arthur, but I have come to this occasion with a heavy heart. Arthur was special to me. I loved him, and I felt blessed in believing he loved me.

Arthur was no ordinary man. He was exceptional in heart and mind, and in his taste for the better things. Our friendship began about thirty years ago when we came together with eight other men to form a dinner discussion group. Without a set agenda and a fixed schedule, we met in the houses of members. Our aim was to examine and decide the great issues of democratic education, religious bigotry, race, poverty, social violence, and the burdens of great wealth. We were a very diverse group, open and blunt in expressing our views. If the intellectual content of a meeting occasionally suffered, the evening was always saved by the good food and drinks that were lavished on the group by the host and his wife. For her part, when we met in the Brown home, Claire helped to build this pleasure tradition to its highest level, and we were always grateful.

After I came to Wayne State in 1972, Arthur and I were able to see each other more frequently, and our good times at lunch became priceless. I found in Arthur all that I admire in men and women, all that makes greatness in the teacher and the taught: ego integrity, inspiration, vision, grace, class, gentleness, and the ability to love.

Arthur was profoundly respectful of the human being, and the intellectual curiosity and pursuits that drove his life also defined his values and goals. He honored learning and achievement, and he let the great tragedy and unparalleled triumph of Jewish life in the world shape the wonderful quality of his own humaneness. So, it was inevitable that he would reject passionately anti-Semitism, racism, and all other insults to human dignity and freedom. It was this core element of values and principles that led Arthur to his founding of the Center for Academic Ethics at Wayne State University.

This giant of a man shared with me some of the best of his caring heart and disciplined mind. As our friendship grew, we were not reluctant to share with each other our deepest concerns and disappointments, our joys and pleasures, our feelings and our tears.

It is for all of this and more that I grieve over the loss of Arthur Brown, even as I well know that his precious legacy to you and to me will live forever.

AGNES BRYANT 1916–2002

I want to thank Joel and Karen for giving me this opportunity to offer a farewell tribute to their mother, and my dear friend, Agnes Bryant. Agnes and her late husband, Warren, and I were good friends from the day we met nearly fifty years ago. We were drawn together, and kept together, through our sharing of love, simple values, the work of the NAACP, and a passion for great music. We loved our children and wanted them to enjoy the fullness of life. We were together through our trials and tribulations, and those precious moments of triumph and ascending to the mountaintop.

Agnes was an exceptionally fine person. She was blessed with an even temperament and a constant smile in her face. She carried the grace of peaceful countenance. We did not have to search for her heart. It was always there with a strong and steady beat. She possessed a broad and active social conscience, and she knew the rewards of a successful professional career in teaching and human rights administration.

I will always remember Agnes, and feel grateful for the bonds of love and friendship that enriched our lives beyond measure.

VERA DANIEL 1921–1991

My family has been brought together today because we loved Vera and she loved us. Vera was family in the best sense, and this fact was well established with all of us: nieces, nephews, cousins, and others. Since she was not a person of worldly possessions and materials, she shared generously with us the most valuable gift of all, love and caring, and without doubt, she expected love and caring in return. This was not a tit-for-tat or measure-for-measure relationship. It was simply love openly expressed, and she hoped, indeed needed, to be loved in return. In her younger days of good health and abandon, she liked a good party, to have family and friends around. She liked a good joke and was always one of easy laughter. She liked to brag. Vera believed in honest work. She worked hard and took pride in the products of her labors. Because she never had much money, she knew both the possibilities and limits of what money alone could do. With very modest means, she always tried to pay her bills and to protect the qualities of trust and integrity that were present in her business transactions. She could get both angry and very sad when let down or offended by disrespect. But she was always believing and willing to try again.

If we loved her deeply, and we surely did, she deserved it all.

My life and Vera's were intertwined for all of our days together. I grew up knowing Vera as a sister, not my aunt. We played together, got into mischief together, and occasionally we were justly punished together. I was the younger, so I looked up to Vera: in the occasional fights that involved me and other youngsters, Vera was always my protector, and she was always the victor in these childish skirmishes.

As we grew older, our relationship ripened and matured, and as the saying goes, we were always there for each other.

I fully expected Vera to live to be an old woman. Except for her smoking habit, she did not mistreat her body and mind; she was relatively healthy for most of her life. Oh yes, she complained about not feeling well, but that was a habit that she could not easily break.

She believed in God and God's infinite mercy, and it was this faith that kept her going when the forces of life seemed unduly burdensome.

She believed in the church and she loved her church family. She was not a laggard in church life, she was a doer, and she wanted to pay her dues.

Vera, or Aunt V, as some of the family children affectionately called her, was also a good neighbor, and I believe that she would have lived on Baylis forever. Here she found the love and caring that were the principal virtues of her own life, and I want to say to her good friend Ro and to all the good neighbors of Baylis who are here this morning, that my family will always be grateful to you.

When Vera reached the point in her illness that it became necessary to place her in a nursing home, it was the most painful change with which we had ever dealt. No such place in its impersonal ways was good enough for Vera, and no nursing home, however good, could reduce our pain. We knew that Vera would not come home again. She suffered terribly toward the end—indeed, for most of the time in the nursing home—not from physical pain but from depression, disorientation, and an inability to manage herself. It was a difficult and trying situation for those who have loved her so much.

When the end came last Thursday morning, I felt the staggering impact of what I had lost: a precious and irreplaceable link to the days of my youth and a love of the noblest kind—constant, caring, and forever forbearing.

This is Vera's special legacy to be shared by all of us for the rest of our days: our friendly neighbors on Baylis; the children of our family; my sisters, my brother, and our mother; my sons and my daughter; our spouses; and other relatives and friends. We are all the possessors of this wonderful legacy.

Let us hold it and carry it with pride, gratitude, and faithfulness in Vera's memory.

LARRY P. DOSS   1928–2001

I want to thank Judy for giving me the privilege of offering a farewell tribute to her husband and our friend and patron saint Larry Doss. I come to this moment with acute sadness, but with the hope that my few words will speak in truth to our enormous debt to Larry and our lasting gratitude for his life and work. I speak for the legions of friends, professional and business associates, and the nameless masses who would proudly stand here and speak for themselves if they could.

God, in his infinite wisdom, love, and power, has endowed a few men and women in the world with exceptional strength, intellect, human skills, character, and the will to stand above the crowd. They in turn bring true honor to these precious gifts of God with their accomplishments and faithfulness in our continuing struggle for common good.

Larry stood tall and securely in this circle. He distinguished himself in every area of his varied interests and work. These include data and systems management analysis, education reform, public schools improvement, school decentralization, coalition building, African American entrepreneurial and business development, political participation, civil rights, community organization, and Detroit advocacy. In all of these areas, his record of leadership and productivity was unexcelled.

I venture to say that except for the impact of racism, a problem that runs in the bloodstream of American life, Larry might have been chairman and chief executive officer of any number of major American corporations, and those few African Americans who hold such positions today are indebted in some measure to Larry Doss, who came before them.

He was person of grace, class, ego integrity, and gentleness. He was an activist and a doer. He was not a classic street fighter, but he possessed all the versatility and steel in his back that successful street fighting requires.

I cannot close this tribute without recognizing what was perhaps Larry's finest personal quality: his generosity and steadfast loyalty to his friends. He did not forget you, and he was always trying to help.

For all of us here today who have shared Larry's dreams for community determination and self-realization, for freedom, and the building of a city on the hill, equally accessible to all, Larry has been our leader, and in a manner of speaking, our chairman and chief executive officer. This is the cornerstone of his legacy and our remembrance of him, and it will remain so forever.

AL DUNMORE 1915–1989

Statement provided to the Detroit News *upon request.*

As a journalist, civil rights activist, and corporate official, Al Dunmore played a sturdy and valiant role in the struggle of black Americans for equal opportunity and equal justice. He was almost unique in the finely tuned skills he brought to his work, and we shall miss him mightily.

BISHOP RICHARD EMRICH 1910–1997

I thank the family of Bishop Emrich for giving me the privilege of participating in this farewell tribute and celebration. The bishop and I became closely acquainted during my years of service with the NAACP, the Michigan Civil Rights Commission, and the Detroit Board of Education. Our work together goes back about thirty-five years. I was young at the beginning.

This was a period of greater hopefulness for change and resolution in black-white relations in America than what we are experiencing today: church and other institutional leaders spoke more clearly to the inhumanity and immorality of racial oppression.

But Bishop Emrich understood what was wrong about racism, and he addressed the problem forthrightly. He did this as a simple expression of conscience, and of his belief that a church leader cannot honorably do otherwise.

While I never raised the subject with him, I think he must have been appalled by some of the misguided doings of the so-called Christian right in our country today, and he could never have been confused by their message and aims.

Bishop Emrich's moral and social conscience and his intellectual integrity brought him to the front ranks of Detroit leadership so that the Episcopal Church and this cathedral grew into the fabric of community life. He was a founder of the Citizens Committee for Equal Opportunity, and he brought to that role the wisdom and integrity that were his special strength.

I was happy to claim Bishop Emrich as a friend. We shared warmth, encouragement, and trust, and I was the better for it.

When I was a youngster in Birmingham, Alabama, I used to wonder about the heart and mind of my parents, who suffered mightily but never discussed with me the life-and-death issues of race that we confronted every day. It was simply understood. I think what helped to keep us sane and hopeful in the darkest days of our despair was the realization that there was always in the racist mob at least one voice that would proclaim: "This is not right."

Bishop Emrich's was one of those voices for me, and I shall always feel deeply grateful.

HENRY FORD II 1917–1987

Statement provided to the Detroit News *upon request.*

Henry Ford II kept a native's pride in the city of Detroit, and he played a critical role in the building of a better city in human terms following the riots of 1967. He believed in affirmative action to advance black employment, and I am grateful for his work.

DEAN CORNELIUS GOLIGHTLY 1917–1976

Some men and women are born to teach, and for them, to teach is an inescapable duty and a continuing source of inspiration. They are renewed by the vital and rigorous process of great teaching, and they are humbled by the belief that teaching and learning are above all a shared experience. Cornelius Golightly was one such person richly blessed, and he was driven by a sense of duty to the end.

Dean Golightly was a man of strong and vigorous intellect. The world of the mind was his place of action. Thought was a necessary function of being alive. He relished the interplay of ideas, both as a means of invigorating the human spirit and as a logical step to constructive action. While he was deeply in touch with the resources of philosophy and logic, he was both gentle and direct in the statement of his views. He often said of himself that he had only a logical mind, which was his explanation for not being as confused or misdirected as others. He used his toughness of mind as a steady and unyielding force to protect all the values that were dear to him and to open the doors of freedom.

Dean Golightly was committed to the service of the university. While the great impact of his public role has been seen and felt through his service as an elected leader of the Detroit Board of Education, he established an outstanding record of service to Wayne State University. In addition to his posts as associate dean of the college of liberal arts and professor of philosophy, he served with distinction as a member of the Community College Liaison Advisory Committee; the Whitney M. Young Jr. Memorial Lecture Series Committee; and the Committee on Admissions, Records, and Registration.

He was a productive scholar, having published more than forty-eight articles and reviews mainly in scholarly journals covering the wide range of his primary interests in philosophy and logic. Notable and characteristic of his published works are "Social Science and Normative Ethics," for *The Journal of Philosophy;* "Race, Values, and Guilt," for *Social Forces;* "Playing the Dozens: A Note," for *The Journal of Abnormal and Social Psychology;* "Value as a Scientific Concept," for *The Journal of Philosophy;*

"Ethics and Moral Activism," for *The Monist;* "Negro Higher Education and Democratic Negro Morale," for *The Journal of Negro Education;* and "Freedom in the Arts," for *The Wisconsin Idea Theatre Quarterly.* And so the list goes, representing splendid evidence of this scholar's energy and commitment.

With all his seriousness, perhaps in spite of it, or because of it, C. L. Golightly was well known, recognized, and respected for his sharp wit and good humor. The gentle and humorous barb was not so much an attack on his opposition as a means of his own defense, and to keep us in good spirits even as we were forced to examine our own frailties. He lived with the irresistible urge to demonstrate that however painful the process of thinking may be for some, for him, it was an exquisite joy.

This rare teacher and individualist greatly prized his own and the freedom of his community, and he worked for that freedom as a person, as an academician, as an American, and as a black man. And I can think of no finer tribute that can be paid in words than the following from the works of Robert G. Ingersoll: "Surely there is grandeur in knowing that in the realm of thought, at least, you are without a chain; that you have the right to explore all heights and all depths; that there are no wall nor fences, nor prohibited places, nor sacred corners in all vast expanse of thought; that your intellect owes no allegiance to any being, human or divine; that you hold all in fee and upon no condition and by no tenure whatever; that in the world of mind you are relieved from all personal dictation, and from the ignorant tyranny of majorities. Surely it is worth something to feel that there are no priests, no popes, no parties, no governments, no kings, no Gods, to whom your intellect can be compelled to pay a reluctant homage." This then is our tribute to the good, tough, gentle, strong, civilized, and civilizing influence in our lives given generously by Cornelius L. Golightly.

IRENE GRAVES 1904–2002

With the death of Irene Graves, this community, a wide circle of devoted friends, and the many students who grew up under her tutelage have suffered a huge and irreplaceable loss. There simply is no way to measure fairly the scope and depth of the many contributions Irene Graves made to improvement of the social and political fabric of our community. She was an achiever and a doer with a winner's spirit and determination. She did not get in any fight, contest, or competition when she did not intend to win, and most of the time she did win. If it were NAACP Freedom Fund Dinner tickets or general memberships, Irene Graves was unrelenting in her striving for growth and results. She thought nothing of calling at 7:00 in the morning and putting the question directly: "Do you have the twelve NAACP memberships that you promised?" You got those memberships if you intended to sleep late again.

She loved the French language, its sound and precision, and she taught it to her eager students with a passion. She understood that to be valid in purpose and achievements, learning must be a shared experience.

In the more intimate side of her life, one could get close-up but not too personal. She loved deeply her distinguished late husband, Willis M. Graves, and she insisted that his major civil rights victories in the courts were justly recognized. The Graveses were opposites in personality, but they found the key to making their differences a source of enrichment to their lives together.

Irene was truly a lady of distinction, an original if ever there was one. She reminded us of no one else. She loved beauty in people, music, and art.

Chacona and I are grateful beyond words to have been the beneficiaries of Irene's love, caring, and constant support. We know that we will always share the abundant blessings of her life, even as she slips away into eternity.

FORREST FLOYD "FOOTS" GREEN 1915–2007

We have come here tonight painfully aware of the great loss we have suffered in the passing of Foots Green. We celebrate the life and work of our dear friend knowing that our sense of loss and the grief that comes with it is not the way we would have it. It is simply God's will.

Foots Green was no ordinary man. He was a giver and not a taker, and he tried in every way he could to improve the quality of our lives. He possessed a remarkable sense of humor and did not take himself too seriously. I cherished the element of humor that he brought to the table, understanding, as he did, that grace is an essential part of a good life.

Although I knew and loved Foots for slightly more than fifty years, when I was asked to speak here tonight I had to struggle a wee bit to find the right words and the frame of thought that would best remind us, all of us, of the rich legacy Foots has passed on to us. I thought only of the soul of this man. What made him great and good?

In searching for the words and thoughts that marked Foots's role and place in our journey together, I came upon those elegant and beautiful words that Joseph Brackett Jr. put together in 1848. Brackett called his thoughts "Simple Gifts," and I wish to close with this tribute to Foots and his family.

'Tis the gift to be simple,
'tis the gift to be free,
'tis the gift to come down where you ought to be,
And when we find ourselves in the place just right,
It will be in the valley of love and delight.

When true simplicity is gained.
To bow and to bend we shan't be ashamed.
To turn, turn will be our delight,
'Til by turning, turning we come round right

'Tis the gift to be loved and that love to return,
'Tis the gift to be taught and a richer gift to learn,
And when we expect of others what we try to live each day.
Then we'll all live together and we'll all learn to say,

'Tis the gift to have friends and a true friend to be,
'Tis the gift to think of others not to only think of "me"
And when we hear what others really think and really feel,
Then we'll all live together with a love that is real.

MAMIE GREEN 1921-1997

All that I know and appreciate about class, integrity, and grace in the human being was amplified, brightened, and made ever more sterling in the life of Mamie Green. She was in all respects the perfect embodiment of these splendid qualities, and with the added feature of her physical beauty, she was clearly an original. She possessed a basic sense of what was right, proper, and decent. She knew who she was, and there was never any extra motion, or need for exaggeration in her behavior. She did not raise her voice. She was always secure in her person—the mark of a truly cultured individual. It was these well-stated qualities that defined Mamie Green's ego integrity. They gave her that enduring, vibrant, yet elusive quality of class, which many others would like to claim but do so only falsely. We could see of this the basic goodness, integrity, class, and grace in her devotion to and love of her family and friends.

I met Mamie and her husband, whom we affectionately call "Foots," in the early 1950s shortly after I came to Detroit to take the job of executive secretary of the Detroit branch NAACP. We quickly became friends, and I have held them closely up to this day. They supported me in my work and through my days of great personal sorrow. I have watched the Green sons grow up and become the exceptional men they are today. She was proud of them. I must tell you, it is another distinction of Mamie Green that she was the only one who could call her husband by his nickname "Foots" and make it sound beautiful.

The passing of one so true and special as Mamie Green puts us in closer touch, although with great pain, with what is good, precious, and sublime about life, and why, although merciful sometimes, death is rarely a wanted companion. I loved Mamie and I held her in highest esteem. I want you, Foots, and your sons, Darryl, Forrest, and Saul, along with all the members of this strong family, especially the grandchildren, to know that as we mourn, we must also come to the celebration of God's gift to us in one so rare and wonderful as Mamie Green.

ROBERT C. HAWKINS 1925–2000

I want to thank Billie for inviting me to say a few words in farewell tribute to her husband, Bob Hawkins. Bob was a prince in whom there were no arbitrary boundaries to human love. He was kind and strong, sturdy in values, loyal in friendship, hopeful in spirit, tough in mind, and gracious in manners. He was no ordinary man. He was devoted to Billie and their daughters.

Bob and I met and became friends when we were fellow students at Morehouse College, and early on, one could see that Bob was the quintessential Morehouse Man—a man of dignity, self-confidence, leadership ability, and an active social conscience. He was in all respects a good man who was remarkably free of arrogance and smallness. He recognized our friendship and shared interests by sending to me on regular basis newspaper clippings and other information items that he thought would be of special interest to me. When we look at all of the sterling qualities that distinguished and set Bob Hawkins apart, we can see clearly why we must celebrate his life, indeed, why we must thank God for such a splendid gift.

RUTH "LADY RUTH" JACKSON   1902–1975

Of all the enduring and blessed benefits of life, the gift of friendship is among the brightest. I speak, then, of a friend, for many friends, and to friends. We cannot speak adequately, or in any way sufficient to console our grief, but it helps to say something. We pay tribute of heart and mind to a great lady, one whose noble stature among friends and family fully honored the nobility and essential truth of life's purpose. We honor one whose sense of self—beautiful as it was—was bound to the lives of others. She wanted it that way. We speak of a tireless and devoted churchwoman who knew that the church must virtually be everywhere if it is to be anywhere and that it works through the hearts and minds of its members. She loved Tabernacle, her church home, and its strong and vibrant leader, Dr. Sampson.

She brought a deep respect to learning, recognizing that the perfectibility of man, and any measure of peace in the world, depend on the development of the mind and the undergirding of firm religious discipline. She ventilated her spirit by reading and writing.

This remarkable woman would rather light a candle than curse the darkness. She was a passionate mother whose gift of love to her daughter was unqualified and unrestrained. It was a source of everlasting joy. With it, she embraced a circle of younger friends, touching and being touched with laughter, cares, and personal inspiration. It was not enough to give her the usual title of respect. With deep affection, we called her "Lady Ruth," and this is the way she will be remembered.

MILDRED JEFFREY 1910–2004

Mildred Jeffrey was no ordinary person, and the great social causes that consumed her life and defined her personhood—civil rights, women's rights, collective bargaining, public education, equal employment, the elimination of poverty, and the search for peace and these other challenges of our democracy—reflect some of the grandeur and nobility of her life.

Surely, the poet was listening to Mildred when he said, "There will never be a generation of free men until there are free mothers."

In our unrelenting struggle for civil rights and racial justice in America, Mildred was always there, leaving the imprint of her voice and action on every piece of civil rights legislation adopted in the past half century.

Few know of the critical mission she served with our good friend, G. Mennen Williams, in the primary campaign of then-senator John F. Kennedy as he aspired for the Democratic Party's presidential nomination in the spring of 1960. As some of you might recall, Senator Kennedy, while on the campaign trail in West Virginia, was asked if he supported the freedom riders and the sit-ins. The senator offered a qualified reply: Yes, he said, if the demonstrators were orderly. The senator's statement served only to deepen the suspicions of black Americans about his candidacy. However, with the sensitive counseling of Soapy Williams and Mildred Jeffrey, Senator Kennedy was persuaded to send his private plane to bring a black delegation from Detroit to his Georgetown home for the purpose of clarifying his views on civil rights. Mildred was on that plane and in that meeting, which resulted finally in a meeting of the minds between blacks and Senator Kennedy on civil rights issues. Mission accomplished, Mildred went on to the NAACP national convention in Minneapolis, Minnesota, where more of the civil rights work in the 1960 campaign was carried on.

In 1963, I attended the funeral of our dear friend Medgar Evers in Jackson, Mississippi. Medgar was state director of the NAACP. It was a terribly sad occasion, in which I was made painfully aware that in my post with the Detroit branch NAACP, I had never really faced the dangers with which Medgar had lived every day. I felt more strongly than ever that nothing, no further assassinations or other dangers, could be permitted to turn us around. There were thousands of friends who had come to pay tribute to our fallen friend. There had been talk of a march through the downtown streets of Jackson following the funeral. Once mentioned, there was no question but that we had to do it. As we began to assemble in front of the church, I took my place in the middle of the street and with others faced the hundreds of angry Mississippi policemen and state troopers. After a while, I turned to my left and there found the beautiful face of Mildred Jeffrey. Spontaneously, impulsively, with deep emotion and no regard for local tradition, I lifted her completely in my arms. Mildred and I have always understood that in that moment, we were in touch with all that our struggle has been about, and we never stopped holding each other.

Those of us who have shared the special blessing of Mildred's love know that we have suffered an irreparable loss and that we shall not see again the likes of Mildred Jeffrey. She was wonderful, simply wonderful.

A SALUTE TO MY MOTHER AND GRANDMOTHER:
Clara McFarland Johnson (1908–1991) and
Elizabeth McFarland (1888–1978)
(Published in *African American Family*)

My mother and her mother were domestic servants for almost all of their adult lives, first in Americus, Georgia, and later in Birmingham, Alabama. They knew the expectations, traditions, and social pains of this lowly work. Because of failing health, my mother was forced to quit in her early seventies, and my grandmother was finally stopped by a stroke in her late sixties.

In my young age, I did not fully appreciate either the trials or the possible triumphs of their labor. I knew it was honest work; otherwise, they wouldn't do it. I also came to know that along with some of its essential drudgery, the domestic service of these good and strong black women brought bread to our table, medicines when we were sick, a roof over our heads, and clothing and books for school. And they managed to bring Christmas joy and surprises in the midst of our poverty. It is a miracle that so much was done with so little. And this is not the full story.

The longest period of my mother's domestic service was spent with the Houston family in Birmingham, Alabama, where there were two children: Billy and Emily. Mr. Houston was a top-level manager with Southern Bell Telephone Company. Mrs. Houston was a housewife. I saw the Houstons as a decent family who occasionally did nice things for my mother and invited me often to come to work with her so I could play with their two children. Two things happened to get me straight on this cozy relationship. First, riding one day in the family car with Mrs. Houston, Billy, and Emily, I overheard Mr. Houston telling Mrs. Houston a derogatory story about "a nigger woman." I never forgot that incident and what it said about black-white relations in Birmingham, and the family for whom my mother worked. I was further awakened to the reality of racism when I turned thirteen and Mrs. Houston abruptly stopped inviting me to play with her two adolescent children.

I began to think about what my mother must have been going through, must have been feeling in her work relations with the Houstons and the other white families she served so faithfully, as did her mother also. In the custom of the South, they did everything: cleaning, cooking, laundry, ironing, and childcare. There was no systematic, organized, fair, and rational approach to labor and compensation as we now see in a good part of domestic service, where a number of middle-class African American families themselves are the employers.

As I reflect on this experience in the light of today's understanding, I want to salute my mother and my grandmother for so much that they took away from their work in unintended benefits and triumph over the racism that operated at the core of southern life. In spite of the exhausting burdens of their work, they lived long lives—my mother reached eighty-three, and my grandmother died at age ninety. They brought the full measure of love and devotion to their families. They cultivated some of the better middle-class habits of their "white folks," and they saw what was ugly and wrong in racial oppression and injustice. All of this must have strengthened their resolve to help me out of their meager earnings first to go to Morehouse College, and then to Atlanta University.

On the day of my graduation from Morehouse, with my mother and grandmother sitting in the audience, I felt a deep surge of emotion and tears that I could not hold back. I rejoiced in the knowledge that this was a day of triumph for them as much as for me.

MARTIN LUTHER KING JR. 1929–1968
(Presented at the Martin Luther King Jr. celebration at the
Episcopal Cathedral Church of St. John on January 15, 1995.)

I am very pleased to participate in the service in which we celebrate and express our gratitude anew for the life and work of one of the truly great men in human history—Martin Luther King. I am humbled to be invited to the pulpit of this historic church. You have good reason to be proud of your history, where you stand now and have stood in the past, the diversity of your membership, and the conscience that has made Christ Church the special congregation that it is. So, you honor me with your kind invitation.

I urge you to continue standing here in full recognition of your place and responsibility in the life and trials of this remarkable city we call Detroit. Our city and others like it speak to who we are. They are the true test of our civilization. They are the worst and the best of what we are; as one poet said, "They are the priesthood of the arts." I take this moment to say a word about our city because so many in our neighboring communities go out of their way to put Detroit down, saying, "I haven't been down there in years." Well, I ask, Where is "down there"? Wherever it is, the people who live there are us, all of us, and we cannot escape the challenge of our common destiny here. This indeed is where King stood.

In coming to our consideration of this legacy of Martin Luther King Jr., it is worth noting that no other American or world leader has been so widely honored in our country and abroad for his work for racial and social justice, for peace, for children, and for breaking the shackles of human poverty. It is a rich and enduring legacy made all the more inspiring because it comes from the life and tragic death of a young African American.

I am frequently asked two questions about Martin King by reporters and others who know of our relationship. The first is, What was King like as a student a Morehouse College? And the second question is, What would King say today if he were alive about this or that issue? I would like to quickly comment on the first question, and then share with you my response to the second.

Martin King was born in an educated, middle-class black family in Atlanta, Georgia. His mother was a Spelman College graduate, and his father, an active community leader, was a Morehouse graduate and a pastor of one of Atlanta's largest black congregations. He led a successful campaign to force Atlanta's largest department store—Rich's—to abandon its practice of speaking to black customers by using their first names.

Martin and I entered Morehouse College as freshman in September 1944. Martin, however, came as an advance student with early admission and graduated as a member of the class of 1948 at age nineteen. It has been often mentioned that Martin was a "B" student at Morehouse. He went on, however, to Crozier Theological Seminary and Boston University, where he earned top academic honors. At Morehouse, Martin was quite a regular guy, though always well-dressed. He liked to tell a good joke and to hear one. He was not a campus leader; I was, and I organized and led the campus chapter of the NAACP. But we all know that Martin was exceptional and would indeed succeed in his chosen work. All of us who came under the spell of Benjamin Mays knew that much was expected of us, and we had to become leaders. At our commencement, Dr. Mays stated that the class of 1948 was the best that Morehouse had produced under his presidency, and all of our classmates agreed with Dr. Mays's assessment.

Let me share with you just a brief excerpt from a piece I wrote about Mays and his influence on the class of 1948:

> Another approach to this reality was provided us by Dr. Mays when King and I were students at Morehouse. In our freshman year, Dr. Mays delivered a series of lectures on the theme of free men in a semi-free world. The central and overriding challenge that he underlined in these lectures was that while we as young black men may be forced to live under a system of racial oppression, even to accept various patterns of racial injustice and segregation, we must not accept any form of racial segregation that was not forced upon us. And more important, we must not permit anyone or any system to enslave our minds. I think that this principle stands at the highest level of education and freedom. It is this freedom of mind and spirit that produced the miraculous triumph of Nelson Mandela, who after twenty-seven years of wrongful imprisonment walked through his prison walls a free man, unscathed and unscarred, freed of hatred and the burdens of bitterness.

Let me now offer a brief response to the second question so often directed to me. What would Dr. King think and say were he still living? I must confess that I have been less than fully responsive to this question because the fact is that Martin King still lives with us in his work, and he speaks to us today in a clear and unequivocal voice. He lives in all of the monuments that have been erected in his name throughout this nation; he lives and speaks in all of the academic programs, schools and institutes, endowed professorships, church-related and community social programs that bear his name. No one has yet developed a complete record of all such tributes, along with the great body of King's written and recorded works in which he yet speaks, reminding us of the large burden of unfinished work that lies ahead of us.

ERNEST MARSHALL 1908–2000

I have been acquainted with the Marshall family for nearly forty years, and in most of that time, we have shared a warm and abiding friendship. I have seen Ernie and Louise in their unfailing devotion to family friends, and to each other. As a couple, they have been so tightly bonded that we have not thought of one without the other. I hope we will go on in this pattern of our thinking and remembrance knowing that this is in part the way of eternal life.

Ernie was a valiant companion in the vineyards of teaching and learning, and he brought a great heart and special insights to the role of educator. He seemed to have been born to the profession of education, so for him it was always the right challenge and the right commitment to give the best of himself to the growth and development of the students whose lives he touched in countless numbers.

For several years, Ernie and I worked together in the Detroit Public Schools' Division of School-community Relations. He was director of the Department of Equal Opportunity. Indeed, he was its primary builder, and in that position, Ernie put his integrity on the line every day. He was tough, unrelenting, and always fair. In other respects, I saw in Ernie Marshall the much-welcomed qualities of grace, dignity, and good manners, and I have no doubt that these splendid characteristics of his personality, along with the precious gift of Louise's love, kept Ernie living to the ripe age of ninety-two.

The legacy of this good man, Ernest Marshall, is therefore very substantial and secure. And you, Louise, and your son, Michael, and the rest of us have the interests of that legacy to share for the rest of our lives. So let us rejoice!

BISHOP IRVING MAYSON   1925–1995

I want to thank Alma Mayson for giving me the privilege of offering a few parting words in tribute to her husband, our very dear friend and a truly distinguished community and church leader.

Irving Mayson was a rare individual: strong in heart and spirit, bright in hope and intellect, faithful to his principles and vows, and undaunted in his quest for racial and social justice. He was a good man for whom the civilizing attribute of good humor helped to keep the conflicting forces of life bearable.

Often, when I would call him on the telephone, he would answer by saying: "Good morning! You are looking very good today. You know that I have one of those telephone instruments that enables me to see you." Now, I always wanted to believe that—not the instrument part, but that I was looking good—and I liked that line enough that I began using it with other friends.

Apart from the special and very important role that he played in this church, I believe that Irv Mayson's finest contribution to his time and nation was in his unrelenting and courageous efforts to break the shackles of racism and racial oppression. He knew the cruelty, the heavy social costs, the madness, and the immorality of racism both in and outside of the religious establishment in America, and he believed it to be a matter of personal duty, honor, and dignity to fight and fight, and to keep on fighting to end this shame and sin in our country. And he fought to the end of his life.

I found joy and inspiration in honoring Irving Mayson because I knew him to be fully worthy of honor. I saw in him the perfect harmony of heart and mind, and I loved him.

So, I am proud and grateful to be able to stand here today and say to Alma, their son and daughter, and other members of his fine family that God has blessed us generously in the life of Henry Irving Mayson; and his shining legacy will live forever.

WADE H. MCCREE 1920-1987

Wade McCree was a first-class citizen, and his distinguished record of community service is marked by a passionate belief in the citizenship rights and responsibilities of every man, woman, and child, unfettered by any arbitrary barriers of race and economic disadvantage.

Thinking about Wade and the uniqueness of his life, I recalled the bright yet unsparing words of W. E. B. DuBois spoken during the late years of his life. He said, "Life has its pain and evil—its bitter disappointments: but I like a good novel and in healthful length of days, there is infinite joy in seeing the world, the most interesting of continued stories unfold even though one misses the end." So Wade has missed the end—as will the rest of us—but not without preparedness, not without great achievements, not without being captured by the voice of great music and literature, and surely, surely not without knowing the special joy of the love of family and friends. The end, then, has come as fate would have it; but let me tell you about the record of community service made by Wade McCree with grace, diligence, and at times, incredible fortitude.

He was a life member of the NAACP, and whenever he felt his counsel was needed, he did not hesitate to speak. His conscience and concern for justice were carried in all areas of his work.

He discreetly and effectively took advantage of his wide circle of contacts in guiding countless numbers of young blacks to new opportunities in breaking the barriers of race and color in the corporate world.

In 1957, the late president of the UAW, Walter P. Reuther, called upon Wade to serve as a founding member of the newly established and independent UAW Public Review Board.

He was a member of the board of the Detroit Symphony Orchestra.

His devotion to learning and high standards in education led to his continuing involvement in the affairs of the United Negro College Fund.

In 1963, deeply disturbed about the very low black student enrollment in Michigan universities, Wade McCree moved with the then dean of the Wayne State University law school, Arthur Neef; Melvin Chapman; and Edward Cushman, along with a few others, to form an organization called the Higher Education Opportunities Committee (HEOC). With the primary purpose of increasing minority representation in Michigan colleges and universities, HEOC grew in strength and effectiveness under Wade's strong leadership, and today this organization is unexcelled in its service.

Finally, I would like to speak of my warm and close association with Wade McCree in another organization, which we helped to establish. It was the Pioneers, a group of twelve to thirteen men, which we dared to call a service club. For all that was lacking in service, we made up in a good deal of eating, and I must say a fair amount of good things to drink. If the world was not listening to our ideas for improvement and remedy, it was not our fault.

In all of this activity, Wade McCree shared the sterling qualities of his intellect, his learning, his commitment, his storytelling and good humor, his sense of class, and above all, his ego integrity. I didn't know anyone else quite like Wade, and I shall always carry his memory with gratitude.

The words of the Swedish Nobel Laureate Par Lagerkvist seem to me to be a fitting tribute to so remarkable a friend and companion:

> Then the walls be broken down
> By gigantic angels
> And freedom, freedom be proclaimed
> To all souls,
> To mine,
> To yours.
> Then all fetters shall be broken asunder
> With a sound giddy and shrill,
> So shrill that none can hear it,
> But we see the fetters cracking like crystals.
> Then the age of perfection will be at hand,
> And all the heavens filled with peace,

The peace of razed walls,
The peace of the ascending heavens,
The peace of freedom
Without end.

WILLIAM H. OLIVER 1915–1994

I met Bill Oliver and Alice shortly after I arrived in Detroit in the summer of 1950 to take up the duties of executive secretary of the Detroit branch NAACP. We were all young then, especially Alice. I had gone to Bill as director of the UAW's fair practices and anti-discrimination department to seek his help with the NAACP's annual membership campaign. With Bill's assistance, I also met Walter Reuther and requested his support. Both Walter and Bill gave major support to the campaign, and thus was the beginning of a long and fruitful relationship between us. In a fairly short span of time, I came to know and to develop close relations with others in the leadership of the UAW: Walter's brother, Roy, Emil Mazey, Brendan Sexton, Andy Brown, and Guy Nunn; and later, Jack Edwards, Marc Stepp, Jimmy Watts, Horace Sheffield, Lillian Hatcher, Doug Fraser, and Leonard Woodcock. In these relationships and with Bill Oliver at my side, I was drawn closer and closer to the UAW until I came to feel that I was a part of the UAW. This is the way it was with Bill Oliver and the NAACP. The NAACP was a part of his life, and his life was devoted to the principles of the NAACP and his union.

With the strength of his commitment and dedication, Bill Oliver became a major force in the local and national affairs of the NAACP, serving on the board and several committees. And, he did not quit until he was physically unable to do it. He fought to the end to express his voice and his conscience.

Bill's leadership for the UAW's anti-discrimination department commanded national attention and respect. It was what one should expect of a great union like the UAW, and it is good to know that this quality of courage, integrity, and strength continues in the department's present leader, Joe Davis.

Great trooper and warrior that he was, Bill Oliver had in Alice the loving companion that he needed and deserved. As all of their friends know, Alice called Bill "sir," but we also know that, as good wives can do, she put his large ego in check and gave a quiet and dignified touch to their entire life together.

I loved Bill. We were good friends from day one. We had good times together, and we shared our trusts, our dreams, some disappointments, and some triumphs. And I am mighty thankful for the time we have had to travel this path together.

May God bless you, Alice, and give you peace and comfort in the days ahead.

ROBERT MOSELEY 1920–1992

When our dear friend Damon Keith called last Wednesday morning to tell Chacona and me that Bob Moseley had died suddenly, we were overcome with a sense of shock and grief. No! No! Not Bob Moseley! Like others perhaps, we had come to believe, quite wrongly, that Bob would always be here just as we had known and loved him. He was a dear friend to us, such that we knew that with his death, we were suffering an irreplaceable loss. And such is the grievous loss of the Detroit branch NAACP. He was a champion second to none, and he was always there helping to guide the Freedom Fund Dinner to each year's greater success. He was effective because he was a good person, a good man—calm, giving, steady, affable, reliable, and gracious. The NAACP and the Freedom Fund Dinner were a vital part of Bob's world, and we were uncommonly blessed to be there with him.

To you, Laura, your children, and grandchildren, I say that for one so special as Bob in his qualities of person, mind, and spirit, we know that even as we grieve, we must celebrate his life and thank God for the gift.

ROSA PARKS 1913–2005
Part of statement provided to the Detroit Free Press.

When I learned of Rosa Parks's death, several thoughts rushed through my mind. First was the huge debt that all of us must share with limitless gratitude to this great lady of simple virtues.

I thought also about the precious value of courage, from which there is no honorable escape, Mrs. Parks taught us, for those who care about freedom and human dignity.

I thought about how much Rosa Parks had given of herself to teach, bring honor and belief to the indispensable role of the individual in shaping the course of our destiny. She was indeed our patron saint and she will remain so.

For all of this, I praise God.

CLAIRE PINKETT 1924–1994

To Claire Pinkett's family, Pastor Adams, and friends, I am grateful for this privilege to pay tribute to the wonderful person we have known as Claire Pinkett. Claire was no ordinary person. She was a great friend who was willing to express her love every day. One did not have to search for her heart. Its pulse was always clear and strong, as was her mind. Claire carried the countenance of a cheerful warrior, a gracious and graceful woman; and she used these admirable qualities to demonstrate the art as much as the skills of an exceptional secretary.

I shared the benefits and was continually encouraged and strengthened by Claire's devotion to the NAACP. In the years of my presidency, she was always there, giving her best in praise and criticism. Above all, she never let me suffer for the need and warmth of her friendship.

When Bill Pickard and I made our final call on Claire last Saturday morning, knowing that the end was near, I think we received from Eddie and Claire's daughter more than we could give. Their spirits were reassuring, and I left this parting scene knowing more than ever that God has blessed us generously in the life, love, and work of Claire Pinkett.

LONGWORTH QUINN SR. 1908–1989

I am grateful for the privilege Dorothy Quinn has given to me to say a farewell tribute to her husband and our friend. I met Longworth Quinn in the summer of 1950 shortly after I arrived in Detroit to assume the duties of executive secretary of the Detroit branch NAACP. At that time, he was the business manager of the *Michigan Chronicle.* As he moved to the position of executive head of the *Chronicle,* and finally to semiretirement, he left two indelible marks in the record of his leadership and service: one, he kept the *Chronicle* alive when other publications were falling by the wayside; and two, he kept the *Chronicle* in the forefront of the black struggle, always saying editorially what had to be said and always printing the facts of racial injustice when the daily press would not. I think he had an enduring romance with the life and role of the black press in the same way that Langston Hughes expressed his love. It was a vital part of his life, and the *Chronicle* drew strength from his devotion.

And so did the Detroit branch NAACP. Longworth was a champion, a loyal contributor, and a thinker of the movement.

His unique contribution to the birth and growth of our annual Fight for Freedom Fund Dinner was published in the *Chronicle* week after week in every name of each dinner subscriber. He also handled special publicity for the dinner from the beginning up to his death.

It is therefore fitting that Longworth Quinn will be memorialized in the Wayne State University Journalism Institute for Minorities, and I express to the Quinn family the gratitude of the university in being able to participate in this lasting tribute.

For all of us who have shared and claimed the bonds of friendship with Longworth Quinn, who have relied on his dedication and faithfulness in community service, who yet understand the realities of racial oppression in our country today as well as yesterday, and who admire the qualities of excellence in character, toughness of spirit, and gentleness of heart and manner that were the sterling attributes of Longworth Quinn, the loss we have sustained is irreparable, but we must be thankful that in God's mercy, we have a rich legacy to share forever.

HORACE L. SHEFFIELD   1916–1995

When I received word of Horace Sheffield's death last week, I felt a deep and staggering sense of sadness. I was struck instantly with the realization that this nation, this city, and the cause of African Americans and other oppressed people here and abroad had suffered an irreparable loss. Horace was a big person who broke through the barriers of convention, status, and racism to become, in the right sense of the term, a great American, and a Detroit citizen of the first rank. Over the years, he gave the best of his heart and mind to labor's cause, to the NAACP; to the Detroit Alliance of Black Organizations (DABO) and its national counterpart, whose founding he alone inspired; to the fight for our schools; to the fight against violence and crime in our community; and a number of other battles that had to be waged. During my three terms as president of the Detroit branch NAACP, we launched with the active support and participation of Horace Sheffield the campaigns to achieve fair banking practices, nondiscriminatory insurance rates in Detroit, and the "Buy Detroit" campaign. He helped to shape our strategies and to sustain our will in these battles.

Horace Sheffield was a good person, a good man, and a loyal friend who was always there. What quickly came to my mind when speaking to a reporter about him last week was that Horace was always ready and willing when necessary to put the full weight of his intellectual and moral strength on the issues that really mattered to him. He was a man of intense passion who caused me many times to reflect on the question: If a person is not able to bring the passion of relief and some emotion to the compelling issues of social injustice and human dignity, for what and where else will one bring passion, feeling, and emotion?

I always marveled at Horace's ability to bring fresh enthusiasm and energy, and to sustain that investment of himself to the urgency of new ideas and programs that he thought should be implemented. In these encounters, he was known to call night and day. He never stopped trying to make a difference and working for the solution that had to be found. He never lost faith in the rightness of the civil rights movement in America, and he pushed us continually to recognize the common alliances that were necessary to the achievement of our goals of freedom and equality.

This is the legacy that Horace Sheffield, a prince and valiant warrior, street fighter and statesman in the same flesh, has bequeathed to his three daughters and son, and to his lovely wife, Joyce. That the rest of us can continue to embrace and share such a legacy, in the name of Horace, is God's everlasting gift to us all.

DAUPHINE WALKER SHIVERS 1931–2005

No one has stood ahead or above Dauphine Walker Shivers in devotion to the great principles of the NAACP and the continuing struggle of

African Americans for freedom and equality. Dauphine was always in the thick of the battle, never flinching, never showing weariness, and never giving up. She was above pettiness and self-aggrandizement.

She played a decisive role in building the growth and development of the Fight for Freedom Fund Dinner. She was a leader in the small group of women who demonstrated continually what a strong, organized group of women can do in any cause. One of Dauphine's strengths and a true expression of her character was seen in her graceful, quiet demeanor and respect for everyone while addressing the major issues of the NAACP. She was kind, considerate, and always the lady in the larger sense. That is why we loved her and held her in high esteem.

Toward the end of her life, Dauphine tried still to maintain that inner smile on her face, and she gallantly fought off death until she had nothing more to give. For these good and faithful contributions, we will always feel grateful to Dauphine. We will never forget her, and we will always praise God for such a perfect gift.

DR. LIONEL SWAN 1906–1999

I want to say especially to Lionel Swan's children, grandchildren, and all other members of his family that he richly deserves the splendid tributes that are being spoken here today. For Swan was a giant of a man whose ideas and ideals were always operating on a lofty scale, and he looked for this virtue in other men and women as well. He was dedicated to learning and achievement, and he brought high expectations to the education of his own and all other children. He disdained mediocrity and gave no ground to so-called black English and the false notion that African American children need something more than belief, challenge, and opportunity to match the educational attainments of children, whatever their status, anywhere in the world.

Swan loved his family, and he kept his arms around them. He gave generously and never stopped giving to the friends and the causes that claimed the best of his heart and mind. To these, he was faithful to the end.

All of us who knew Lionel Swan well and shared the warm embrace of his friendship will remember him for his love of a good story; for the fun he found in "wolfing," as we call it; and for his mastery of bridge.

What a terrible opponent he could be, and just as fierce and unrelenting an advocate. We saw in Swan the marvelous strength and character that made him an effective leader in the medical profession, the NAACP, the Howard University alumni, his fraternity—Phi Beta Sigma—and the Detroit community as a whole. He was a citizen of the first rank. And I want to note in particular that the NAACP's famed Fight for Freedom Fund Dinner in Detroit would not have been so successfully launched in 1956 without the enormous contribution made by Lionel Swan.

On a more personal note, I want to share with you that when Chacona and I reached the decision to be married, we called on Swan to ask his blessings. His positive response was instant and heartwarming. He asked where we planned to be married, and we told him that we had not yet decided. And then he said, "Why not be married here in my home?" We immediately accepted Swan's invitation, and we were married in a brief ceremony on his back lawn on August 30, 1980. It was a very beautiful day!

When I think of this event and so many other precious moments that I was fortunate to experience with Swan, when I think of the grand legacy of this good and extraordinary man, I know today better than even before why I have loved him, and have held him closely through all the years with gratitude and honor.

JUDGE SAMUEL A. TURNER 1926–1994

Sam Turner was one of the finest human beings that I have ever known, and he shared the best of himself in the long friendship we enjoyed since our student days at Morehouse College.

He was a man of genuine distinction: a fine intellect, solid integrity, a commitment to fairness and justice, a gentle demeanor, perseverance, loyalty to friends, a believer, a Detroit citizen of the first rank, a loving and faithful husband and father. I loved him and held him always in high esteem.

As I think about the sterling qualities that truly distinguished Sam Turner, one simple virtue stands out: he was a good and patient listener. When we think of how much the world needs the exercise of this virtue, we can appreciate even more what a special person Sam Turner was.

Yesterday, I spoke briefly with Mrs. Josephine Harreld Love about Sam Turner, and when I said to her that Sam was a real Morehouse Man, this well-known daughter of a Morehouse father and teacher asked, pulling my leg: "Well, what is that?" When I recovered, I said, "Well, Sam was simply the best of whatever we hope that a Morehouse Man will be."

So I say to you, dear Carmen, and to your proud and strong sons, Adam and Jeffrey, you are richly blessed in Sam's legacy, and may God bless you to find comfort in that legacy and to celebrate it in all the days ahead.

ABRAHAM ULMER 1927–1997

I want to thank Trudy for the honor and privilege of expressing a farewell salute to my dear friend Abe Ulmer. At my age, one grows more and more conscious of losing friends, especially one so rare, sturdy, good, and faithful as Abe Ulmer, and however much we are guided and sustained by our Christian belief, our pain and grief at this moment are almost unbearable.

Abie and I became good friends when he was courting Trudy, who has always been wonderful and beautiful. I attended their wedding thirty-five years ago, and I have rejoiced in the triumph and glory of their love of each other.

When I seek to offer any measure of Abe Ulmer's life and work, I think first of the wisdom of W. E. B. DuBois and how fittingly it describes the character and ego integrity of Abie. On his seventieth birthday DuBois said, "I have met life face to face, I have loved a good fight and I have realized that love is God, and work is his profit; that his ministers are age and death."

With his wisdom and a strong heart, Abe Ulmer has left an inextinguishable mark on his times. He put his life with Trudy's on the line when he organized and led marches against housing segregation and job discrimination in the early 1960s in every major suburb surrounding the city of Detroit. He fought and broke the patterns of discrimination that had been the practice of Detroit's largest home-loan bank. And he held his troops together in the face of real dangers because he respected them and he was first to the line of battle.

It was our common and united struggle to break the chains of racial oppression in our city and nation that drew Abie and me together, but it was love and shared faith that kept us together through all these years.

Abie was a golden friend—golden in love, trustworthiness, faithfulness, helpfulness, and golden in his laughter. So that I—we—are now left with golden memories.

I thank God for such a rich blessing, and I shall hold you Trudy, Philip, Rodney, and Abie's sisters in my heart forever.

REVEREND JAMES WADSWORTH 1923–1986

When I spoke here at Fellowship Chapel some time ago as part of an anniversary tribute to Jim Wadsworth, I asked rhetorically if anyone in the audience could truly say the he or she had met someone who could remind us of Jim. For such were the originality, unique personality, and rare character of Jim Wadsworth that to know him was to know the only one of his kind.

He dressed well and liked to look good. He enjoyed good food and fine champagne, and knew that he deserved them. He admired intellectual ability and loved good music. He honored the power of great preaching in the Baptist church tradition, and he was such a good listener in conversation that he was able often to build his own sermons on the ideas shared by others. He admired neatness, cleanness, and order in his own surroundings, and in the lives of others. He spoke quietly and softly and could not be shaken to a point of looseness, or hopelessness.

Jim was made of granite, honor, love, truth, hope, faith, charity, and all of those splendid qualities that God has invested, to his best. To have known and loved such a friend was to know how truly wonderful and matchless is the gift of life itself.

So I shall miss him mightily, his sound and the touch of his heart and mind. He joined Nicholas Hood in conducting the marriage ceremony for Chacona and me. On a night of personal crisis for me, he provided shelter and counsel, and in all the days in between, he was a constant friend.

I cannot help, then, but to grieve over this terrible loss. But, as I reflect on Jim's life, I know that his work is done, and I rejoice in the knowledge that in Virginia he found love and held dearly the perfect companion to the end.

IRMA WERTZ 1912–2007

I met and got to know Irma Wertz in the period of the 1960s when I served the Detroit Board of Education as Deputy Superintendent for School-Community Relations. This was a time of great turbulence in our public schools. The community was heavily engaged with the issue of black control of black schools, recognition of African American culture in the schools' curricula, school integration, and school decentralization.

Irma Wertz emerged in this environment as one of the brightest, most articulate, and courageous of those community leaders working for school change and improvement. She recognized that good and successful schools were an absolute requirement if Detroit were to survive as a healthy and productive community.

Irma possessed many strengths, and I was always taken by that impish quality that inevitably came through in her interactions with others. It helped to keep us sane.

I am grateful for the opportunity to salute this remarkable lady and claim her as a friend.

IRA WHITBY 1889–1986

The report of Ira Whitby's death brought on me a sense of genuine sadness, and I was only comforted somewhat by the family's request of me to speak briefly on behalf of the Pioneer Club. Ira was a pioneer, and in all respects, he was one of the best of our group.

The Pioneers were supposed to be a small service organization, but the club was more social than program oriented. Among the members were Charles Butler, Horace Sheffield, Jim Wadsworth, Wade McCree, Ed Hodge, Leonard Proctor, and the late J. J. McClendon. The Pioneers enjoyed good conversation in which they settled some of the world's great problems, but the real centerpiece that attracted us to the monthly meetings was the food, those wonderful meals that the wives put together. With the Whitbys, this was always a rich and enjoyable experience. We received not only all that Mrs. Whitby could give, but for extra measure, we got the presence and special touches of daughters Norma and Janice. No one enjoyed these Pioneer fests more than Ira, and he was proud of the flattering treatment we received in his home.

In the meetings of the Pioneers, I came to know the steadiness of Ira Whitby's values, his solid-gold character, his salt-of-the-earth goodness, his ready appetite for a funny story, and the smile that was always in his countenance. You had to love a man like that, and we did.

As we mourn Ira's death, we are reminded that we should always celebrate the life of such a rare individual, knowing how richly blessed we are to be touched by it. I hope that the fullness of this blessing will remain as a happy treasure to be shared by all the members of this family.

Letter from Joseph Hudson about the Formation of New Detroit

Joseph L. Hudson Jr., former CEO of the J. L. Hudson Co, spearheaded the creation of the New Detroit Committee after the 1967 Detroit riot.

Dear Arthur,

You put a challenge to me in your request that I write you some thoughts as to how the New Detroit Committee was formed, what were the various interactions, and now, almost forty years later, what stands out as to "markers in the sand."

The first point that I remember is that we could not find any examples or road maps to follow. There were no urban coalitions throughout the country, the public and political sectors (federal, state, and local) had been rejected by much of the population, few so-called community leaders had any meaningful dialogue with significant members of the black community.

So what should we do? Governor Romney, Mayor Cavanagh, and Cy Vance said, "Go at it, figure out how Detroit should go from here"; and they asked me to chair such an effort. Their request probably had one sound rationale. I had not been previously identified in too many leadership activities in the community and thus did not bring along a lot of baggage.

Within about ten days, I had selected thirty-nine individuals who might compose a starting board of this urban coalition, soon to be named "New Detroit." I received 100 percent acceptance of the thirty-nine invitees over a four-day weekend.

The individuals came together within a week to ten days, pledging their personal participation, offering staff, financial, and creative support, and then commencing the process—first learning how to listen.

Sincerely,
JLH
July 24, 2006

Letter from William Patrick
about Joining New Detroit

William T. Patrick Jr. served as the first president of New Detroit, Inc.

Dear Arthur,

You asked me how I came to be part of New Detroit.

First, let me back up a moment to contemplate my thoughts and feelings as our town was engulfed in flames and devastation during those fateful days in late July 1967. During those days, I would go to my office high in the Michigan Bell building each day and look out the window to see the smoke rising from various locations in the 12th Street area as fires and destruction held sway. It left me with the dreadful feeling of frustration and futility as I would sit there and realize that, however much I wished to play a role in curbing the disturbances, there was nothing I could do. I felt utterly powerless.

After the flames died down and the rebuilding process began, there was a continuance of this aching to do something to help. It did not matter how small or insignificant. There was just the driving urge to do something, which I shared with many people. Our town and our citizens were in trouble, as unfortunately was the case in other cities all about our country during that racially charged hot summer. There were many who wanted desperately to help.

In the news media, I followed reports of the formation and convening of the New Detroit Committee in response to the joint call from Governor George Romney and Mayor Jerry Cavanagh, and I was heartened with the realization that important forces in our metropolitan area were being mobilized in an herculean effort to bring the city back from the brink and to seek solutions to the misery of masses of people living in dehumanizing conditions of poverty and want. This was heady stuff, and there was a glimmering of hope.

The New Detroit Committee represented all segments of our urban community. It included earnest and impatient young militants, older people who had been in the struggle for improvement for much of their lives, the leaders of labor, the heads of the major institutions, and the captains of the great industries of Detroit. They numbered thirty-nine strong at the beginning. Joseph L. Hudson Jr., chairman of the J. L. Hudson Company, one of the finest retail establishments in the country, was named chairman of the committee. Staff for the new organization, some fifty strong, came from people in the member institutions. The committee was made part of the Metropolitan Fund headed by Kent Mathewson. The rebuilding of the city was launched.

Then one day a few weeks later, I was summoned to the office of Bill Day, president of Michigan Bell, who informed me that Joe Hudson wanted me to go over to New Detroit and head up its staff operation, and he asked me if I would be interested. I eagerly assented and went immediately to meet with Hudson to be appointed head of the day-to-day operation. The next day I reported to the New Detroit offices to start my official duties, and I ushered in the beginning of more than three years of great effort to erase the causes and scars of the rebellion and to return Detroit to its place as one of the great cities of the world. A short time thereafter, when the committee was incorporated and became New Detroit Inc., it was separated from the Fund and I was made president. The years I was with New Detroit were memorable and purposeful, and I treasure my association with all facets of the group.

July 26, 2006

A Commitment to the NAACP

Remarks by Arthur L. Johnson upon his installation as president of the Detroit branch NAACP at Tabernacle Missionary Baptist Church on January 23, 1987.

I am honored to have been elected to serve as president of the Detroit branch of the National Association for the Advancement of Colored People (NAACP), and I am grateful for the trust of my fellow NAACP members and friends who have made possible this opportunity. I promise that I shall do everything within my power, using the best of my heart, mind, and physical energy to unite and mobilize the forces of this community behind the NAACP, to toughen the will and muscle of the organization, and to make real gains in removing from the path of black people, especially black children, the killing effect of racial oppression.

In this task, I shall call on everyone to participate: white and black, young and old, rich and poor, union member and businessman, the handicapped and able-bodied, the educated and those who cannot read. I shall ask all to give what they can of their means and time. And yes, I shall seek the return of the buppies who have escaped to nowhere. Our mission is to free ourselves and our country.

Racism is still rampant and a virulent force in our national life. Its open manifestations, as seen in recent incidents of racial violence in the North and South, provide us with clear evidence of the problem before us. I come, then, to this responsibility with the belief that we can and must do a great deal more to hasten the realization of our goals. To this end, I have already moved, with the support of our board, to establish six task forces in the following areas:

1. Jobs and economic development
2. Education and health issues
3. Member participation and activities

4. Youth and young adult involvement
5. Fiscal and membership development
6. Public communications and image

These task forces will take a fresh examination of where we are, with the aims of determining the most critical problems and issues confronting the NAACP and the black community. They will then seek to outline a set of realistic goals, which we shall work to achieve.

We shall not try to do everything, but we shall do what we must to change the conditions in our community. And, for those who may yet ask the question, Is the civil rights movement alive? we shall answer as we have through the years—we shall go to court, we shall protest, we shall demonstrate, and we shall be heard.

We know that our work is cut out for us. The black community is heavily burdened by a generalized economic weakness and poverty conditions, which afflict more than half of our men, women, and children. In such conditions it is impossible for blacks to find self-realization in the best terms, to educate their children, provide adequate health care for their families, and to support development of their neighborhoods. In a very tragic sense, we have here, as Kenneth Clark has described it, the experience of a mugged community where teenage pregnancy, high infant mortality, a high crime rate, and black-on-black violence are the most painful signs of social disorder and dysfunction.

Our forebears did not willingly accept racial oppression, and it is time for us to undo it for ourselves, our children, and black generations to come.

Our struggle as African Americans has become the struggle of our city. I welcome the responsibility; I believe that we have in the survival of the city a fair test of our civilization. Therefore, those who profess to help the black cause and who seek to stand above white racism must address the needs of the city, or they do little of any consequence to achieve change and reconstruction in race relations.

I have noted in other places that the weak state of our city's economic health, the calculated mistreatment of its image, and the alarming scale of economic disinvestment in Detroit are in large part the result of conscious and unconscious racism. Whether we wish to recognize the fact or not, these conditions are the symbols of our own apartheid.

We must attack these oppressive conditions at their roots, and what better way to begin than by determining where and how we shall get a firm handle on our own economic resources and will spend our money where it will do the most good for our community, our children, our neighbors and the city.

Finally, I want to say a more personal word to you, my friends, who share the mantle of leadership and continued faith in this work. We are a strong and good people, fully entitled to the enjoyment of *freedom now* with all other citizens. Let us, then, take heart from some of the words of DuBois reminding us of "the divine gift of laughter which helps to make the world human and loveable, despite all its pain and wrong, loving a good fight, we can meet life face to face, knowing that love is God and work is his prophet."

"Buy Detroit" Campaign

Remarks by Arthur L. Johnson at NAACP press conference on December 12, 1989.

On December 12, 1989, we launched another phase of the Detroit branch NAACP "Project Freedom," which was announced a little more than a year ago. It is a "Buy Detroit" campaign. The aim of Buy Detroit is to strengthen business-commercial activity in Detroit in all areas, to invigorate further the economic life of Detroit, and in so doing, to expand viable job and business opportunities for African Americans and others in our city.

In constructing this campaign, we have been moved by a number of considerations. First is the fact that the city of Detroit has been "malled" almost to death, creating heavy economic burdens for the city and its residents. In many ways, Detroit has been abandoned, primarily, we believe, because of its majority black population. Racial isolation and polarization have come to mark the face of this region more than any other urban center in the nation. The impairment of this central city's health has weakened the health of the entire southeastern region, and this process of social and economic deterioration will continue until we have come to our senses as one community.

For our part in the NAACP, we cannot accept such conditions as being in any way desirable, necessary, or inevitable. Furthermore, we not only believe that we can make a major difference, but that we must.

Thus, in addition to other program measures we have undertaken in Project Freedom, involving the practices of Detroit banks, the issues of discriminatory automobile insurance premiums, black business development, and fair share campaigns, we are now putting into action the Buy Detroit campaign.

This is not a campaign against the suburbs, where blacks and whites engage in commercial trade and a number of black business ventures are thriving. Such a misguided effort would defeat our purpose. Buy Detroit is simply "pro" Detroit on the basic premise that the economic good health and well-being of this central city are essential to the health and well-being of the larger region. Indeed, the suburbs can ignore this principle only to their own peril.

Therefore, we are, and shall be, appealing both to Detroit and suburban residents to shop and dine, and to do business in Detroit as much as possible. We are especially urging suburban residents who now feel far removed from Detroit to enter with us into the spirit as well as the work of rebuilding a great city where all citizens can lay claim equally to its life and enjoy the fruits of their labors.

For much of the past two years, we have had a strong committee of NAACP volunteers led by the distinguished founder of the Detroit Association of Black Organizations, and a board member of the Detroit branch, Horace Sheffield Jr., doing the necessary research and planning of this project. The committee, our cause, and our city deserve the best support we can bring to this endeavor, and I thank you for your participation.

Elected to the NAACP Presidency
for a Third Term

Remarks by Arthur L. Johnson upon installation in his third consecutive term as president of the Detroit branch NAACP, January 20, 1991.

Judge Keith, my colleagues on the branch executive committee who have just been installed with me today, members and friends of the Detroit branch NAACP: I want to express to you my genuine appreciation in being elected to a third consecutive term as your president. I accept all of the obligations that are associated with this important office at this critical time in our struggle and history. You deserve the best that I can give you, and I do not intend to spare myself in responding to the need.

I want to express to Judge Damon Keith our gratitude for the role he has played today in these ceremonies. He was due in Cincinnati in connection with his court duties, but he stayed here to give us the helping hand that we needed of him. Most of you know Damon Keith as the great judge that he truly is—sensitive, generous, tough, hard-working, courageous, and unswerving in his devotion to what our nation's constitution says of opportunity and free speech. We are proud of him, and we proudly claim him as one of our own. Now with all of this, I know Damon Keith as my best friend, and I thank God for enabling us to grow together and to share as much as we have. It is a rich blessing.

I want to congratulate all of the members of the executive board who have been elected or appointed and installed today. You are a great team with which to work—each one of you—and in working together and keeping our eyes on the main thing, indeed, on the prize, we can and will make a difference. I was never more inspired by the experience of what one individual—man or woman—can do in changing things than by the deeply moving example of our brother Nelson Mandela. Let us keep the powerful and loving image of this great man along with that of our patron saint—Martin Luther King—ever before us.

When I came to the presidency of this branch in 1987, I said to you that I wanted us to narrow the focus of our attack, to be more strategic in the definition of our program goals and objectives, and to achieve a greater discipline in the use of our limited resources.

I asked you to adopt "Project Freedom"—a plan of action in which we said that our main objective was to break the stubborn shackles of economic oppression that keep black Americans deep in the bowels of poverty, unable to support adequately the education, health, and social needs of the black family and community. We pointed out that the patterns of separation and distance between black and white America, in terms of income and wealth, were widening instead of being reduced.

We stated our goals in Project Freedom as follows:

1. To expand our attack on job discrimination at every level.
2. To destroy whenever possible the institutional vestiges of economic discrimination.
3. To expand the thrust of the NAACP's "Fair Share" program.
4. To support the development of black business enterprise and economic development of the city of Detroit.

We have met and are continuing to meet the challenges of Project Freedom with the following actions:

• For the first time in the history of the branch, we have established an office solely concerned with complaint investigation and adjustment.

• We have conducted a highly successful campaign to change the lending, promotional, and development financing practices of the Detroit banks.

• And we now have in motion a lawsuit against AAA of Michigan that is designed to break the pattern of discriminatory automobile insurance rates by the auto insurance industry in Michigan. In this work, I salute Butch Hollowell, in particular.

• We have successfully negotiated with General Motors a number of constructive program changes and measures that will be helpful to black dealers and suppliers. Here I salute Sharon McPhail for her diligence in advancing the goals of our Fair Share program.

- Finally, we launched in December of 1989 our "Buy Detroit" campaign under the strong and faithful leadership of Horace Sheffield. In this major undertaking, we have already struck pay dirt in the improved performance of a number of Detroit businesses, most notably Crowley's in this past Christmas season. We are committed to this campaign for the duration of the need.

This is not all—by far—of what we have been doing:

- We have the brilliant achievement of our act-so program.
- The organ donor program
- The branch awards program
- The sip-ins
- Fashions for freedom
- The magnificent Freedom Fund Dinner
- The golf tournament
- And the Christmas Seals campaign.

I applaud in particular the fine contributions to these programs by the following members: Jesse Goodwin, Lavern Ethridge, Rebecca Davis, Voncille Green, Lavonna Davis, our late friend and companion, Betty Lackey, Irene Graves, Evelyn Case, Gilda Keith, Corrine Houston, Horace Stone, Helen Love, Mel Chapman, Nate Shapiro, Jim Clark, Tom Adams, Leona Stallworth, Darin Walker, Claire Pinkett, Lois Williams, Beulah Work, Leon Atchison, Myrlen Washington, Richard King, Lionel Swan, Bill Pickard, Mary Blackmon, Butch Hollowell, Charles Boyce, Robert Neal, Dauphine Walker Shivers, Lottie Caudle, and Joe Davis.

To all of you and others whom I have not named, we owe you our applause and deep gratitude.

As we look ahead, I urge that we keep our attention focused on five critical areas of the problems that yet confront us. They are:

1. The severely depressed economic conditions that continue to be suffered by African Americans in Detroit and throughout this nation.
2. The heavy burden of attrition and academic failure in our public schools.

3. The signs of failing health in the black community, i.e., drug addiction, the infant and adult mortality rates, suicide rates, and the lowered life expectancy of young black males.
4. The unyielding force of racism in America.
5. The persistence of national government policies and practices that operate to continue all of the liabilities above—a disproportionate representation of African Americans in the ranks of the poor, uneducated, sick, crime offenders, the nation's armed services, and the victims of early death and criminal violence.

Along with these gigantean tasks, we must also do everything within our power to improve the quality of life and to advance the growth of our city of Detroit. This city's struggle and our own have become one. Our work is cut out for us. We shall remain faithful to our purpose and goals, always ready to do what we must, remembering what DuBois once said: "Love is God and work is his prophet." With this faith and God's help, we shall succeed.

Rodney King Verdict and the Detroit Branch NAACP Twelve-Point Plan

Statement by Arthur L. Johnson, president of Detroit branch NAACP, during a press conference at the branch office on May 7, 1992.

All of the citizens of Detroit can feel a measured sense of relief that the life of our community has not been traumatized by any acts of violence in response to the disaster of the Rodney King jury verdict. We were horrified by the verdict and deeply saddened by the violence and destruction that followed in its wake. Both aspects of the Los Angeles experience have exposed for all the deeply rooted forces of racism in our country.

The city of Detroit has been spared the worst of what might have been, largely because of the tremendous contributions of Mayor Coleman A. Young in changing the face and ways of the Detroit police department, along with the will and spirit of this city. Many among us have used the term *wake-up call* in reaching for the meaning of the Los Angeles experience. In whatever way we have been moved in the Detroit area, it is abundantly clear that a new "call" to action now confronts us.

We must do all that we can, not tomorrow, next month or next week, we must do it today.

In the spirit of the common efforts that must be made to rebuild the infrastructure of our city and to break the shackles of racism, we are today offering a twelve-point plan for action and progress in which all concerned individuals and organizations can participate.

NAACP 12-point "Call to Action"

1. We call on African Americans and others to give highest priority to the needs and legitimate aspirations of Detroit's youth by investing community funds toward employment, cultural/leadership development, increased opportunities for recreation, and arts and social programs. The NAACP-

sponsored Affirmative Action Community Task Force for Black Employment (ACT-BE) and other branch programs will continue to address these needs; and we invite other community organizations to join these initiatives.

2. We call on all Detroit area residents to support the "Buy Detroit" campaign to rebuild the economic base of Detroit and expand critically needed job opportunities. African Americans in particular must make more effective, strategic use of their own economic resources in fighting the forces of racism and achieving self-determination.

3. We call on religious leadership, city officials, law enforcement agencies, youth, community residents, and community based organizations to expand and intensify our war against the intolerable levels of crime, drugs, and violence plaguing our communities. We call on community residents to support a variety of programs that actively address anticrime and antiviolence efforts, including SOSAD (Save Our Sons and Daughters), The Alliance, the Community Coalition against Crime, and others.

4. We call on Detroit area schools through their administrators, faculties, students, board members, parents, and community members to upgrade education programs aimed at promoting respect for all people, diversity, and multicultural understanding. We urge in particular the inclusion of programs on conflict mediation and a human rights curriculum that reflects the commitment to multiculturalism and Afrocentric education.

5. We call on New Detroit Inc. to redouble its efforts, in concert with the NAACP and other agencies, to bring to the surface and eliminate the structural, institutional, and systemic inequalities that are the daily burdens of Detroit's African American residents. Among the worst examples of these inequalities are the discriminatory practices in the sales of goods and services, racism in economic investment decisions, and the redlining practices of automobile and housing insurance companies.

6. We call on the Detroit media to play a larger and more aggressive role in bringing to public light the hidden practices

and forces of racism that systematically work against the well-being of the city of Detroit and its predominantly African American population.

7. We call on the public officials and politicians of this state, whomever and wherever they are, to stop the dirty, mean-spirited, and racist bashing of the city of Detroit and its leadership. Political leaders can and should be criticized, rejected, or supported by the citizens who have the right to vote. That is the way of democracy.

8. We call on the Detroit police department, the courts, and all other agencies and members of our criminal justice system to maintain law and order in this community by making the system work fairly and evenhandedly for all citizens, and rejecting at every turn lawless and illegal conduct by law authorities themselves.

9. We call on Detroit Renaissance to redouble its efforts and to quicken the pace of revitalizing the city of Detroit, its neighborhoods, and downtown services as a necessary step to reducing Detroit's staggering unemployment rate and repairing the city's image.

10. We call on African American leadership, other people of color, and whites in the suburbs and the city to bring the problem of racism to the top of their program and action agenda.

11. We call on the leaders of the public and private sectors, and the Chamber of Commerce, to join a national call for immediate state and federal action to reduce human suffering and to aid the growth of economic opportunity in Detroit and other major, central cities in America.

12. We call on all citizens to register and vote as a principle of good citizenship. It is specious to claim that we do not have viable choices.

Bibliography

Bennett, Jr. Lerone. *Before the Mayflower: A History of Black America.* Chicago: Johnson Publishing, 1982.

———. *Forced into Glory: Abraham Lincoln's White Dream.* Chicago: Johnson Publishing, 2000.

Boyle, Kevin. *Arc of Justice: A Saga of Race, Civil Rights, and Murder in the Jazz Age.* New York: Henry Holt, 2004.

Davis, Allison. *Leadership, Love, and Aggression.* New York: Harcourt Brace Jovanovich, 1983.

Davis, Michael D., and Hunter R. Clark. *Thurgood Marshall: Warrior at the Bar, Rebel on the Bench.* New York: Birch Lane Press, 1992.

Drake, St. Clair, and Horace R. Cayton. *Black Metropolis: A Study of Negro Life in a Northern City.* New York: Harper & Row, 1962.

DuBois, W. E. B. *The Souls of Black Folk: Essays and Sketches.* Chicago: A. C. McClurg, 1903.

———. *Dusk of Dawn: An Essay toward an Autobiography of a Race Concept.* New York: Harcourt, Brace, 1940.

Dyson, Michael E. *Open Mike: Reflections on Philosophy, Race, Sex, Culture, and Religion.* New York: Basic Civitas, 2003.

Frazier, Edward F. *Race and Culture Contacts in the Modern World.* Boston: Beacon, 1968.

———. *Black Bourgeoisie: The Rise of a New Middle Class in the United States.* New York: Collier, 1973.

Green, Dan S., and Edward D. Driver. *W. E. B. DuBois on Sociology and the Black Community.* Chicago: University of Chicago Press, 1978.

Jacobs, Jane. *Cities and the Wealth of Nations.* New York: Random House, 1984.

Locke, Alain, and Bernhard J. Stern. *When Peoples Meet.* New York: Progressive Education Association, 1942.

Logan, Rayford Whittingham, ed. *W. E. B. DuBois: A Profile.* New York: Hill and Wang, 1971.

Mays, Benjamin Elijah. *Born to Rebel: An Autobiography.* New York: Scribner, 1971.

Mumford, Lewis. *The City in History: Its Origins, Its Transformations, and Its Prospects.* San Diego: Harcourt Brace Jovanovich, 1961.

Rampersad, Arnold. *The Art and Imagination of W. E. B. Dubois.* Cambridge, Mass.: Harvard University Press, 1976.

Rowan, Carl T. *Breaking Barriers: A Memoir.* Boston: Little, Brown, 1991.

———. *The Coming Race War in America: A Wake-Up Call.* Boston: Little, Brown, 1996.

Sugrue, Thomas J. *The Origins of the Urban Crisis: Race and Inequality in Postwar Detroit.* Princeton: Princeton University Press, 1996.

Thernstrom, Abigail, and Stephan Thernstrom. *America in Black and White: One Nation, Indivisible.* New York: Simon & Schuster, 1997.

Williamson, Joel. *The Crucible of Race: Black-White Relations in the American South since Emancipation.* New York: Oxford University Press, 1984.

Young, Coleman, and Lonnie Wheeler. *Hard Stuff: The Autobiography of Mayor Coleman Young.* New York: Penguin, 1994.

Zinsser, William. *Writing about Your Life: A Journey into the Past.* New York: Marlowe, 2004.

Index

Page numbers in italics refer to photographs

Keith, Cecile, 154

Keith, Conyers, Anderson, Brown, and
Wahls, 150

Keith, Damon, 52, 73, 167, 192, 243; chair
of membership campaign of Detroit
NAACP, 151; core convictions, 147–48;
deep sense of responsibility to help
others, 147; and Detroit riots of 1967,
105, 106; 1970 Freedom Fund Dinner,
75; friendship with Arthur Johnson,
145–57; leadership for Freedom Fund
Dinner, 151; at meeting with federal
officials regarding civil rights legislation,
76; meeting with Kennedy in 1960, 77,
78; member of Coleman Young's "kitchen
cabinet," 133, 135; on Michigan Civil
Rights Commission, 82–83; in NAACP,
42–43, 52; at NAACP membership
committee meeting, 1956, *146;* "Soul
Food Luncheon" in chambers of, 2003,
146; status of legal legend, 145; struggle
to obtain federal judgeship, 150–54; style
of approach to problems, 149; support
for Cavanagh, 63; at United Community
Services meeting, 1984, *148*

Keith, Debbie, 154

Keith, Gilda, 154, 245

Keith, Rachel, *146,* 154–55, 157, 167,
168, 179

"Keith decision," 145

Kennedy, John F., 97, 191, 213; assassination,
79; attitude toward civil rights work in
South as presidential candidate, 77–78,
78; Civil Rights Bill, 74, 79; and March on
Washington, 76–77

Kennedy, Robert, *76,* 85, 191

King, Martin Luther, Jr., 2, 33, 59, 76, 89, 157,
192, 195, 243; assassination, 85, 110–12;
and Detroit "Walk to Freedom," 65–67;
eulogy, 216–18; "I Have a Dream" speech
in Detroit, 67, 110; "I Have a Dream"
speech in Washington, 74, 149; "I've Been
to the Mountain Top," 112, 195; love as
source of power and energy, 193; and
March on Washington, 74; at Morehouse
College, 23–24, 31; opposition to Vietnam
War, 110; "Why I Am Opposed to the
War in Vietnam," 110–11

King, Martin Luther, Sr., 23, 24, 31, 32

King, Richard, 245

King, Rodney, jury verdict, 247

Knox, Patti, 120

Ku Klux Klan, 2–3, 10, 79

Lackey, Betty, 245

Lagerkvist, Par, 221–22

Lane, Artis, *130*

Latin Quarter, Detroit, 73

Lee, Canada, 28–29

Lee, Everett, 177

Lee, Sylvia, *127*

Levy, Bert, *129*

Liebermann, Samuel J., 40

Locke, Hubert, 103, *129*

Lofton, Ernest, 142–43

Lokumbe, Hannibal, 178

Louis, Joe, 6

love, as essential element of the good life, 193

Love, Helen, 245

Love, Josephine Harreld, 229

Lucas, Louis, 96

Luck, Michael, 168

lynchings, 3

MacKenzie High, Detroit, 87

Macomb County, Michigan, 99

Malcolm X, 192

Mandela, Nelson, 192, 195–96, 217, 243

March on Washington, 67, 74, 76–77, 79

Marshall, Ernest, eulogy, 218–19

Marshall, Louise, 218

Marshall, Thurgood, 43, 71, 96, 100, 101,
157, 192

Martin, Fred, 133

Marx, Richard, *76*

Mathewson, Kent, 236

Mays, Benjamin, 6, 26–27, 30–31, 33, 35,
70, 192, 217; and intellectual culture of
Morehouse, 18–19, 20; philosophy of
nonviolent disobedience, 89; signed flyer
from 1976 event honoring, *21*

Mayson, Alma, 219

Mayson, Irving, eulogy, 219–20

Mazey, Emil, 222

McCarthyism, 80

McCay Hill School, Americus, Georgia, 4

McClain, Clementine, *127*

McClendon, James J., *70, 75,* 231

McCree, Dores, 197

McCree, Wade, *75,* 150, 151, 153, 231;
eulogy, 220–22

McCutcheon, Aubrey, 96, 97

McFall, Benjamin, 65, *75*

McFarland, Elizabeth, 1–2, 4–5, 11, 12, 33,
34, 35, 158, 172; salute to, 214–15

McFarland, Vera, 2, 3, 4, 11. *See also* Daniel,
Vera, eulogy